THE LION AND THE FOX

THE LION
AND
THE FOX

The rôle of the hero in
the plays of Shakespeare

WYNDHAM LEWIS

METHUEN & CO LTD
11 New Fetter Lane, London EC4

Originally published by Grant Richards Ltd, 1927
First published by Methuen & Co Ltd, 1951
Reprinted 1955 and 1966

Printed in Great Britain by
John Dickens & Co Ltd, Northampton

" *Essendo, adunque, un Principe necessitato saper bene usare la bestia, debbe di quelle pigliari la volpe e il leone ; perchè il leone non si difende da' lacci, la volpe non si defende da' lupi. Bisogna, adunque, essere volpe a conoscere i lacci, e leone a sbigottire i lupi. Coloro che stanno semplicemente in sul leone, non se ne intendano* " (MACHIAVELLI : Il Principe, cap. xviii.).

" *Ne voilà-t-il pas une belle preuve qu'un prince doit être un fripon, parce qu'Achille a été nourri, selon la Fable, par un animal moitié-bête et moitié homme ! Encore si Ulysse avoit eu un renard pour précepteur, l'allégorie auroit quelque justesse . . .*" (VOLTAIRE : Correspondence).

" *. . . want cannot be withstood, men can do no more than they can do : what remained then, but the fox's case must help, when the lion's skin is out at the elbows* " (NASH).

CONTENTS

INTRODUCTION

PART I.—TUDOR ENGLAND AND RENAISSANCE ITALY

PART II.—MACHIAVELLI

7

CONTENTS

CONTENTS

PART VII.—THERSITES AND APEMANTUS

PART VIII.—RENAN'S CALIBAN AND CHAPMAN'S DUKE OF BYRON

PART IX.—APPENDIX

SHAKESPEARE AND RACE

INTRODUCTION

i. *Shakespeare as an Organism*

THE master-subject of Shakespeare's plays has its origin in the machiavellian obsession of his time : or rather, that is the form the deeper conflict takes. The figure used by Machiavelli to express this conflict is that of the *lion and the fox* ; these two animals are chosen to represent the two forces in opposition, although his doctrine was directed to combining them. In Shakespeare, as in most of his contemporaries, with one foot in the old world of chivalrous romance and the other in the new one of commerce and science, they were imperfectly combined : for his was not an emancipated and scientific mind, like that of the great Italian in question.

Parts I. and II. are occupied with establishing an historical background. In Part I. the time factor or historical environment is considered ; tudor England is co-ordinated with renaissance Italy, the nature and extent of the italian influence fixed. Part II. is devoted to Machiavelli.

These two parts (as also the Appendix, which would have taken its place with them but that it seemed to delay too much the arrival at our central theme) are not directly concerned with Shakespeare or his plays. In Part III. the rôle of the hero or king in Shakespeare's plays is discussed. That part of the essay concerning itself directly with the text of Shakespeare begins in Part IV.

The Appendix may seem unnecessarily remote from the ostensible object of the book : but it greatly serves to effect the necessary isolation of Shakespeare's personality ; it disposes of the claims of some vague *blood*, of a legendary flesh and bone, on this singular mind ; and it brings into great relief the essential character of the respective epochs just between which Shakespeare's destiny was set.

The pages dealing with english history and the italian

renaissance have no pretension to be anything but a rough
sketch, in which some of the most easily accessible material
necessary for coping with the questions raised in the ensuing pages is assembled and offered to the reader in place
of merely referring him to a group of textbooks. The reason
that the reader is not simply referred to textbooks is this.
First of all, if it is my good fortune to be read by a variety
of readers, of unusual intelligence, but to whom the few
books required are not easily accessible, and who are in
any case repelled by what is called history, then my brief,
unvarnished collection of notes may be welcome. In the
second place, the more general information is digested into
the scheme of this essay for the purposes of this essay;
and as such is offered to the reader.

Shakespeare's works are luckily so well known that
anything you have to say for which they can be taken as
a text has at the outset one great obstacle removed from
its path; where an english-speaking public is concerned
Shakespeare offers unique advantages from that point of
view. I should myself, apart from anything else, be interested to perpetuate those advantages—not for us but for him;
although the services that such a writer as Shakespeare
renders a community in stabilizing its consciousness, and
giving it that rallying-ground of thought and illusion
which it requires in order to survive, are immense. So we
had, at the last, certainly better say *for us*, whose speech
for so many generations has been the same as his, rather
than *for him*, who owes us nothing.

Where that seemed necessary I have given the references
for the passages I quote: but I have left them in the body
of the text, because in that way the reader is spared the
rather disturbing fluctuation of the eye from the text to
the bottom of the page and back.

One of the standard questions about Shakespeare has
reference to his *heart*—whether he supplied his readers
with " a key " in his *Sonnets*, and if he did, whether that

INTRODUCTION

made him *less* Shakespeare even than he is by the time the baconians have done with him. Browning, old machiavellian romantic that he was, would not hear of a national poet appearing without a highly misleading mask, and the entire diplomatic apparatus of a studied duplicity. So he said: "If so, the less Shakespeare he!"—meaning if he left no keys lying about on his demise.

To this question of the *heart* of the romantic lover of the *Sonnets*, the doctrine of impersonality is allied and related. For if Shakespeare is the perfect *mirror* of the advice to the players in *Hamlet*, he is one of the star exemplars of art's self-effacing aloofness. His, too, is the infinitely supple mind; to his blank and non-committal countenance you could truly say:

> " Your wit is of the true Pierian spring
> That can make anything of anything."

There is another attribute that the standard picture of Shakespeare must display—namely, what is necessary to symbolize *the feudal poet*. It is with such literary conceptions and historic tags that the popular idea of the personality of the national poet is built up. I think that the machinery for reviving this defunct elizabethan only spirits him away, unnecessarily conspiring with the snobbish madness that substituted a minister of state for the Bankside business man. Also interest in his personality—or impersonality, which is much the same thing—obscures the very active features of the wonderful mind exhibited in his plays. I am setting out to show in the following essay how—with all the noble proportion and harmonious adjustment that made his achievement so incomparable—bellowing at you from the windy corner of every scene in the great tragedies is a human personality for whom such playful theatrical or finicking disguises as are thrust on him by his interpreters would have been pushed aside with as much distraction as Charles Duke of Byron at the moment of his pathos would have shown a laundry bill. Each of the figures of his tragedies, Timon, Lear, Coriolanus, are vast keys to unlock a giant's meditative fastness. It is because the scale of his mature creations is so superhuman that it has been possible to describe them as standing aside from life, or as arabesques of unwieldy passion dispassionately projected. They are, it is true, immense shadows, rather than realities in a cheaply concrete sense ; and their roar is muffled by the great lines that interpret it. And it is true that in this control of these creatures Shakespeare showed all the *sang froid* that we associate with the great technician, the tactical transference of the individual experience into a series of prepared puppets. But such puppets are born, not made, by a most painful gestation. It will be my business here to relate the spasms of these scowling and despairing monsters to a particularly concrete figure, or to a mind experiencing things according to identifiable personal laws.

It will also come into my scheme to show how, contrary to the aristophanic function, the comic spirit in Shakepeare was Puck-like and anarchic, and not at the service of reactionary superstition. For the curses of Caliban and Thersites are *Shakespeare's* curses : and far from being a feudal poet, the Shakespeare that *Troilus and Cressida*, *The Tempest*, or even *Coriolanus*, shows us, is much more a bolshevik (using this little word popularly) than a figure of conservative romance. That the person behind all this material, which is so harsh and turbulent, should have been missed it is difficult to understand, except that his inalienable status as the national poet required some little manipulation. The official critic, for the same reason as the doctrinaire impersonalist, would prefer that Shakespeare wore his mask. Anything not quite respectable can in that way be put down to his divine impartiality. That the wild and subversive matter that we know fermented and broke out in the personal life of Marlowe, as in many other people of that violent age, was equally in that sweet and gentle Ford (as a horrified lady that I shall presently quote from calls him), and in " Sweet Will " as well : that the coming revolution, the first in Europe, was at work in these elizabethan minds : that Cervantes, " laughing away the chivalry of Spain," would have been incapable of such ferocious laughter as breaks incessantly, in a most unseemly way, from the english national poet, is certain. In Achilles, Ajax, Hotspur, Coriolanus and the rest you get what *Shakespeare* thought of the chivalry of the physical hero. Falstaff is his Don Quixote, not his Sancho Panza.

But contradicting this such figures as Othello and Antony appear. But the different uses of these heroes I examine at length in the ensuing pages.

Over all the plays of Shakespeare is the shadow of Machiavelli, as it is over all the other plays of the tudor stage. Chapman writes :

> " there are schools
> Now broken ope in all parts of the world,
> First founded in ingenious Italy,
> Where some conclusions of estate are held
> That for a day preserve a prince, and ever
> Destroy him after, from thence men are taught
> To glide into degrees of height by craft
> And then lock in themselves by villany."

Ingenious Italy, and its academies of manslaughter and deceit, played its part in the mind of Shakespeare, as it did, more heavily and differently, in that of the " sophist " Chapman.

In this essay I confine myself almost entirely to a consideration of the tragedies and histories. Each of the great figures of this *theatre of character* is to be regarded as an organ of an organism that we know as Shakespeare. On this principle it will be seen that the quixotic organ was more developed in Cervantes than in Shakespeare ; and there is no need to point out how very much more complex the Shakespeare organism is. We could say, on the physiological analogy, that the quixotic organ in Shakespeare was differently situated, and that Sancho Panza had grown so big that he perhaps should rather be regarded as the Englishman's " Knight," on whom a simple, heroic and devoted child-figure attends. For Prospero and Caliban are not the pair that provide the parallel.

INTRODUCTION

ii. *Shakespeare's " Impersonality " and its Consequences*

If we could understand Shakespeare — not make a Hamlet-problem of him, but realize the problem that does exist for the understanding in such a highly organized mind, and approach even its solution—we should also have established, critically, a new human identity immune from the vicissitudes of the war of person and no-person. We should, in short, have secured this magnificent person from the chances of the fashionable campaign against the personality.

That there is something equivocal and of a very special nature in the figure of this poet has been felt constantly ; and people have always tapped his pedestal, inquisitive and uneasy, and peered up into his face, scenting a hoax. The authenticity of that face even has been doubted : it has been called an " obvious mask," the " face of a tailor's dummy," and many other disobliging things. For there, in place of the massive bearded mask popularly expected of a Homer or an Æschylus, is a delicate egg-like countenance, serene and empty. The very sleeves of his doublet have been testified by a tailor to be wrong : the left sleeve is on his right arm, the right sleeve on his left, this Bond Street authority has pronounced, and signed his statement. The sense of mystification, of something not properly explained, found its most famous expression in the Bacon controversy, which gave rise to this discussion about his face and sleeves. His plays were handed over by the baconians to the man who " wrote on science like a Lord Chancellor." And the begetters of this theory have been accused of a snobbery that felt that a Lord Chancellor, at least, should be found in order worthily to account for the production of these epics of national life.

But this uneasy and almost incredulous feeling is natural enough if you consider one by one the circumstances of the case. First of all, the English are very confident of their great practical capacities, but do not regard themselves as much of a hand at the things of the intelligence. " For thinking" they "have no great turn" they would, with some little pride, agree with Matthew Arnold. And it is natural enough that they should have felt that there was something strange about their having such a poet as Shakespeare to represent them. They may be sometimes lulled by such statements as Mr Saintsbury's that "Shakespeare was nothing if not english," but they do not believe it really. And then there is the disquieting statement so often made that *Shakespeare is universal*. *Universal* bears an uncomfortable affinity to *international*. How can you be a typical Englishman and at the same time be "universal"? they ask themselves doubtfully. And it is then that they look up at the mask appearing in the folios, reproduced in his statues, and wonder if there is not something wrong somewhere. Perhaps, although he came from Warwickshire, he was a Welshman, blown by some cambrian raid as far as Stratford; or he may have been a Pict (hence the supernatural in *Macbeth*): perhaps even he was a Jew: but whatever he was, there was something queer and unnatural. That has been the general english feeling. Again, he was not a scholar. It is true that Cervantes was not either, nor Molière—but such analogies do not help: two blacks do not make one white. There seem to be, again, in his plays, no slips of taste or social judgment of the critical and peculiar kind that a watchful snobbery would detect. And he has a polish and ease in finding words for princes, great commanders, and ladies of the court that is unusual, and that a reading even of Castiglione might not give. Yet he was a sort of peasant—his face we have already alluded to, with its unfortunate emptiness.

He seems to have been inconspicuous. "Sweet Will" or "gentle Shakespeare" is about all that can be got out of his contemporaries by way of description of this "myriad-minded" omnific individual. In the same way that Thomas Cromwell seems to have been of an anonymous presence, as it were, though generally pleasant in contrast to his flourishing titanic namesake, Oliver, so Shakespeare cannot have worn his personality on his sleeve. There are many things, too, only half uttered or only used by baconians. One of them is his name, SHAKE-SPEAR—there

INTRODUCTION

is a fantastic name for a man to have, when you come to
think of it!—which did not escape his hostile contemporaries (*cf.* the "shake-scene" of his Oxford rivals).
But those who do not wish Bacon to have him, point out
that Shackspur or Shaxpur was probably his proper name
(*chaque-espère* also coming in handy).

Of all those difficulties the really insurmountable one is
that he (so near to us in time, and so much part of our
blood and speech) is so very "great": and, what is more
difficult, universally admitted to be one of the rarest minds
of which we have any record.

If Shakespeare had belonged to a country politically less
important than England his name would be sufficient alone
for its prosperity. He would be its principal commodity
and source of revenue. A relatively small community could
indeed live on it.

In the ensuing pages no questions of controversial
scholarship are involved : it is only proposed to examine
the internal evidence afforded us by some of the plays as
to the personality behind this "mask" : to arrive at some
idea as to whether Shakespeare saw the world as the expression of *techne* or of *tyche* : to consider what was the
nature of Shakespeare's identification of his personality—
if such existed—with that of his characters, if any : and to
carefully avoid, in the process, any speculation that would
disturb the concentration required in such a ticklish
research.

> "... nice philosophy
> May tolerate unlikely arguments,
> But Heaven admits no jest. ..."

So, awfully prepared, this very high study can be entered
on, the invasion of only so much of that vast bibliographic
kingdom marked *Shakespeare* as is comprised within the
purviews of a reading of his work being contemplated.

Shakespeare is the greatest elizabethan—or in Swinburne's chivalrous dialect he is "that veritable king of
kings and lord of lords among all writers and all thinkers of
all time." In any case, with him something unexpectedly

surpassing came to birth. Only to mention the great Marlowe, and think of his *Jew of Malta*, or Webster, and remember his *Duchess of Malfi*, or Chapman, with his *Revenge of Bussy*—you get at once a sense of the vital disparity between Shakespeare and his great contemporaries, and see what sort of lacuna would have been there if Shakespeare had died too young to produce his characteristic work.

This magical quality of unmatched perfection that makes comparison with others difficult, and robs people in consequence of their favourite sport, is no doubt in the long run irritating. A comedo, even with the uncleanly, and everywhere anything *sticking up*, is a standing invitation to man's destructiveness or his hysterical gouging, scratching, squeezing, flea-hunting, stone-throwing fingers. Or in another way the famous " natural magic " of Shakespeare, " the cloud-capped towers " and the rest of his divine bag of tricks, is liable always to engulf the magician, too, when, one of these days, as usual, they are disintegrating under his wand. This is all the more to be feared as he does not possess any recorded or very tangible personality —as regards that he is a thumbling : he could easily be whipped into a witches' cauldron, and has too much the secret of a disincarnate life to be likely to trouble about any gross survival. To attach Shakespeare to his contemporaries is to do us, though not him, a service, therefore, by making him more concrete. On the other hand the tendency of some scholars to make his personality (or such as he has got) disappear in the other direction—namely, by diminishing too much his isolation, by a process of distribution and allocation among his contemporaries—is to be deplored.

The feeling that Shakespeare might suffer a sea-change, or an earth-change, at any moment ; that he is not a stable thing, is liable to float away on a fragment of island or what not, is encouraged by his destiny. We have already seen all his plays given away to Bacon. Certainly popular— and even in some cases expert—belief in the very existence of Shakespeare was at one moment shaken. And that suspicion that he is not real is in the back of people's minds, always hanging over him. Even without that, such a complicated person as he would be in hourly danger of disappearing into nothingness and becoming a ghost, haunting, without dimension, only the glimpses of the moon.

The thing about his work that makes it natural for Sir J. Robertson to analyse his " originality " as he has done (describing him as a kind of sensitive plate suddenly endowed with a soul by reading Montaigne) is an interesting one to fix. It is of the same character as another feature of his genius that would incline the student sometimes to turn from his smooth felicity, or even rough felicity, to, let us say, the more muscular verse of Webster, or the more muscular and amazingly ardent prose of Nash. Or it is the same thing that will make the student turn from the ultimate perfections of the art of a great civilization to the asperities and barbarous grandeurs in less-developed cultures. For the fact is—and that has to be so if you think of it—that the penalty of such maturity and complexity as Shakespeare's mind exhibits is a sort of ease that is too felicitous to be telling—as a more dogmatic, one-sided or passionate expression would be. He is if anything too much everything to be any particular man ; and sees round and behind things so much that he presents them too completely, *too* universally.

This is the origin of the fixed dogma of his impeccable impersonality or lack of personality. It is in a sense Hamlet's disability taken into the problems of art. Not that there was any hesitation, or uneasiness, there : it works out rather in the contrary sense in art—everything became too easy. And he was perhaps too universal a man to draw men.

All this being so, anyone who defines in the body of Shakespeare's work a personality and traces of passion and opinion is rescuing him for us from the abstract in which he might eventually disappear where less important men would survive.

INTRODUCTION

iii. *The Time-Race-Class Machinery, and its End*

In Shakespeare's time every influence of the old and new world met and parleyed : and if we were making Shakespeare the most acute and typical child of his time we should have no difficulty in showing that his universality was inevitable—that the complete eclecticism and confusion of his time gave him that universality in the ordinary course of things. He was far enough north and far enough back to live half in norse saga : near enough Rome and the tuscan schools, and late enough in our era, to be well dipped in a by that time well-articulated antiquity : in the two or three generations coming before him the tudor court swarmed with Italians, the papal and protestant influences were both vigorous and picturesque ; Machiavelli, immensely influential, represented for his period the fine flower of a cynical opportunism, and chivalry and physical adventure were still flourishing concerns. And Shakespeare did, indeed, perfectly express his time, only he expressed it a little too perfectly to be its child. If you allow yourself the luxury of being superstitious about this splendid figure, you will feel that nature may have constantly flung down, century after century, this glittering cipher, this touchstone, until at last the conjunctions were as they should be and she swept in the trumps. And yet the severest natural science could not require a more self-effacing instrument to show how relative, unsubstantial and psycheless even the most notorious *personality* can be. Since in a time the only object that remains with any clearness is such a personality as Shakespeare's, as represented in his work, and as symbolized by his name, it is equally legitimate to feel that it is he and not the time that is a reality ; or that he is a reality independent of his time : this all the more so if you are more interested in things than in the manner in which they happen to be manufactured, or if you regard the manufacture as a pointless activity unless at the end some positive thing is the result.

As the tragic and comic were mixed in Shakespeare's plays, so they were mixed in his mind : and at some time one was in the ascendant, then the other would have its turn. But neither was ever absent ; it dogged its other half like a shrinking or growing shadow.

In studying some aspects of his plays, as we are about to do, keeping this in mind we shall be less surprised at the fundamental contradiction that is evident everywhere through them. We find him at one moment firmly planted in the bosom of one of his demigods, and then the next he is sneering at him in the person of his fool. " What is it that drives men, at certain times and places, to seek and find expression for the tragic or the comic vision of life ? " Mr Cornford asks, but refuses in that place to debate. When we find these two things " driving " simultaneously in a great and mature production, as we do with Shakespeare, it is difficult to avoid debating it if we are going to examine the work at all.

One of the great difficulties of any discussion about Shakespeare to-day is, first, to avoid any appearance, even, of assailing his great position in the intellectual world, for no one else could fill it if it were left vacant, and hardly anyone is so unchallengeable as he : and secondly, still maintaining that, to show the forces of disintegration at work in his mind. Out of one half of his mind, we might say, the modern world could be seen issuing, with its mean, colourless and violent *hubris* (on whom nature retaliates by gigantic, dull and muffled wars). Out of the other and civilized half we could almost step into the attic theatre— taking, if you like, the crude and humble mediæval stage on the way.

In Shakespeare there is, as in no doubt every elizabethan, some of the " cold muck " of Calvin, as there is the maturer spirit of a distant child of Rome. It was partly again this spirit of social revolution so ardently stirring in his time that impelled him to accept the comic and democratic framework where the heroes of antiquity were concerned— as it was the italian democratic infection that no doubt caused Cervantes to take chivalry by the throat. But as he was nearer to the sources of civilization than Shakespeare he embraced what he had intended to assault, or both

INTRODUCTION

buffeted and caressed the object of his satire. Shakespeare, on the other hand, is more relentless, although even with him there are returns to " grandeur." For always at the bottom of Shakespeare's mind there is negation and chaos ; the *tyche* has its will of the *techne* :

> " Life's . . . a tale
> Told by an idiot, full of sound and fury,
> Signifying nothing."

But at the bottom of Cervantes' mind there would be found a more constant piety, and a kind of reconciliation.

So if you see in Shakespeare at once the " mirror of chivalry," " the glass of fashion and the mould of form," and the comic-demon Thersites ; if you hear (but pretend not to) the envious snarl of the rabble, then (with a pleased shiver) the thunders of Jupiter Tonans, then what you interpret with satisfaction as the distinguished intonation of " the aristocrat " and his nietzschean invective in *Coriolanus* : if you observe things of such different worlds as Queen Mab's chariot and Cleopatra's barge, or two images of our world engaged in a perpetual encounter, it is the usual thing to try to reconcile them. " This is not Shakespeare's drama, but merely that of the world he depicted, that does not change much from age to age." The mirror is held up to nature, and there are two fighting forms reflected there—mazdean, moral or not-moral ; at all events, a dark and a light, a black and a white. And as the great national poet of England must be a " white man," whether that involves morality or not, it would be otiose to inquire on whose side his interests would lie—if he were not, unfortunately, merely a " mirror," and so unable to speak.

To be a " mirror " at all, it could be pointed out, is ethically dubious. It could be shown that any mirror that was really a mirror, and which told the truth, would have been smashed long ago. And then it could be suggested that this particular mirror was a very lively one, giving a very purged, not to say peculiar, view of the hegelian " contest " in progress. But in these pages it will be contended that Shakespeare entered furiously into the contest of the two

23

halves of which he was composed. He was alternately as black as night and as white as snow, or both at the same time. Renan describes himself as a " tissue of contradictions, one half of me engaged in devouring the other half, like the fabled beast of Ctesias who ate his own paws without knowing it " : a description that could very well be applied to Shakespeare. The perfection and equilibrium of his mind is the proof of the beautiful matching of the opposing forces.

PART I

TUDOR ENGLAND AND RENAISSANCE ITALY

CHAPTER I

THE NATIONAL SITUATION OF ENGLAND UNDER ELIZABETH

THE political status of England is of importance, since it determined the attitude of the court to the new southern cultures and affected the opportunities possessed by England for absorbing them.

The " spacious days " of Elizabeth's reign were under the great economic shadow of Henry VIII.'s wastefulness. Froude's " patriot king " was not a good predecessor to have, from many points of view. This full-blooded monarch, for instance, " had twenty or thirty palaces, on all of which pulling down and building up was perpetually going on. He built huge ships which would not sail, huge palaces . . . some left to decay. If he could have got at it, he would have spent all the private wealth of all his subjects, and he made every effort to get at it. . . . The smaller monasteries went . . . soon the greater monasteries went. . . . A long array of waggons carried off the gold, silver and precious stones which had accumulated round the shrine of Becket. . . .

" After these exploits he seems to have hardly dared to ask his people for money. But there still remained a way in which he could most effectually attack their pockets. He began to issue base money. He soon became shameless, for his mint kept issuing baser and baser coins. . . . He is the only english sovereign who has committed this peculiarly mean . . . crime, for Charles only thought of it " (Rogers : *The Economic Interpretation of History*). The money got down to 60 per cent. below par. When Elizabeth had it sorted out in the process of rejuvenating the currency the slag was used for road-mending, we are told.

So elizabethan England came after the devastations of " a Vitellius and Nero," according to Rogers, a " patriot king," according to Froude ; in any case a very lavish man, who debased the currency very much indeed.

Before the formation of the great trading companies, of the kind of the Merchant Adventurers, England was in a state of economic vassalage. As well as being the " wool farm of the Hanse," she was the silver mine of Rome, it appears. Rogers believes that the greater part of the silver of Western Europe came at that time from England. The breach with Rome of the sixteenth century was probably precipitated by the silver payments made to the papal court constantly draining the resources of the english state. In the heyday of roman power in England the pope received annually the equivalent of the royal revenue.

In pre-tudor times the english dependence on the imperial system resulted in the english getting their famous longbows from the Baltic, and gunpowder and arms from Germany. At the beginning of the age of Elizabeth, and before the english participation in the looting of the New World, England was still in a position of political, as of economic, inferiority : it was only with Cromwell that the days of english power in Europe began.

By Shakespeare's time the movement into the town throughout England, precipitated by the rapacity of the great landowners, was universal. London itself grew like a mushroom, contemporary accounts showing it to have been for noise, and the clash and press of its narrow streets, an inferno like the modern Paris. Owing to the debasement of the coinage already referred to, and the cheapening of silver consequent on the inpouring of that metal from the New World, the age of Elizabeth registered a rise of 300 or 400 per cent. in prices over former periods.

The English silver trade languished with the opening up of the New World. The ruin of the flemish trading cities struck the iron industry a mortal blow. It is supposed that the foreign trade of England, and by implication the currency, was not a fifth what it had been a century before. " Everyone was distressed who had fixed or quasi-fixed incomes. . . . The Oxford and Cambridge Colleges were terribly distressed. They cut down their chapel services, for all that may be said about Elizabeth's advertisements, to the meanest forms. They ceased to buy books. They abandoned wine for small-beer. . . . The varied and more unctuous feasts of two or three generations before were exchanged for plain beef and mutton, with rations of salt fish. The spice-box was locked up except on gaudies. . . ."

If England was badly off Ireland was in a far more pitiable condition, so that by Swift's time he could write : " There is not an acre of land in Ireland turned to half its advantage, yet it is better improved than the people ; and all these evils are effects of english tyranny, so your sons and grandchildren will find it to their sorrow."

A few decrepit merchant ships was all that Henry VIII. discovered in England when he came to the throne. Hoys and fly-boats drifted out of the Thames to Antwerp and back. Complete stagnation reigned. There was no fleet, and it had not occurred to anyone that such a thing was necessary. When Henry was excommunicated Ireland rebelled, and his papist subjects plotted his overthrow ; he then built himself a fleet, which, except for certain unfortunate miscalculations, did what was required of it. But Henry's fleet lay rotting in harbour during Mary's reign ; the coast forts were neglected or dismantled, Calais was lost ; and so the reign of Elizabeth inherited, in a military sense, the results of Mary's catholic fervour, while financially it received the burden of Henry VIII.'s extravagance.

" How was it," Froude asks, " that the genius of our scandinavian forefathers suddenly sprang again into life ? "—that is, at the time of sixteenth-century maritime enterprise in England. He puts this strange ethnologic fact, as he considers it, down to the reign of terror in the time of Mary. The protestant English, driven out of their country, took to the sea, and naturally, once there, the old viking sea-wolf came to life again.

As regards this re-emergence of the sea-wolf in the english race, piracy, between the norse invasions and the days of the Spanish Main, had never ceased ; and the sea-wolf instinct, where it asserted itself in any seafaring man, had enough opportunities of satisfying itself any time during those intervening centuries. The Hanse, English, Dutch or French, all together or separately, covered the sea with pirates at all times, and did their country's business as much in that way as by more legitimate methods of commerce. The *Victual Brothers* and the *Rovers of the Sea*, for example, in Henry VI.'s reign, made naval war on England much more effectively than the more pretentious and famous armada of Philip; and, later, the international pirate states of Algiers or Morocco were as powerful on the sea as Carthage—only not as traders, but as trade destroyers. The universal insecurity of the highroad in the Middle Ages (necessitating the waste-space of two hundred feet on either side of it) was as nothing to that of the high sea. When Edward III. claimed the overlordship of the waves a " king's peace " was supposed to be established—a bastard, watery *pax romana*. But its claim was premature, and its effectiveness never interfered with the traditional norse sea-lawlessness.

So Froude's romantic picture, requiring a mysterious resurrection of the piratic soul of the north, would seem to be far-fetched.

But what did characterize the age of Elizabeth, and that certainly carries it back to the early norse days of personal adventure, was an unlimited and, for a modern state, unparalleled development of personal initiative. A period of lawless and, for the most part, unrecognized military activity opened. The state services lapsed and its management and defence passed into the hands of private persons or trading companies. The states and their rulers were as vacillating and inactive as their subjects were enterprising; for religious revolution had opened a chasm at their feet, and every government was chary of venturing on a warlike action of any sort for fear of precipitating a world-war of religion. So every state remained officially at peace, while fleets of privateers of all nations hurried hither and thither, making private war. The Robinson Crusoe type of Englishman came to life, the little, independent, heavily armed, practical child of the genevan Bible, in direct communion with God, and ready to take on his shoulders, in consequence of this usurpation of authority, at any moment any responsibility whatever.

The plundering and raiding of the spanish colonies after and before the armada, chasing of plate-fleets and so on, was done by the coastmen of the West of England principally —mixed with huguenots, and irish and italian adventurers, the latter as pilots. With or without letters of marque, independent gentlemen of a seafaring turn—puritan or otherwise—would equip a ship and go yachting in the Bay of Biscay or off the flemish coast, where they could have sea-duels with other gentlemen they met on the high sea, of similar tastes. More spectacular gentlemen like Raleigh would pay, often, not very useful visits to distant parts of the world. His transatlantic trips were costly and unproductive usually, but no doubt more agreeable than they would be to-day.

Elizabeth put every obstacle in the way of military preparations to meet the spanish invasion; the ships of her regular fleet had only two days' ammunition, the crews were ragged, on half rations, and sick with infected food. The officers who provided arrowroot and wine out of their own pockets for the men were reprimanded after the defeat of the Armada for their action. Elizabeth's very laodicean disposition would not take any interest in the theological dispute, but the fanaticism of the puritan would not appeal to her, and the instinct of the european rulers wrestling with the problem of heresy told them that the downfall of one discipline must, in the end, involve all. The armada itself was never intended as anything but a demonstration, and it was the powerful groups of private citizens who turned it into a desperate encounter, dealing a spectacular blow to a trade rival.

English finance (more " patriotic," naturally, than the reigning house) by operations on the continental bourses stopped spanish credit. By this means for a year the armada was prevented from sailing for lack of funds. When this difficulty was at length overcome, and the fleet, under Lima, was able to sail, it was the same financiers who equipped an english counter-armada and defeated it.

THE LION AND THE FOX

The Hamburg Company provided one hundred ships, for instance. Drake, the greatest english seaman, was in command of this great privateer fleet. From that time forth the financial interests were supreme. They cut King Charles's head off when he tried to blackmail them too much, and backed the Protector, who represented their interests. Cromwell was, no doubt, more than anything else a stupid ruffian, whom they pushed forward to do the more brutal and spectacular part of their work. History *à la* Carlyle, written as though in anticipation of the Boy Scout Movement, with its exaltation of every brutal puppet that caught the bloodshot eye of that great sensationalist, is for the eternal infants' class merely. It would be pleasant to think that before long a more scientific type of history may be available.

CHAPTER II

THE EMPIRE

IN the councils of Philip, the Netherlands, the Hanse and France, the exigencies of their various economic systems played, of course, a major part in the staging of those spectacles preserved for us as "history." Sixteenth-century Spain was the economic vassal of Flanders and Germany, just as, under the Stuarts, english policy was controlled by the subsidies of Gondomar ; though the english financial system, apart from the independent treacheries of the Crown, was english.

In 1553 the Adventurers and Staplers had taken charge of the king's debts, and in return the king had supported them against the Hanseatic League. From the history of discovery we learn that the great voyage of Magellan, perhaps the most daring and romantic of all those early voyages of the first circumnavigators—designed to give the Moluccas to Spain, by discovering the western route to them—was financed by Christopher de Haro, the Haros being " the Rothschilds of that day." They were a firm of jewish Antwerp traders, whose ships, like those of the Jew of Malta, were on every sea. In both the East and West Indies their commercial factors and agents were to be found, who kept them informed on all matters of interest, in trade, politics and the latest geographic finds and possibilities. Luis de San Angel, a spanish Jew, was similarly responsible for the even more celebrated voyage of Columbus. Magellan's romantic circumnavigation was undertaken at the expense not of the spanish Crown then, but of a jewish merchant : and it was all about *pepper*. Pepper was the thing that, more than any other substance, can be said to be at the bottom of the British Empire. It is usual for the economist-historian to insist on the high sense of " patriotic " duty of the early merchant, his high sense of being engaged on a sacred national work, delight-fully identical with personal enrichment. Many merchant princes are very emotional, and a keen sense of the service they are rendering the state by making money out of it is a well-known feature of their psychology. But it requires a great deal of sophistic practice in the manipulation of history to disentangle the " patriotism " from the personal gain, or to show how one is really identical with the other.

Wool, sugar, turpentine and pepper: pepper, sugar, turpentine and wool, can, of course, be sung to the tune of the national anthem; but to get the most out of that solemn air words should be picked more carefully. In any case, where you have such authentic figures of unmercenary romance as Drake or Hawkins, there is some reason to leave such forms as that of Sir Christopher Pack out of your picture. The romantic figures are more suitable for a child's history (for which purpose each age is careful to furnish the necessary quota); but that other sort of history which certainly should be written, side by side with the Greens', Gardiners', and so on, would lose its point by stealing the romance from its neighbour.

To get material for ships and armaments, to dispose of woollen cloth to people in cold countries, to get sultanas, nutmeg, but, above all, *pepper* (in order to pickle the meat on which the elizabethans lived through the winter) —to these considerations can be traced this fantastically large edifice of empire—India, pepper; Virginia, dyes; Newfoundland and Canada, material for ships, and salt fish (Bristol fishermen first stake this out); the West Indies, sugar. If you followed the economic explanation entirely you might say : " What huge sub-continents to get a few sacks of sultanas out of ! " Later the great struggle with the Blefuscu of Swift added other colonial elements to the grocers' or cloth merchants' dream. And then other younger grocers and emigrant clothiers, as energetic as their ter-rible, puffing John Bull fathers, began retaliating from the colonies. The fuss now is over and the dream approaching its conclusions. For the prodigious, housewifely marketing operations of the first days have been substituted, meantime, the abstractions of imperialism.

That there were other dreams as well is certain enough ; but the number of complete puritans in England at any time before the Civil War must have been surprisingly small. Of pure religious fanatics, in such a country as England was then, there could not have been many, though there were enough to keep things in an uproar in Mary's reign and provide her with heretics enough for her zealous nature. There were many reasons to urge people out of England. Raleigh, for instance, left in search of El Dorado because of the persecution and espionage to which he was subjected at the time of Kyd's arrest, when his " atheism " was a source of curiosity to the authorities.

In 1599 the London grocers formed the East India Company. This was necessary if England was not going to be deprived of pepper—or made to pay through the nose for it—by venetian, portuguese, spanish or other rapacity. The new route to Asia round the Cape of Good Hope spelt the ruin of the italian republics ; and the pepper famine and other grocery grievances at length stirred England into maritime action in the East ; and the grocer, once roused, proved a very lion in the competitive scramble for the spice-lands. Clive and Warren Hastings (ferocious as they were) are merely the *personnalités d'apparat* of a later day to that of the original ferocious elizabethan grocer. India, whatever complications may have ensued for England since, meant, in the first place, *pepper* (chutney and curry are all that are left to testify to this earliest destiny) ; and the explosive heat of this commodity communicated itself to its peppery english purveyors.

CHAPTER III

POLITICS AND THE ELIZABETHAN STAGE

SHAKESPEARE'S time was an extremely rough one; he seems to have steered fairly quietly through it, and outlived most of his contemporaries, except Chapman, by twenty years. Most were crushed or worn down in early life. His plays are full of this violent bustle and adventure. Between the antique and the ogival, between the attic stage and Jean Bodel, Shakespeare writes for the *scène pour petite société*. But in this restricted space, by whirling the spectator and characters from place to place, and skipping lightheartedly over months and years, he produces a theatre that is essentially one of *action* in the modern sense. By *exterior* agitation and movement he arrives at what the classic stage reached by *interior* stress. He substitutes variety for intensity of truth, seeks the complicity of the audience, makes a divinity of natural physical action, and governs by surprise. It is by remembering this that the psychology of many of his figures can be most easily understood. Technically, Hamlet, for instance, is a *time*-phenomenon. He could be regarded as a Greek got on to the bustling, elizabethan stage, and acting as a brake on the action by maladjustment to the altered time-sense, or rather absence of time-sense, he finds.

The New World that had just been broken into would have suggested, if the other conditions even had not favoured it, the expression of an exterior life of movement and great dislocation and dispersion. But the english playwright was an entertainer, in the first place; though Thomas Cromwell is reported to have relied on interludes for influencing opinion on religious matters, the plays performed at the Bankside were for a partly italianized nobility and a rough pit audience fresh from the excitements of animal-baiting, who wished to be entertained.

POLITICS AND THE ELIZABETHAN STAGE

But a political impulse, especially as the stage became more an institution emancipated from court patronage, was ready enough to turn the properties of the entertainer into political weapons.

In 1605 Samuel Calvert writes in a letter that "the players do not forbear to represent upon the stage the whole course of this present time, not sparing either king, state or religion, in so great absurdity, and with such liberty, that any would be afraid to hear them." Chambers says that by the seventeenth century the theatre was so much of an institution in London that vindictive measures of suppression were probably no longer feasible.

James's queen, according to Beaumont, the french ambassador, went to the play to laugh at her husband ridiculed on the stage. But both Jonson and Chapman went to prison in 1605 for *Eastward Ho!*—acted by the Children of the Queen's Revels. In 1606 Chapman's *Byron* was suppressed, following other suppressions, and a general inhibition of plays ordered. In the light of what we shall have to say about Chapman later on, this fact has considerable significance. In 1604 a standing order against the representations of any "modern christian king" is quoted.

But that contemporary political fires were smouldering beneath all these seemingly aloof façades of elizabethan tragedy is proved, even Shakespeare's *Richard II.* being involved.

" 'Shortly,' he [Essex] wailed to Elizabeth on 12th May 1600, 'they will play me in what forms they list upon the stage.' And when the last mad step of rebellion was taken in February 1601 it was a play, none other than Shakespeare's *Richard II.*, to which the plotters looked to stir the temper of London in their favour. The curious thing is that in this case, although Essex and more than one of his followers lost life or liberty, no very serious results seem to have followed to the company involved, etc." (Chambers).

As to the censorship (in the hands of the Master of the Revels, a subordinate of the Lord Chamberlain), Chambers says that Sir George Buck was on the look-out especially for political criticism, and that in 1611 that would consist of criticism of the king and court. Any passages speaking without sufficient respect of courtiers and court ladies, knights and so forth, were dropped on by him. The theme of *tyrannicide* was one to which he was especially sensitive, and no dwelling on that was tolerated.

The comic spirit, as exhibited in Aristophanes, was exercised against innovations or intelligence, and served the conservative bourgeois spirit with its compelling laughter. The comic spirit in England has usually been more anarchic, and is certainly so in Shakespeare. Shakespeare himself and Chapman are both, intellectually, in the camp against which Aristophanes directed his attacks. And Chapman was a great favourite with the aristocratic patron of the theatre. This is strictly in character with the traditional dilettantism and affected political anarchism of the english aristocrat.

Those were the conditions controlling the impulses to political expression on the part of an elizabethan playwright. As to the abstract or ethical appeal, the elizabethan stage was secular, and had little to do with religious controversy. The playwright had none of the responsibility of a greek playwright, for instance. Greek theology was formulated not by priests nor prophets, but by poets (*cf.* F. M. Cornford: *Greek Religious Thought*). The poet and the philosopher in Greece were so strictly called to account for what they said because of this. Euripides was attacked because a character in one of his plays said : " My tongue has sworn, my mind has made no oath." This condoning of perjury could not be allowed in a man who was recognized as having a decisive influence on the public conscience. It is, of course, because the reality of this sort of indirect influence is not recognized to-day (although the priestly influence hardly any longer exists) that the press is allowed the terrible licence that we see. But the elizabethan stage was apparently immune from these responsibilities, and not reckoned as of sufficient importance to need very close watching.

So in general the elizabethan was a secular, non-political,

and individualized theatre; from the time of John Heywood (writer of *Interludes*, 1520-1565) this " other pole of
all art "—namely, the Individual and Personal—prevailed.
" In contrast to the Mysteries and Moral Plays which
represent the General only from one point of view . . .
there appears in Heywood's plays the other pole of all art "
(Ulrici : *Shak. Dram. Art*, vol. i.).

The origin of this aloof, secular, non-political general
tone of elizabethan drama is certainly to be found in its
origins, whatever limited licence subsequently prevailed.
And before considering Shakespeare's political instinct
in greater detail it will be well to look a little more into
the social setting of these stage "mirrors of life." The
people responsible for their manufacture, and those who
subsequently would gaze into them with the clear desire
of seeing a flattering reproduction of their persons, were
originally kings and nobles. The tudor stage, arising in
the luxurious fashions of the despotic court of Henry VIII.,
was in the strictest sense a servant of the nobility. It
had been the habit first of Richard III. (John, Duke of
Lancaster) to keep a company of players, and other great
nobles followed his example. These players wore the
badge and livery of the lord they served, like any other
domestic of his household. They received twenty shillings
a head from an earl, ten shillings a head from a baron,
for each performance. So when the independent companies
of players of Shakespeare's time started business in their
" round O's " (built, as the " Rose " was by Phil Henslowe,
as a speculation), molested in every way by the city
authorities, they again could only survive under the pro-
tection of some noble—as "the Earl of Worcester's men "
or " the Lord Admiral's."

Chambers says on the subject of the status of the players :
" Its constitution [that of a company of players] had a
mediæval element, by which the derivation of playing from
minstrelsy is strongly recalled. The nature of the licence
which it must hold, at any rate if it desired to secure itself
from the arbitrary discretion of local justices, was determined by statute. And this licence, whether it took the

form of a warrant from a nobleman with the confirmation of the Master of the Revels, or of a royal licence by patent, was always such as to set up a relation of service between the company and a " lord." Nor is this relation to be dismissed as a mere empty formality. Probably the players of many country nobles and gentlemen continued to the end to consist of the ordinary household servants, who played only at Christmas and other times of recreation, and mainly at their lord's expense. With the regular travelling companies, and particularly with the London companies, it was different. Financially, at least, they were independent. But even of these the " service," though largely a legal fiction, was not wholly so. The Statute of Retainers, kept alive by the Proclamations of 1572 and 1582, forbade the maintenance of retainers who were not in some real sense household servants.

The players " wore the lord's livery and bore his badge. A practice of offering up a prayer for the lord's well-being at the end of a performance was probably of ancient derivation, although whether it survived in the public theatres may perhaps be doubted. There are instances, moreover, which suggest that, if the lord had need of players for the celebration of a wedding or other festivity, it was to his own servants that he would naturally turn. Thus Leicester had his company with him on his expedition to the Netherlands in 1585."

CHAPTER IV

ITALY AND EUROPE

THE english clown, the pugnacious pierrot of the circus, is a figure familiar in other countries. Charlie Chaplin, the only creative personality that the cinema has produced for itself (coming in its first days, before superproduction changed, in standardizing it, the character of the screen play), was the swan-song of the english clown. The political colour of Chaplin's creation was identical with the old spirit of the circus clown. That personage had as a foil the dignified boss of the circus, whip in hand, whom it was his task to circumvent and "score off." Thus he provided the public with a traditional version of the war of Capital and Labour, Authority and Anarchy.

The elizabethan actor was originally an acrobat as much as a player, and his physical strength and dexterity made him a favourite with foreign audiences as well as english. Bands of english actors, doubling their trade as players with that of "instrumentalist," morris-dancer, clown or acrobat, resembling in that the Italians, took their art over the frontiers of countries which were not at the time accustomed to regard the English as a nation lost to anything but a dull oblique rapacity joined to a frigid moralizing.

In Germany for instance, in Shakespeare's time, the repertory of plays was partly english: a *Hamlet, Prince of Denmark*, a *Titus Andronicus*, and a *Romeo and Juliet* were played there. Between 1590 and 1620 Robert Browne took over relays of actors to Germany. Fynes Moryson, a Cambridge student travelling in Germany, describes how, at the Frankfort fair, "both men and women flocked wondering to see their [the english players] gesture and action, rather than hear them speaking english, which they understood not." *Gammer Gurton's Needle*, and some plays of Marlowe, were given at Frankfort in 1592.

Louis XIV., in 1604, then four years old, sees the english players who have come to perform at the french court : and afterwards " se prendre à parler, disant : ' Tiph, toph, milord : et marchant à grands pas.' " There appears to be no record of their having gone to Italy ; nor is that very likely, as taking coals to Newcastle is not a business proposition : and the Italians would have been as amused at elizabethan pseudo-italian diabolics, though not so patient and pleased, as they were with the carolingian heroics of the strolling minstrels of that time.

Contrariwise the Italians never got a foothold in England, as they did in France. They came occasionally : from Mantua representatives of the *commédia dell' arte* (comedies and somersaults) arrived in the seventies and eighties of the sixteenth century. A Martinelli came in 1578. In 1573 the lord mayor of London was duly horrified at the "unchaste shamelesse and unnaturall tumblinge of the italian women."

But the italian influence came into the english theatre not, as in France, by the establishment of italian companies, or in technical example, via the *métier* of the actor, but rather through the influencing of the playwrights by italian models. But in general the influence of Italy was, in England as elsewhere, immense : and it is to that subject that I now will turn.

If celtic chivalry provided the feudal nobility, pre-eminently of France, with a soul and background of legend, Italy provided the worldly and brilliant age of centralized government, succeeding feudalism, with its art, manners and ideas of life—of a very different order. In Shakespeare, as in the more typical and explicit drama of Cervantes, you see the Roman and the " Celt " (*cf.* Appendix) fighting for ascendancy.

It was in the beginning of the fourteenth century in Italy, too, that a parallel, and in one sense an opposite, movement to that on which Dante set his seal by his great poem in the vernacular was started. The movement of the classical revival, or renaissance, resulted in a greater respect and more living interest than formerly in the classic tongues—latin and greek. But at the same time, with the invention of printing, and the increasingly secular spirit flourishing in the rich italian city democracies, although more people busied themselves with scholarship, and as compared with the preceding age, the scholarship became otherwise scientific, the popular spirit gained ground.

Shakespeare is a phenomenon of vulgarization. If it had not been for Poggio Bracciolini, and the other codex-hunters, Shakespeare would not have existed as we know him. Poggio, or Pope Nicholas, founding the Vatican Library, is part of the personality of Shakespeare; all this italian intellectual ferment heated and civilized the north sufficiently for things to be created and acted in London as though it were for the moment a magical city in a Mediterranean island. It is not certain that Morgante was not necessary for the pupping of Caliban. Alberti—with his ball-playing, sculpting, dancing, engineering, trick horse-riding, painting, love-making, vulgarizing, fortress-planning —was an essential part of the Shakespeare scene. It is all one incandescence.

It was to " celtic " England that feudal Europe was indebted intellectually and imaginatively. The gothic continental world, twelfth and thirteenth century feudal France, reacted of course, on England : but it was partly the debtor of England, and indeed that for its trump card, chivalry. So the ascendancy in that time was " celtic "— that is to say, politically, english. Pulci and Boiardo, with their comic epics, if their work was used by an english playwright, were only returning, in a sense, to the place from which it was originally launched, the " celtic " stuff of earlier romance.

The flower of european civilization — and the only portion of it that can hold its own for a moment against the productions of the East, or of asiatic or egyptian antiquity—is to be found in the italian renaissance. The schools of painting of Northern Italy, from Giotto onward, contain scores of significant names ; the rest of Europe only a handful in comparison. The power and perfection of the italian work has never been equalled elsewhere in Europe. But this great flourishing period of culture was still, as such things have always been in Europe, a kind of breathless dilettantism. With a pathetic haste, and in a worldly competitive rush, these few generations of men trod on the heels of each other's achievements. They brought to birth gigantic and disparate masterpieces, which had too little congruity with the life around them. Tintoretto would paint his huge canvases in two days, and these wall-paintings are full of imposing architectures that did not exist, and were placed in surroundings that they dwarf, or that do not suit them. No sooner was some great task started than it was assailed, and the first man to whom it was given superseded, or he was presented with a baffling multitude of colleagues. St Peter's, in Rome, engaged the attention from start to finish of such different personalities as Bramante, Michelangelo, Raphael, Cellini, Peruzzi, Sangallo Fontana, Maderna and Bernini. This haste (which a recent authority shows extended to the construction of its many buildings, vast blocks of stone imitated by the superposition of smaller stones upon each other, and by a disguising of the sutures ; or by a lavish imitation of materials where the real thing could not be obtained in time, or was beyond the means of the patron) gave the sudden renaissance flowering the appearance of a theatrical entertainment. The society for which it was organized was not secure enough or deeply enough established to give it such an immemorial foundation as is required by the perfect productions of such a culture as that of China or Egypt. In the baroque of the jesuit counter-revolution it lapsed without disguise into an immense theatrical display, hardly more solid than the scenery of a ballet or court entertainment. It rose frothing but stark into a false imperialistic opulence, whose charm was its grimacing untruth, in which the *beauty of vulgarity* was patented, and which we weakly parody to-day.

Always these bursts of dilettante culture in Europe grow feebler and shorter ; they are cut short by wars ; or a little shifting of the political centre, and they snuff out. The death or failure of a single individual is enough to give them a mortal blow wherever they occur. They have nothing behind them, they are an affair of *individuals*, fortuitously cropping up where favourable circumstances for a moment present themselves. They are not more concrete than the pictures made by words, they are literary purely. Their little heroic attempt at "civilization" is played against an alien background, with whose life, progressively diminishing in significance, they have no connexion.

But of these revivals the italian renaissance came nearest being the real thing, and gave Europe its only, and probably its last, opportunity to match itself seriously in the fields of art and civilization with the older cultures. And this movement of classical revival, and adaptation of Greece and Rome to a "modern" environment, produced some specifically european art forms and plastic conceptions, not unfortunately given any *suite* or perpetuated. The mixed population of renaissance Italy certainly produced a mass of work in building and all the concrete arts superior to anything roman. But still they must be regarded as the continuation of Rome. The augustan critic, Vetruvius, was the canon of the renaissance architect: and roman art, preserved in wall-painting, gems and medals, is reproduced, with a difference, in the "golden age" of the renaissance—that is to say, the period coinciding with the unearthing of the full archæological material required for the imitative expansion of this period. Raphael died from a fever contracted while he was superintending excavations in Rome : but by that time the documentation was complete. At the beginning of the fifteenth century Poggio only knows of six statues recovered from roman antiquity at Rome. But before long the reconstruction was effected. Renaissance art must thus be regarded from the *school* point of view as a continuation of roman art.

That in the art of the renaissance, with the encouragement of a line of cultivated and ambitious popes, the secular pagan spirit did really come to life again is certain. Even the harsh and masculine strength of the oldest Romans seemed to come up, as though through a suddenly opened *mundus*, for a moment. Michelangelo is like a tremendous throw-back to the roman past. With his harsh energy and worship of power he is an ideal roman, even to the insensitiveness and harsh emptiness of his statues, and the immense athleticism of his genii and pictures of the *Creation* or the *Judgment*. The psychological kinship of the primitive roman stock with the Norseman is illustrated in these gigantic and martial masterpieces, so " northern " in type, so european and so unlike any other non-european art. Of course it could very easily be argued that it was the asiatic element in the italian population that made the exquisite expression of all this possible, and there is much evidence to support anybody relying on ethical explanations. The painting of Venice again is, of course, saturated with the gorgeous impressions derived from the venetian commerce with the East, and the semi-eastern origin of its inhabitants is evident. But the character of much tuscan art makes it easy to class it not only as european, but almost as germanic, whatever means it took to get itself produced.

The polytheism of the saints and the worship of the mother-goddess, that provided subjects for the renaissance painters, the embarking on a sensuous and concrete pagan expression, broke the spell of the abstract fanaticism that had ruled for so long. But at the moment that, once more under roman rulers, Rome declared itself for the old life of the first and only flowering of the northern races, the rest of Europe, too far from the cultural sources, organized that barren Reform, that here in England only allowed twenty or thirty years of precarious life to the great elizabethan stage, and then closed down on it for good.

The last great pagan goddess, descended ultimately from Helena, the mistress of Simon Magus, a gnostic *æon*, can still be worshipped best in the pictures of Leonardo or Luini. There she is " imprisoned " in the loveliest matter that has ever been discovered for a northern goddess. But in every way this strange ebullition of a race seeking refreshment in its wonderful origins produced a human type particular to Europe, but only expressed by Italy. Its very robust and concrete physiology has not been insisted on as it might. The byzantine asceticism and stiffness suddenly gives way before the tide of normal animal life and superb vitality.

Raphael's Madonnas are healthy massive country girls; Luini's celebrated Madonna is the essence of divine candour and simplicity ; Titian's Venuses are very opulent animals indeed. Michelangelo's, Mantegna's or Tintoretto's people are superb types of aryan heavyweights. If you compare these figures with the male figures of the Ajanta caves, the unmuscular male Egyptian of antiquity or the clumsy, bearded warrior-dwarf of mesopotamian art, you see how Italy also represented the type of european male in its full magnificence. There are, of course, many exceptions where chlorotic beauties, and emaciations of a delicate perversity, occur ; but on the whole it is very noticeable how healthy and physically successful the type represented in italian renaissance art is : probably, excepting the greek and the negro, the most normally balanced physical human type of which we have a record. Even the portraits of the nobles are of very solid nobles ; very energetic, like a fresh aristocracy, in its first generations ; with little of the french or Stuart fineness and fastidious grace or the dreamy blue pallor of Gainsborough's delicate oligarchs. It would seem almost, to look at these pictures, as though all the animal health of Europe, too, has flowed up from the latin soil.

The extent of the literary indebtedness of England especially to this well-head of life need not be insisted on. In another place I have gone very thoroughly into that. But the entire european stage is indebted to Italy : the *commédia dell' arte*, imposing itself on the french taste, made it possible for french comedy to exist. Molière was an italian-trained playwright ; as an actor he had an italian actor for master. One could multiply this indebtedness of Europe to Italy indefinitely.

It was the greek mind, operating in the græco-roman

mixture, that helped to destroy the roman element, as once before it had done. There had been something always in Greece that had never existed in Rome, which did not become merged or transformed, and which was as active as ever, once both these systems were dug up and once more given life for a moment.

The most roman thing about the Greeks, their gymnasium and sporting ideal, combined with the roman one of law and conquest, found together a more responsive soil in England than elsewhere. But the scepticism and spirit of inquiry of the Greeks broke up the roman efficiency of which this athleticism was an ally.

No better type of the semi-roman mind developed freely in England could be imagined than Sir Isaac Newton. Space with him became a plan of massive highways : the celestial bodies circulated as safely as possible in the henceforth well-disciplined and blandly illuminated universe. The health and athleticism of a sane exterior life observed in the plastic thought of Italy is a proper accompaniment for newtonian laws of matter. And even with Newton the direct initiative came from Galilei. The power of lucid order with which this great Italian bound up the less experimental, less " scientific " discoveries of Copernicus and others, found in Newton its culmination. A roman peace reigned in physical science for two hundred years after this great series of calm imperial fiats had regulated the visible universe.

To-day, as though the never-properly-silenced paradoxes of the greek sophists had been released once more, or all the perplexing questions of the mind (allied with new forces of nature and their troubling physical interpretations) had been marshalled for its overthrow, the imposing newtonian structure is no longer secure. Quite another type of order has set about charting the universe and its world-ways.

On the one hand to-day we have Newton's superseded structure (still there and still *useful*, though nothing more, or a " beautiful myth " if you like)—a material universe ruled by immutable grandly conceived roman laws of absolute space and time. In opposition to it rises a universe far more vivid, co-ordinated from the infinite facets of individual experience. In the first, the newtonian system of classical mechanics, each man is ruled by the changeless laws of the revolving suns. A musical ride of the spheres (with music by Kepler) is in progress. In the second, the system of the Relativity theory, to a complex geodesic frame of flowering events each man contributes his widow's mite of necessary reality.

So the fine order of our civilized ideas is in disarray. The façade put up by our very practical, very roman grandfathers is cracked from top to bottom. With the triumph of this subtler science the day of anglo-saxon, and generally of west european, ascendancy is finished. In the day of Shakespeare the anglo-saxon ascendancy was just beginning. Yet the art of the theatre, of which he was the great ornament, perished immediately at its hands ; the commonwealth—not the court of Elizabeth and the tudor stage —giving the cue to the intervening anglo-saxon life with which we are familiar.

But long before Shakespeare's time England was being italianized. Henry VIII. used in everything italian models, and was himself surrounded by Italians. His " master of ceremonies, his foreign secretaries, his artists, musicians and actors, were all Italians, as was the architect of his father's tomb and the chief historian of his father's reign." The magnificence of Cardinal Wolsey was on the same italian model. The statecraft of Thomas Cromwell was to the letter machiavellian doctrine. Sir Thomas More translated the *Life of Pico della Mirandola* that it might be an example for Englishmen as to how to live. The tudor courtier conducted his disputes and duelling according to the precepts of Guazzo and Saviolo. Few of the gentlemen of Elizabeth's court were unable to speak Italian. Elizabeth herself was an excellent linguist. On one occasion, it is reported, the entire assembly of Elizabeth's ministers conducted a negotiation with the venetian ambassador in his native tongue.

Earlier still, italian engineers had been constantly

employed by the english government for the founding of cannon, and whenever scientific skill was needed in the appliances of war. And, both in art and in science, italian ascendancy in France was as great as in England. François I. surrounded himself as much as Henry VIII. with italian artists, especially in the latter part of his reign at Fontainebleau: Rosso, Primaticcio and Cellini being among the italian workmen employed constantly by him. We find in France again the same reliance on italian engineers for the scientific side of war. Piero Strozzi and Marini were the engineers employed by the Duke of Guise in his famous defence of Metz against Charles-Quint. When, later, Guise decides to take Calais back from the English, he sends Strozzi, in disguise, to report on the state of its defences. This was in the reign of Henri II. : but the italian influence became still more marked as time went on.

It was the famous " free captains " of Italy who created the new art of war : Alberico da Barbiano is the first name in modern warfare as opposed to mediæval, and all the new european states were compelled thereafter to transform their military systems—or such as they had up till then possessed—on these more scientific models, turning them into the mass-structures of modern armies.

It was above all, and in the first place, as men of science that the Italians imposed themselves on Europe. Later, with the renaissance, came their pictorial and applied art. And their political philosophy came hand-in-hand with their canons of elegance and the social arts. But it was with natural science and engineering that they first recommended and established themselves. Throughout the period of their ascendancy, whether as architects, politicians, conversationalists, men of letters, or what not, it was always as *men of science* in one sense or another—as people applying to those various tasks a scientific method and intelligence—that they must be regarded.

The uses to which science is put, like the uses of wealth, depend of course upon the disposition of its possessor. In Italy itself, its home, it took a humanistic form. Not only were men like Alberti and Leonardo at once men of science and painters, architects and sculptors ; but *science* was understood as a universal principle of exact experiment. As much in the painting of a picture as in the construction of a fortification, the artist *and* the man of science would appear. Modern science was therefore not, in its earliest italian phase, a thing to cut the world in two : into human and non-human ; the " scientific " and the " non-scientific." The conduct of a business negotiation, the deciphering of a codex, the painting of a picture, arranging a cavalry attack, courting a sharp-witted woman, choosing a doublet or making a thermometer, were all on one plane of reasoned effort, objects of exact analysis, offering the intelligence a similar delight.

Coluccio Salutati, secretary of the florentine republic (1375), was " the first to write diplomatic and business documents like works of art, and he wrote them with singular success. Galeazzo Maria Visconti is said to have declared himself more afraid of one of Salutati's letters than of a thousand florentine knights ; and it is an undoubted fact that, when the republic was at war with the pope, the letters written by Salutati . . . had the effect of stirring to revolt, in the name of liberty, many territories belonging to the Church. . . .

" And Salutati's work had very noteworthy consequences even in the future. The enlistment of literature in the service of politics increasingly bound up the former with the public life of the Florentines, and prepared the way for a radical transformation in the latter. . . . This led by gradual steps to the political science of Machiavelli and Guicciardini, that owes to learning not a few of its merits. . . ." (Villari).

So with the increasing wealth and power of the democratic italian city-states an entirely new type of mind gradually substituted itself throughout Europe for the feudal mind—a scientific one, concrete and realistic. In place of the dreams and abstractions of the " celtic " mind, which were unable to express themselves exteriorly at all, except in music, you get the pictures and sculptures of tuscan and venetian artists, the experimentalism of

Leonardo and Alberti, and the great practical achievements of Galilei or Toricelli. The obscenity of Panormita and Poggio (which is generally regarded, censoriously, as exhibiting the " bad side " of the classical ardour of reunion with Greece and Rome) could surely be regarded rather as the high spirits of the low-born of the feudal age (as of any age, and which had always existed) promoted into the regions of classical scholarship and debate : the learned exploitation of a popular art, rather than the creation of a new one. It was much more the people who, in this democratic time, had corrupted the scholars, than the wicked scholars who were corrupting the innocent people. Poggio, for instance, in his *Invectives*, abuses his literary antagonist, and is abused in turn, like a fishwife—only in the purest latin. In Poggio's case this can of course be regarded as the high spirits of a very successful codex-hunter, and of a fine man of letters savouring the violent picturesqueness, as Rabelais did, of popular speech, and juggling with all the grossness of the gutter in the horseplay in which the learned, when they have occasion to be pleased with life, are apt to indulge. The theory that Poggio should not have used such disgusting language in a beautiful villa, surrounded with the lovely objects of the collector, is a stupid one, I think : but it is part of the great system of shocked astonishment which for long has been the only recognized manner of approach for the historian to this very favoured period of history.

The flowering of the feudal age, characterized by the *chansons de geste* and the *fabliaux*, could be described as the " celtic " period in Europe. That was the age of romance, of exaltation of the sexual passion, of aristocratic love and its accompanying poetry. Its theatre was France, although one of its most powerful impulses was derived, as we shall see, from the small " celtic " countries—Wales, Brittany and Ireland. And the epoch that the italian renaissance inaugurated can be described most accurately as an epoch of science. It is in terms of science that the italian renaissance should be properly regarded.

Instead of the chivalrous bravery of the *preux*, the

isolated hero of the " celtic " dream, you get the large dis-
ciplined armies of centralized governments, and the devices
of the italian engineers. It was science that mediæval and
renaissance Italy was teaching Europe, as, to some extent,
Rome had done earlier.

Without Italy it is unlikely that Watts would have invented the locomotive, any more than a Tasmanian or an
Esquimaux. Italy is so " artistic," and so full of museums,
of renaissance pictures and beautiful buildings, that it is
usually forgotten how much more scientific and commercial
the renaissance Italians were than " artistic " even. They
were indeed everything—except " celtic." And we have
to-day every opportunity of observing how necessary it is
that science should be associated with other faculties, and
not be allowed to remain in its pure state. The italian
man of science was an artist as well : but the people to
whom he taught his science—the populations especially of
largely germanic blood—usually were not. They became
men of science, but did not become artists—which is very
unfortunate, as, in the sequel, has been proved by the
Anglo-Saxon and the German.

The magnificent display of plastic and pictorial art of
renaissance Italy has dazzled the senses so much that
the western mind is apt to forget the general truth of how
much science there is in the first place in the arts of architecture, painting and sculpture ; and so, how the italian
population of the time was pre-eminently practical, commercial and scientific, and *therefore* " artistic," it should
perhaps be said ; although that is a very difficult conclusion
for the contemporary European to understand.

The contradiction most insisted on in any historical
survey of this period is that of the beauty of the art on the
one hand, and the badness and corruption of the society
on the other. But there is another contrast which provokes in a quieter way as much surprise, only as it is not
accompanied by a sensation of horror and scandal it is
not usually insisted on so much. That other contrast is
the contrast between the " artist " activities of many
renaissance men and the " scientific " activities which they

carried on simultaneously. Leonardo da Vinci is the most eminent example of this supposed anomaly. These misunderstandings are of a piece, and should be regarded as twins. It is the false interpretation that the North European gave to science that made him separate it from its " artistic " envelope or social skin : that part of science that gives science a meaning, in short. At present this is beginning to be seen ; but so many interests are ranged against its evulgation that it is likely to become an academically accepted principle only, disregarded in practice. What in all probability will in the end become the officially accepted version will be somewhat as follows. "The Italians were so immoral," it will be said, "because they were so 'artistic.'" Now that science has been separated from and purged of art, it is possible to be scientific and highly moral at the same time. Were art reinstated as a recognized part of the scientific impulse, without which science were admitted to be meaningless, then we should slide back into the antique mud of our beginnings.

In reality the names associated in our minds with the most violent corruption, like that of Borgia, represent people using merely all the high activities of the renaissance for their own purposes, of the most ordinary description ; not at all peculiar to renaissance Italy, but found in every time and place. Indeed, as Professor Muntz says, mediæval Italy was at the least as corrupt as renaissance Italy. The corruption of manners at the time of the renaissance was not at all new. It was only the " renaissance " that was new. Such classic scandals as that of Pope Joan, who gave birth to a child while engaged on some church function, are a picturesque reminder of the state of affairs in the Dark Ages, half way between the roman decadence and the renaissance decadence.

Even the mass of scholars and philosophers, some of whom have given a handle to the enemies of the intelligence by their rather second-rate rabelaisian high spirits, were very few of them remarkable at all, as Villari took so much trouble to point out. The transactions of the platonic academy were characterized, except in the case of Ficino, by a surprising absence of intellectual resource ; and, for all the enthusiasm spent in and around it, nothing new was said or done. And to place against the murders and incests of the Borgias, you have the disgust of the greatest men of that time, the Michelangelos and Savonarolas, in whom these murders and incests, the general absence of good faith, public and private, and the extinction of political liberty that eventually ensued, produced a truer disgust and despair than that of the subsequent historical expert.

When italian science first captured Europe, however, it came hand-in-hand with, or enveloped in, the forms of art : taught by Italians, it was taught as art. They taught the social arts and the fine arts at the same time as their practical discoveries. This polished life was accepted and eagerly copied ; and France adopted the polish and maintained it, whereas with the English the polish was of less account than the machinery that produced it.

The French are usually thought of as a naturally *polished* nation : though of course, in fact, they got all their polish from Italy at this period. Feudal France must have been especially uncouth. The natural grace of the Valois facilitated the process of social sophistication : but the original Gaul, prior to this, was at least as rough and violent as his neighbours, or as those Russians whom Peter the Great decreed should have their hair cut before entering a town. And just as the polish has been more successfully retained in France, so in the french countryside, better perhaps than elsewhere in Western Europe, the savagery these italian graces superseded can to-day be observed intact.

PART II
MACHIAVELLI

CHAPTER I

THE OPPOSITE EXPERIENCES OF POGGIO AND THE ENGLISH MILORD

ENGLAND manufactured an art of her own with a breathless rapidity under the fecundation of the renaissance. It was of a far more ambitious description than the *commédia dell' arte*. It was not a cunning amusement, politely acrobatic, full of the measured sobbing of the civilized clown, but unexpectedly wild, providing the renaissance with its primitive antiquity. It was a new and rude but remarkable people expressing their destiny under a foreign and ultimately greek stimulus, and providing M. de Voltaire, later on, also, with something to discover, a new great-people, expressed by a new barbaric great-poet.

The elizabethan play is indeed so savage, and in that sense childlike, that no english audience to-day can get any meaning or pleasure out of it. For our deliberate child-obsession to-day, and worship of infancy, is in the same category as the traditional interest taken in flappers by the elderly gentleman, or as King David's desire for a youthful body to warm his bed and keep his old blood moving round. It is the very opposite of the primitive and the simple. The elizabethans, with their worship of adventure, of the terrible *male* italian tiger, of braggadocio and coarse fun, were the real children. That is, of course, not the sort of childhood that we worship—but rather an insipid and civilized variety : and the elizabethans are altogether too childish for us. But the italianate *Faithful Shepherdess* of Fletcher, on the other hand, is too civilized for the average contemporary english audience : for there is civilization and civilization, as there is child and child. And we are not so much civilized as fatigued, stereotyped and inert, A stiffness, partly of the old puritan

59

pasteboard, and partly of age, is beneath most english
shirt-fronts, whatever the physiological age of the wearer,
at an average play ; or else its wearer is relaxed to some
snobbish decay. The mind of the same playgoer has been
drilled out of, and watered down from, other franknesses
as well. It is no longer a possible earth for such wild seeds
as the tragedies of Webster or Shakespeare. At the most
the moneyed crust of our time affects a pedantically cynical
wildness that is often whorish enough, but so overlaid with
a sweetening of sentiment (just as its rendering of childhood
will run essentially to the insipid) that its representative
is able to rival in repulsiveness the miltonic prude. The
version of a *Faithful Shepherdess*, in short, that the contemporary english Chloe provides, is as revolting as any
version of *Comus* must of necessity be : so that you will
be inclined to think that in such natures *the natural* is
for ever extinct, oscillating in a " moral "—" immoral "
see-saw, either extremity matched in an unalterable
dreariness of caption, something like a duty presiding at
both ends.

"We are told on high authority," says Swinburne, in
his foreword to Middleton's plays, that " the greatest glory
of England is her literature " and that " the greatest glory
of english poetry lies rather in its dramatic than its epic or
its lyric triumphs."

The first statement, to begin with, has an unreal sound ;
for England's political history would not encourage such
an expectation. The unprecedented material success of
the English must overshadow, rather than advertise, their
intellectual triumphs. But that the English—traditionally
so close, cold, silent and immature as compared to their
famous neighbours—should excel in dramatic literature
especially, seems even more to require some explanation.
"How is it that Italy at the renaissance did not produce
a great theatre of tragic masterpieces to match the italian
pictorial production ? " might be asked. " For are not the
Italians peculiarly adapted to ' passionate ' expression ;
active, fiery, intelligent, with a vast armoury of coloured
and expressive gesture belonging to them, handed down

from father to son; passionately fond of spectacles; their lives traditionally seething with vendettas, running into bloody tragedy much more readily than english life can ever have done? "

No doubt many things contributed to this; but there is one generalization that, although it requires the complicity, to make it live, of a great many factors (without any one of which, indeed, it might have been inoperative), can be insisted on as the principle of this paradox. The natural astonishment at the existence of this wonderful drama wildly leaping up in England at the opening of the modern period will be dispelled if it is regarded as a phenomenon of infancy. This generalization, it is unnecessary to say, does not apply to all great tragic expression; but it certainly applies to some extent to the tudor stage. It is because, precisely, the English were not " born artists," as we say of the Italians as a people; because they were very near to a savage condition, very fresh to life, especially to the civilized life of the renaissance, that this great art occurred. It was because that vivid and dramatic life was not going on to the same extent off the stage in England that it occurred on the stage so naturally. The english public were in the nature of (distant) spectators of this wild italian reality. Wicked, hot, diabolically cruel, romantic and so forth, this distant cynical ebullience seemed to them. The dumb, clumsy and cold (all these predicates meant relatively) english nature, repressed by climate—distant from the source of life, culture and light —vented itself in mimic violence, in " passionate southern love," gasconades, terrible revenges, marvellous intricacies of " policy," in its fifty years of dramatic dreaming. Shakespeare was England's greatest dreamer, and he dreamed somewhat to order. So the machiavellian nightmare necessarily occupied an important place in his art.

The gentlemen who watched *Romeo and Juliet* or the *Duchess of Malfi* presented in their native town, written by native playwrights who had never been out of England, must have been very critical of the italian local colour, as of so much else about these plays which must have seemed absurd to them. They would especially appreciate the diabolism emanating in reality from themselves, brought back with them from the source of all tudor *chic*, although no doubt laughing a great deal at it.

" We can imagine," Vernon Lee writes, " how the innumerable english travellers who went to Italy greedy for life and knowledge, or merely obeying fashion . . . how the italian clothes, rehearsing italian steps and collecting italian oaths, the Faulconbridges of Shakespeare, Mr Gingleboys of Beaumont and Fletcher, sent to Italy to be able gracefully to

> " ' *Kiss the hand and cry " sweet lady !* "
> *Say they had been at Rome and seen the relics ;*
> *Drunk your Verdea wine, and rid at Naples* ' :*

how all these privileged creatures ferreted about for monstrous crimes with which to horrify their stay-at-home countrymen ; how the rich young lords, returning home with mincing steps and high-pitched lisp, surrounded by a train of parti-coloured, dialect-jabbering venetian clowns, deft and sinister neapolitan fencing-masters, silver-voiced singing boys decoyed from some church, and cynical humanists escaped from the faggot or the gallows, were expected to bring home, together with the newest pastoral drama, lewd novels, platonic philosophy and madrigals set in complicated counterpoint, stories of hideous wickedness and of the murders and rapes and poisonings committed by the dukes and duchesses, the nobles and senators, in whose palaces they had so lately supped and danced."

But these " privileged " travelling English would still be, from the point of view of the Italian, provincials. The English had from the start, in Europe, their evil reputation for enormous dullness, as a community. This is, for instance, Poggio's experience as a traveller—in the opposite sense—the Italian in England :

" In England, however, while with Cardinal Beaufort, he found himself isolated in the company of wealthy uncultured nobles, who passed the chief part of their life in eating and drinking. During those dinners, which sometimes lasted four hours, he was obliged to rise from time to time and bathe his eyes with cold water, in order to keep himself awake . . . the novelty of the country and the variety of customs and characters, all of which he noticed and which occupied his mind, were not sufficient recompense for the slight account in which the learned were held there, and he, therefore, sighed for his native land " (Villari).

We are reminded of the disobliging opinion expressed by David Hume, the philosopher, a couple of centuries later, of the english nation : his reasons identical with Poggio's.

CHAPTER II

MACHIAVELLI IN ELIZABETHAN DRAMA

THE master figure of elizabethan drama is Machiavelli. He was only known through the french of Gentillet, if that : but he was the great character of supreme intrigue that, however taken, was at the back of every tudor mind. Elizabethan drama—" the first terror-stricken meeting of the England of Elizabeth with the Italy of the late renaissance "—was more terrified of Machiavelli than of anybody. The Borgias, Sforzas, Baglionis, Malatestas, Riartes were of far more importance to the elizabethan dramatists than any of their own eminent countrymen. Familiarity bred contempt in the long run. But during its flourishing period the english stage went constantly to the schoolmaster of manslaughter, Machiavelli—and his political paradigms chosen in conformity with his Borgia worship—for its thrills.

Had there been thirty years ago in Europe a theatre as impressionable and active as the elizabethan, it is certain that we should have had a body of plays reflecting the human-all-too-human doctrines of Nietzsche, with " aristocratic " supermen in the principal rôles.

Mr Bernard Shaw, it is true, produced a " Superman," of sorts ; but his Superman was dressed in Jaeger underclothing and ate nuts, instead of being a blond beast, its jaws dripping with human blood. The nietzschean frenzy was queerly translated into the genial posing and prosing of a victorian literary puppet, rendered excessively voluble through the " celtic " bias. Certainly no galvanizing horror could possibly be extracted from that or any other figure of Mr Shaw's : the inveterate cackle of the dialogue would alone preclude any thrill. The strangely unreal geniality and playfulness in *St Joan*, again (that seems written to be played by a cast of elderly anglican curates),

64

is a deadly atmosphere for such a heroic subject, of course, and produces a most painful effect. Indeed, as it was presented first in London, it was difficult to escape from the feeling that most of the actors—with all their very "kindly" but, of course, mischievouşly twinkling eyes, and breezy, capable manners—were not in reality of a more elevated calling than that of an actor ; and that for some reason they had decided—attracted perhaps by the " religious " nature of the subject—to take part in that performance.

In any case when Nietzsche came there was no great european theatre—the Scandinavians having produced the last effective thing of that sort : and so the super-humanity influences found other outlets—even such inappropriate ones as Mr Shaw was able to provide—on the principle, probably, of " any port in a storm." Machiavelli, on the other hand, three centuries earlier, was much better served, and precisely in England of all places.

Apart from the theatre, however, Nietzsche had nothing to complain about. Europe was deeply affected by his doctrines, and found a better way, perhaps—certainly a more sensational one—of giving them effect—namely, in real life. In France they were given hospitality by a crowd of writers—Remy de Gourmont is an instance : in Italy Marinetti and Papini collected them ; and many vitalist strongholds ran up the flag of the *Ubermensch*. And—without necessarily dramatizing the central conception, or making operas of Zarathustra—everywhere people were saturated with these bird-of-prey, ruthless, " a-moral " ethics.

Before all that—and in a sense the father of it—was the great shadow of Bonaparte, who provided England with her biggest " scare " since the Armada, and impressed on Europe the image of the type of gigantic material success he symbolized. From his commissariat officer, Stendhal, to the Wall-Street millionaire, this picture of relentless personal aggrandisement served as model.

Mr Edward Meyer has catalogued three hundred and ninety-five references to Machiavelli in elizabethan literature. As to his influence in England, Dr Grosart wrote :

THE LION AND THE FOX

" I have suggested to the biographer of the renowned Machiavelli (Professor Villari of Florence) that an odd chapter might be written on the *scare* his name was for long in England : so much so that he came to be regarded as an incarnation of the Evil One himself."

If three hundred and ninety-five direct references can be found to Machiavelli in elizabethan literature, it is everywhere steeped in his philosophy and what his philosophy represented. Webster, Massinger, Ford, Marston, Tourneur, Middleton are all indebted to him so heavily that either in the form of revulsion or delight they could be called the children of Machiavelli. *The Unnatural Combat, Women beware Woman, Antonio and Mellida, The Insatiate Countess, The Changeling, The Revenger's Tragedy,* etc., would not have existed in the form in which they did without the showmanship and propagandist zeal of Machiavelli.

Marston was the first eminent machiavellian. He was entirely subjugated. The following lines can be cited as examples of his machiavellism :

> " Why, by the genius of that Florentine,
> Deepe, deepe observing, sound brain'd Machevell,
> He is not wise that strives not to seem fool."

This will recall Iago's profession :

> " For when my outward action doth demonstrate
> The native act and figure of my heart
> In compliment extern, 'tis not long after
> But I will wear my heart upon my sleeve
> For daws to peck at : I am not what I am."

Iago is a typical elizabethan *Machiavel*. With him we can associate, as among the best known, Barabas, Aaron, Eleazar, Angelo and Mendoza (in *The Malcontent*). A remark of the latter is among the most full-blooded of the elizabethan machiavellisms, and also relates Machiavelli, in its bombast, to Nietzsche :

> " We that are great, our sole self-good still moves us."

Meyer insists on the influence exercised over Marlowe

MACHIAVELLI IN ELIZABETHAN DRAMA

by Machiavelli. And his successors, Greene, Shakespeare, Jonson, Marston and Webster, inherited this.

Nash, in his *Unfortunate Traveller*, exhibits with great fervour the prevailing fascination. This is his discourse with the " ugly mechanicall Captain " with whom at Turin " it happed me to fall in " :

" Oh my Auditors, had you seene him how he stretcht out his lims, scratcht his scabd elbowes at this speach ; how hee set his cap ouer his ey-browes like a politician, and then folded his armes one in another, and nodded with the head, as who would say, let the French beware for they shall finde me a diuell : if (I say) you had seene but halfe the actions that he vsed, of shrucking vp his shoulders, smiling scornfully, playing with his fingers on his buttons, and biting the lip, you would have laught your face and your knees together. The yron being hot I thought to lay on load, for in anie case I would not have his humour coole. As before I laid open unto him the briefe summe of the service, so now I began to vrge the honorablenes of it, and what a rare thing it was to be a right politician, how much esteemed of kings and princes, and how diuerse of meane Parentage have come to bee Monarchs by it. Then I discourst of the quallities and properties of him in euery respect, how, like Woolfe, he must drawe the breath from a man long before he bee seene, how, like a Hare, he must sleepe with his eyes open, how, as the Eagle in his flying casts dust in the eyes of Crowes and other Fowles for to blinde them, so hee must cast dust in the eyes of his enemies, delude their sight by one meanes or other, that they diue not into his subleties, howe hee must be familliar with all and trust none, drinke, carouse and lecher with him out of whom hee hopes to wring any matter, sweare and for-sweare, rather than bee suspected, and, in a word, haue the Art of dissembling at his fingers' ends as perfect as any Courtier."

And the great *fox and lion* figure which went with this political machiavellian obsession, invariably used to express it, is well illustrated by Nash in the same context :

" Want cannot be withstood, men can do no more than

they can do : what remained then, but the fox's case must help, when the lion's skin is out at the elbows."

But in the long run the English got over their fright, and " saw through Machiavelli "—" Machiavel, thou art an ass ! " (*The Distracted State*) dates from 1641. The English were getting cleverer, It may be that, having suitably diluted his creed for British use, and absorbed him, this " seeing through " would ensue. In *Volpone* (iv. 1) Jonson ridicules the popular scare. Chapman in *All Fooles* ridicules the popular conception of Machiavelli. But while it lasted the rage and counter-rage was immense : and it became a component of all subsequent english psychology, just as the *italian* infatuation has never disappeared.

CHAPTER III

MACHIAVELLI AND THE REFORMATION

BUT Machiavelli, "the bible of the queen-mother" (Catherine de' Medici), the bugbear of the elizabethan stage, was at the same time the great formative influence, at once philosophic and political, throughout Europe; although it was only in England that he found a herd of poets to echo and advertise him. His influence must have been far more potent than that of Nietzsche. His bold ideas, falling on the sensitive and superstitious minds of the people only just out of the dusk of the Middle Ages, full of satanic fancies, had everywhere the greatest repercussion. In 1557 the jesuits burned his works, and the Inquisition decreed their complete destruction. The Council of Trent confirmed the edict of the Inquisition.

Everywhere the vogue (either of repulsion or attraction) was associated with the great religious revolution of the time. Machiavelli was an Italian to begin with, and his chosen hero was the son of the Pope. The movement of revolt against the authority of Rome, denouncing papal abuses and crimes with which the christian spirit, it said, had been utterly polluted, would naturally find in Cesare Borgia, the military and diplomatic champion of the new temporal ambition of the Church, and his outspoken philosophic supporter, material very much to its purpose.

It was from France that England got its Machiavel : and in France the reign of Charles IX. witnessed the greatest act of borgiaism of the renaissance world, the St Bartholomew massacre. That was hatched in the virtual minority of a king directed by an italian mother, Catherine de' Medici.

Protestantism in France seemed on the point of succeeding : the Châtillon faction could rely on a fanaticism superior to the traditional devotion of the supporters of the faith. The events leading up to the massacres in Paris, the alternate capitulations and military resistance of the queen-mother through a number of years, the certainty that the fate of the Crown was implicated with the fortunes of revolutionary church reform, made it difficult to believe that the great assemblage of protestant leaders in Paris, with Coligny at their head, was not the result of a "machiavellian" plan. After so long a period of struggle Catherine de' Medici, it was to be assumed, must have known where she stood with this revolutionary sect. Yet, had not the leaders of the protestant faction been disarmed by her behaviour and that of the king, they would hardly have come and lodged so accommodatingly for the purposes of wholesale execution in a hostile city. And the occasion of their visit—a marriage ostensibly of a protestant prince to a catholic princess—was as good a safe-conduct as, in a civilized society, could be desired.

This terrible super-machiavellian event—if it was machiavellian, as naturally the huguenots believed—staggered the whole of Europe. And the policy of all the later Valois, their grace, their ideas of honour and their particular vices, were for France, as for England, "foreign," in the first place ; and in the second, italian. If it had not been for Machiavelli probably Catherine de' Medici could have effected the Saint-Barthélemy (if she did do so) without anyone regarding it as more than a tragic brawl on an immense scale. It was Machiavelli that revealed in advance, for everyone acquainted with his writings or his legend, the *jeu*. And it was everywhere the papal and the royal interest that was held responsible for machiavellism—since Machiavelli was the great champion of those causes : and all the forces of revolution, both anti-papal and anti-constitutional, would be inclined to magnify the figure of this papal devil, obsessed with the desirability of temporal power, holding up as a model a diabolic Prince.

In England the young courtier, and the playwright depending on the favour of the court, would be disposed to be papal and italian in his sympathy ; but also would no doubt be deeply touched with the revolutionary idealism that so shortly in England would result in the first european

MACHIAVELLI AND THE REFORMATION

revolution in a modern non-feudal state. Between these two emotional poles he would be inclined to vacillate.

A great deal of evidence has also been collected by Mr Edward Meyer relating to Machiavelli's influence in Europe. Two of Meyer's quotations from Goethe—who as a young man seems to have admired Machiavelli very much—are of interest, as the Germany of Goethe's time was somewhat in the same situation as the english italianized romantic school of the beginning of the nineteenth century :

"So ist das Wort der Menschen ein Wort Gottes . . . und mit inniger Seele falle ich dem Bruder um den Hals, Moses, Prophet, Evangelist, Apostel, Spinoza oder Machiavelli" (*1774, from the writer to Lavater*).

"Alles Spinozistische in der poetischen Production wird in der kritischen Reflexion Machiavellismus" (1807, *Tagebuch*).

It was in France that the Machiavelli " scare " seems first to have started, and it was through the *Contre-Machiavel* of Gentillet that he first reached England. The full title of this book (of which *Contre-Machiavel* is the popular name) is " *Discours sur les Moyens de bien gouverner et maintenir en bonne paix un Royaume ou autre Principauté—Contre Nicholas Machiavel, Florentin, 1576.*"

This was translated into english by Simon Patricke in 1577. The first time on the other hand that the book containing Machiavelli's characteristic doctrines was translated into english was 1640. These are the dates of translations of his books into english :

Arte della Guerra (translated by Whitehorne, 1560-1562).

Storia Fiorentina (translated by Bedingfield, 1595).

Discorsi (translated by Dacre, 1636).

Principe (translated by Dacre, 1640).

So it seems fairly certain that it is from Gentillet that most of the elizabethan dramatists would get their notion of Machiavelli. I cannot agree with Edward Meyer that had they been able to read *The Prince* itself their horror would have been turned into enthusiasm, and that they would have recognized how they had misjudged him. But it gives an interest to Gentillet's book ; and if that is really the

THE LION AND THE FOX

source of so much perturbation it is historically of great interest.

Gentillet ascribed to Machiavelli's writings not only the massacre of St Bartholomew but also the whole french policy, from Henry II. to Charles IX. and Henry III., who were generally believed to be well read in "the queen-mother's bible." Gentillet accuses him of having been the author of " Contempt of God, perfidy, sodomy, tyranny, cruelty, pillage, foreign usury and other detestable vices."

Here is a table of Machiavelli's maxims as drawn up by Gentillet, and as read, it seems likely, by Shakespeare and his contemporaries.

Maxims of Part II., treating of the religion appropriate to a prince:

1. A prince, in everything, should try and pass as pious, whether he is so or not.

2. The prince should support what he knows to be false in religion, provided it serves his turn.

3. The beliefs of the pagans disposed them, full of courage and hardihood, to great undertakings: but the christian religion causes people to be humble, weakens their courage and lays them open to attack.

4. The great christian teachers have obstinately sought to stamp out the memory of letters and the civilization of antiquity.

5. When it abandoned the pagan cults, the world became corrupted, and came to believe neither in God nor Devil.

6. The Roman Church is the cause of all Italy's calamities.

7. Moses could never have imposed his laws on his people if his army had failed him.

8. Moses seized Judea, in the same way that the Goths seized part of the Roman Empire.

9. The religion of Numa was the principal cause of the good fortune of Rome.

10. Man is happy so long as fortune is identical with his appetite.

Machiavelli is made by Gentillet for his renaissance contemporaries into something very close to Nietzsche. Sections 3, 6, 7 above are identical with the very keystone and pivot of Nietzsche's political teaching. How the affinity of these two teachers is shown by Marston.

"We that are great, our sole self-good still moves us," has already been referred to. "We that are great" is the voice of Nietzsche, and is accompanied by the core of his reasoning. Gentillet's attack had for its immediate motive to influence the French against the Italians who swarmed everywhere in France: and he pictured them as invariably with this devilish BIBLE in their pocket; just as it was supposed to be the *livre de chevet* of the unpopular italian queen.

Patricke, the english translator of Gentillet's *Contre-Machiavel*, "believed Machiavelli sent from Sathan to France: that he had made a hell of it, where his doctrines were in everyone's mouth."

It will be remembered how in *Henry VI* (Part I., act v., scene 4)—attributed by Swinburne to "the infamous author of *Edward I.*," George Peele—when Joan of Arc claims Alencon as the father of her child, Yorke exclaims:

> "Alencon! that notorious Machiavel!
> It dies, an if it had a thousand lives":

—and the fact that she was supposed to be proposing to bring another Machiavel into the world decided her fate.

This is from Patricke's introduction (quoted by Meyer):

"For then (before the queen-mother brought Machiavelli into France, Sathan being a disguised person amongst the French), in the likenesse of a merrie jester (Rabelais) acted a comoedie, but shortly ensued a wofull Tragoedie. When our countrymen's minds were sick and corrupted with these political diseases, and that discipline waxed stale; then came forth the books of *Machiavel*, a most pernitious writer, which beganne not in secret and stealing manner (as did those former vices) but by open means, and as it were a continual assault, utterly destroyed not this or that vertue, but even all vertues at once: insomuch as it took faith from Princes authoritie and majesty from laws, libertie from the people; and peace and concord from all persons. . . .

"Moreover Sathan useth strangers of France, as his fittest

instruments, to infect us still with this deadly poison sent out of Italy, who have so highly promoted their machiavellian bookes that he is of no reputation . . . which hath not Machiavel's writings at his fingers' ends. . . . Truly it is a wonderful thing to consider how faste that evill weede hath growne within these fewe yeares, seeing that there is almost none that striveth to excell in vertue or knowledge : as though the only way to obtain honour and riches were by this discourse's direction."

By 1609 Machiavelli had been promoted from a proper into a common noun, and is spelt without a capital letter (on the principle of "braggadocio" from the figure in Spenser's *Faerie Queene*). Aretino, sharing this honour with his compatriot, becomes "such aretin"—as who should say "such rice" or "such foolscap." Both had become so important, in short, that they had lost their personalities, and grown into spiritual commodities.

The prodigious scare-cult in a more general way reached its fullest expression in Barnes' *The Divel's Charter*, " a mixture of murder, adultery, incest, homicide, fratricide and sodomy seldom surpassed." I have not read this play, but it will be observed that sodomy is there too ; although for the most part they lag behind in that variety of " frightfulness."

Aretino, the great vagabond blackguard who lived in a venetian palace " by the sweat of his pen," is in no way a *foyer* of interest and excitement, like Machiavelli : but he is so characteristic a renaissance figure that he has his place in even the briefest account of this great intellectual breeding time. In a recently published book (*Pietro Aretino, The Scourge of Princes*, by E. D. Hutton) an interesting résumé is to be found, and the following passage also gives a further picture of the setting that accounts for this particular *fleur du mal* :

" Something evil and corrupt had entered into the civilization of all Europe at this time, and not least Italy. . . . With the fifteenth century we are face to face with the break-up of Europe and european society. Something evil, depraved, venal and mean appears. The pen is bought and sold, futile praise and blame are purchased by popes, kings and prelates, and we see a monster appear, a monster of genius, blackmailing, and blackmailing successfully, every authority, every power. That monster was Aretino. . . . An epoch had appeared which was an anarchy, in which everything was questioned, everything doubtful ; in which anything might happen and anything might be thought to be true : an epoch without principles and without authority : in which a charlatan of genius might do anything, might destroy the unity of Europe or the spiritual and philosophical basis upon which Europe stood, by one multiple weapon—calumny."

So there we have a writer contemporary with us still dealing in renaissance thrills and montrosities : only Aretino is his particular leprous hero.

CHAPTER IV

THE QUALITY OF MACHIAVELLI'S CANDOUR

HOW the diabolical honesty of Nicolò Machiavelli should have shocked the world at large, and earned him an almost infamous notoriety, is easy to understand. Every organized duplicity felt itself unmasked by one of its own servants. It is doubly easy to see how in England the ungentlemanly frankness of this logician should have been regarded as a first-class scandal. Here was a political philosopher, trained in a small-scale imperialistic school amongst the little factious states of Italy, giving away the whole position of the ruler, and revealing even the very nature of all authority. The meaning of all political conquest, and the character of the people engaged in it, transpired with a startling simplicity in the pages of this pedant of crude " power." With Darwin's *Origin of Species*, it is a book that forces civilization to face about and confront the grinning shadow of its Past, and acknowledge the terrible nature of its true destiny. In his cold handbook of the *True Politic Method of Enslavement and 'Expropriation* the real meaning of life by conquest and management, and almost the real meaning in a further analysis of life itself, was shown with that convincing simplicity, in a tone of engaging harmlessness, reminding you of Defoe's style of narration when a cutpurse is speaking. If we compare a few passages from Defoe with passages from Machiavelli we shall understand better the affinity of inner tone in these two voices.

Moll Flanders is describing how she gets away with her first watch:

" The comrade she helped me to dealt in three sorts of craft—viz. shoplifting, stealing of shop-books and pocket-books, and taking of gold watches from the ladies' sides ; and this last she did so dexterously that no woman ever arrived at the perfection of that art like her. I liked the first and the last of these things very well, and I attended her some time in the practice, just as a deputy attends a midwife, without any pay.

"At length she put me to practice. She had shown me her art, and I had several times unhooked a watch from her own side with great dexterity; at last she showed me a prize, and this was a young lady with child, who had a charming watch. The thing was to be done as she came out of the church; she goes on one side of the lady, and pretends, just as she came to the steps, to fall, and fell against the lady with so much violence as to put her into a very great fright, and both cried out terribly: in the very moment that she jostled the lady, I had hold of the watch and, holding it the right way, the start she gave drew the hook out and she never felt it, I made off immediately, and left my school-mistress to come out of her fright gradually, and the lady too; and presently the watch was missed; Ay, says my comrade, then it was those rogues that thrust me down, I warrant ye; I wonder the gentlewoman did not miss her watch before, then we might have taken them."

For the purposes of comparison the fifth chapter of *The Prince* is not too long and is characteristic:

Chapter V

THE WAY TO GOVERN CITIES

WHENEVER those states which have been acquired as indicated above have been accustomed to live under their own laws and in freedom, there are three courses open to those who wish to hold them: the first is to ruin them, the next is to reside there in person, the third is to permit them to live under their own laws, drawing a tribute and establishing within it an oligarchy, which will keep it friendly to you. Because such a government being created by the prince, knows that it cannot stand without his friendship and interest, and does its utmost to support him; and therefore he who would keep a city accustomed to freedom will hold it more easily by the means of its own citizens than in any other way.

There are, for example, the Spartans and the Romans. The Spartans held Athens and Thebes, establishing there an oligarchy, nevertheless they lost them. They wished to hold Greece as the Spartans held it, making it free and permitting its laws, and did not succeed. So to hold it they were compelled to dismantle many cities in the country, for in truth there is no safe way to retain them otherwise than by ruining them. And he who becomes master of a city accustomed to freedom and does not destroy it, may expect to be destroyed by it, for in rebellion it has always the watchword of liberty and its ancient privileges as a rallying point, which neither time nor benefits will ever cause it to forget. And whatever you may do or provide against, they never forget that name or their privileges unless they are disunited or dispersed, but at every chance they immediately rally to them, as Pisa did after the one hundred years she had been held in bondage by the Florentines.

But when cities or countries are accustomed to live under a prince, and his family is exterminated, they, being on the one hand accustomed to obey, and on the other hand not having the old prince, cannot agree in making one from amongst themselves, and they do not know how to govern themselves. For this reason they are very slow to take up arms, and a prince can gain them to himself and secure them much more easily. But in republics there is more vitality, greater hatred, and more desire for vengeance, which will never permit them to allow the memory of their former liberty to rest ; so that the safest way is to destroy them or to reside there.

These are two passages from books hailing from very different worlds, the one treating petty theft, the other the enslavement and destruction of a modern state by a tyrant, from the point of view of the pickpocket and tyrant : and therefore as the most ordinary thing in the world. It seldom occurs to people that the most respectable code possible *seen from outside* would look ugly and lend itself to ethical censure : yet that is of course the case. It is a common-place that, pursued in its effects, far enough and deep enough, the most civilized canons lead to oppression and manslaughter. It is only because his system is individual-istic that that of the pickpocket or tyrant is repulsive to us. But the majority of people are brought up to regard the snatching of watches, and the prison that ensues, in a superstitious light of traditional horror. It is a " crime " to snatch a watch. The murderer is not " human." And the trustful child is accustomed to accept many things ethically indefensible as very much to be admired. Un-ruffled with any sense of guilt, as simple and mechanical as a dog, the human child grows into the usual implacable, self-righteous, treacherous man. With an easy conscience and some relish he proceeds to prey (like the little brute he remains to his dying day) on his fellows. He robs and with luck murders, with fluctuating success : and he imprisons and murders other people for doing the same thing less " correctly " than himself. The patriotic robbery of a neighbour's territory, sharp practice and intrigue of every sort, in his personal enterprises, are highly virtuous if the rules of the game are observed. Childhood is spent in the learning of these rules.

In fact the same prison, banishment or ostracism awaits the man who *refuses* to take part in one form of theft or murder as is reserved for the man who *commits* another sort. To murder for the community (for a lot of people) is a virtue : to murder for yourself a vice.

Conformity to literally anything is, in short, the key to honour : acting within the consent of the majority cannot be wrong whatever you do. The only true standard of right and wrong, all education implies, is the consent of the majority.

The child is made to feel that the individual in himself or in herself is the enemy. And the death or subjection of that enemy is the task of the child. He must learn to kill himself before he can be allowed to kill other people : or he must deaden himself before engaging as a qualified human being in the world-wide occupation of making life mechanical and uniform, and fit for even the vastest herd to live in.

Honour is not your own "good," for there is no you. Honour is a faculty of the gentleman : its exercise consists in doing as much for somebody else (for the Not-You) as is consistent with the natural reluctance to do anything of the sort, and where the circumstances ensure complete safety : in order to get the maximum for yourself, while pretending all the while that the self does not exist, and that the Not-You (or you might say the NOT) does.

There are a few of the commonplaces of what is generally regarded as cynical or revolutionary doctrine : the doctrines and modes of feeling provoking statements like " *La propriété, c'est un vol* "; or " *Il y a des heros en mal comme en bien* "; or "*Nous avons tous assez de force pour supporter les maux d'autrui.*" Yet although in reality no words can be "cynical" or "brutal" enough to convey the truth, it is one of the great conventions of our life always to label such remarks as " cynical " or " brutal," as it is the most established of conventions to refer to a man as "suspicious" who has a low opinion of the good faith to be expected of men. The "right to pessimism," as Georges Sorel called it, will certainly be the last " right " conceded to our kind.

Should anybody, however, in ninety-nine cases out of a hundred, accept these pessimistic statements as true, a curious thing will happen. He will consider that the realization of this universal evil is a sanction for more evil, hence the great danger of truth. Truth does not propagate itself, but is always prostituted. The problem connected with Machiavelli is whether he manipulated truth deliberately for the ninety-nine out of the hundred, " cynically " forestalling what must inevitably happen to his truth, in any case : whether in a sense he contaminated it even as he produced it : or whether he gave truth that depraved appearance in order to awaken disgust.

The strange honesty that characterizes Machiavelli reminds you of a similar honesty often found in the Jew ; it would be called a childlike honesty. The german imperialist philosophers of the late nineteenth century also displayed this to most people startling predilection for truth—for calling war murder, with no feeling for decency in the composition of their military textbooks—which made them such sensational reading ; they developed such a way of publicly and gratuitously confessing to the necessity of violence and fraud. Western opinion at the time was genuinely scandalized ; in America it caused an even deeper indignation, and this clumsy truthfulness resulted in military defeat. As war it was good but as diplomacy it was bad. It was substituting Machiavelli for Cesare Borgia : the philosophy for the fact : the pedantry and exposition for the action. Nietzsche as an expounder of " aristocratic " dogma, with his childlike enthusiasm, suffered from a similar tendency to put the cart before the horse.

To be what Hotspur called a " king of smiles," and to go about well provided with every deadly drug, was essential, Nicolò Machiavelli was never tired of impressing on prospective princes (especially new ones) if *power* was what was wanted. To have *power*—that is to say to become, not by right but by force, the mechanical destiny of other people —you must train your personality with a superhuman severity. You must be as slippery as the eel and as daring as the cat.

" The wish to acquire," says Machiavelli, " is in truth very natural and common, and men always do so when they can, and for this they will be praised not blamed." That is the first thing you must accept. And then—if you are a prince, or in any way in a position of ambitious authority—you must remember these further facts :

" Because this is to be asserted in general of men, that they are ungrateful, fickle, false, cowards, covetous, and as long as you succeed they are yours entirely ; they will offer you their blood, property, life, children, as is said above, when the need is far distant ; but when it approaches they turn against you . . . friendships that are obtained by payments, and not by greatness . . . are not secured, and in time of need cannot be relied upon : and men have less scruple in offending one who is believed than one who is feared. . . ."

THE LION AND THE FOX

In Hannibal's army " no dissensions occurred . . . either in his bad or in his good fortune. This arose from nothing else than his inhuman cruelty. . . . A wise lord cannot, nor ought he to, keep faith where such observance may be turned against him, and when the reasons which caused him to pledge it exist no longer. If men were entirely good this precept would not hold, but because they are bad, and will not keep faith with you, you, too, are not bound to observe it with them."

Of the great Borgia pope, Alexander VI., Machiavelli says :

" Alexander the Sixth did nothing but deceive men, nor ever thought of doing otherwise, and he always found victims ; for there never was a man who had greater power in asserting, or who with greater oaths would affirm a thing yet would observe it less. . . . Therefore it is unnecessary for a prince to have all the good qualities I have enumerated, but it is very necessary to appear to have them. And . . . to have them and always to observe them is injurious . . . to appear to have them is useful : to appear merciful, faithful, humane, religious, upright, and to be so, but with a mind so framed that should you require *not* to be so, you may be able and know how to change to the opposite."

This last passage is among the most characteristic : and to have " a mind so framed " must, he convinces us, be the ideal of the politician, trafficker, despot, or any type, for that matter, of dull " successful " man to-day, smally or largely predatory. " For this reason a prince ought to take care that he never lets anything slip from his lips that is not replete with the above-named qualities, that he may appear to him who sees and hears him altogether merciful, faithful, humane, upright and religious. There is nothing more necessary to appear to have than this last quality, inasmuch as men judge generally more by the eye than by the hand, because it belongs to everybody to see you, to few to come in touch with you. Everyone sees what you appear to be, few really know what you are, and those few *dare not oppose themselves to the opinion of the many*, who have the majesty of the state to defend them : and in the actions of all men, and especially of princes, which it is not prudent to challenge, one judges by the result.

"For that reason, let a prince have the credit of conquering and holding his state, the means will always be considered honest, and he will be praised by everybody; because the vulgar are always taken in by what a thing seems to be and by what comes of it; and in the world there are only the vulgar, for the few find a place there only when the many have no ground to rest on."

The prince, according to Machiavelli, should adopt the animals inevitably reigning in his human composition with some care: and of all possible combinations a compound of the fox and of the lion is proved by experience to be the best. We are half beasts—that we must always remember. The apologue of the centaur Chiron, for instance, is designed to show "that, as they (the greek princes) had for a teacher one who was half beast and half man, so it is necessary for a prince to know how to make use of both natures, and to understand that one without the other is not durable."

The title of this book is taken from this famous apologuic figure of Machiavelli's. With this thought the society in the midst of which Shakespeare lived was saturated, and he is, as a matter of course, constantly making use of it. In Cervantes the struggle of the new spirit of scientific detachment and the old mystical, chivalrous spirit is dramatized in his most famous work. But, although in Shakespeare this struggle is dispersed all over his creation, not concentrated in one master work, as it is with Cervantes, the reaction of Shakespeare to these impulses is with him, too, the most central fact. If you have understood his leanings in that respect you have understood him.

CHAPTER V

"PERIODS OF TRANSITION"

BEFORE seeking, as we are about to do, in the figure that stood for renaissance Italy to the tudor imagination, the meaning of a surprising quantity of the work of the tudor stage, it may be as well first to carry a step further our review of the problem indicated in the last chapter, the general european attitude to the problem that he and his political heroes present.

In the *Life and Times of Machiavelli*, by Professor Pasquale Villari, this problem is dealt with intelligently ; his book is still the best popular guide to matters connected with that period. All the questions that naturally arise from the contrast stated above, this writer puts down to the conditions incident to a "time of transition." The abrupt translation of an entire society from one set of values to another, from the values of the feudal commune to the more generous and elastic conditions of the modern state, from a mystical view of the world to a "realistic" one, is responsible for all the monsters and angels produced by the renaissance. A *sphinx*, from one point of view, was the result of this release of vitality in all directions. The meeting of these two different ages, with their respective passions and characteristics, produced "a mysterious sphinx, which excites our wonder and almost our fear ": half angel and half devil.

This alarm and astonishment expresses itself logically in the following problem: ". . . to behold men who speak and think like ourselves, men who experience genuine delight before a Madonna by Fra Angelico or Lucca della Robbia, before the aerial curves of Alberti's and Brunelleschi's architecture, men who show disgust at a coarse attitude, at a gesture that is not of the most finished elegance ; to behold them abandon themselves to the most atrocious

84

crimes, the most obscene vices; to behold them using poison, etc."—that, says Villari, is what it is difficult to understand.

When Villari wrote, in the middle of the nineteenth century, those contradictions would be more difficult to reconcile than they are to-day, in the first place. For to-day we are in the midst of a "transitional" period, on a vast scale, and which provides us (although heavily disguised in patriotic formulæ or in revolutionary altruism, and therefore more complex and baffling) with contradictions just as notable.

But statements of another order in Villari's excellent book would in any case tend to lessen our surprise. To-day in place of "humanism" we have science. And no one is, in the nature of things, so surprised to observe a man of science (engaged in what is popularly regarded as an "inhuman" study) busy one day with the construction of a device for ensuring greater comfort to the human race and the next day contriving a machine of destruction guaranteed to wipe out at a moment's notice what he was so busy inventing the day before.

Humanistic culture, on the other hand, is a very different matter. If in place of science you have painting, philosophy and poetry, it is much more difficult to reconcile those activities, and the beautiful productions that are their result, with the madness that is inseparable from successful banking operations, and the sensational crimes by which the possession of "power" if possible expresses itself.

But when we consider that the popes and princes who encouraged the arts did so usually not at all for the sake of the arts, as all their actions testify, but for the enhancement of their own prestige: that a courtier was not a master of graceful deportment for the abstract love of grace and beauty, but for the most practical motives: and that learning was a weapon in the service of worldly ambitions, and at the most, in the case of the scholar, an affair of disinterested passion, or a necessity of the mind; then this contradiction in any case vanishes for us.

The renaissance italian captain or tyrant was as alive to

the uses of learning and the social arts as he was to the science of war, which was his invention, and in which, as a theoretician, he excelled. The prince or commander of the army of a state had often started as a free captain ; and birth or training, in this age that has been called that of bastards and adventurers, never mattered less. Muzio Sforza started life as a field labourer : Niccolo Piccinini as a butcher : Carmagnola as a herdsman. We can agree that it must have been " singular to see these men— generally of low origin and devoid of culture—surrounded in their camps by ambassadors, poets and learned men, who read to them Livy and Cicero, and original verses, in which they were compared to Scipio and Hannibal, to Cæsar and Alexander." But they were all acting on a tiny scale the past that was being unearthed, just as English statesmen were modelling themselves at the time of England's great expansion on the statesmen of Roman antiquity. With the more intelligent of them, like Cesare Borgia, this archæological and analogic habit of mind assumed the proportion of a mania. His " *Aut Cæsar aut nihil* " is the same type of literature as is concentrated in the small maniacal figure of Julien Sorel, Stendhal's little domestic Napoleon. Borgia's motto itself is reminiscent of the title of a book popular before the war in Germany : *Worldly Power or Downfall*.

For every type of relatively small adventurer there was an antique model. If the free captain had not had the benefits of a court or university training, then some man of letters of his acquaintance would no doubt find a model for him : " You are just like Scipio, Muzio ! " this admirer would no doubt exclaim. Cesare Borgia was quite capable of finding a hero for himself, and he went straight for Julius Cæsar ; although, with his name, there was probably not much choice. The republican would call himself Brutus, the *littérateur* would be Cicero, and so forth. They attempted to bring to life the heroes of antiquity, and recall in their own lives the events recorded in the codices, and it was this immediate application of everything to life in italian renaissance society (like the substitution of a cinema for

a history-book in a school) that made the italian influence
so vivid in the rest of Europe. Renaissance Italy was very
exactly a kind of Los Angeles, where historical scenes were
tried out, antique buildings imitated and roughly run up,
and dramatic crimes reconstructed.

How the association of learning and political crime came
about is shown by Villari as follows :

" Those were days in which every Italian seemed a born
diplomatist : the merchant, the man of letters, the captain
of adventures, knew how to address and discourse with
kings and emperors, duly observing all conventional forms.
. . . The dispatches of our ambassadors were among the
chief historical and literary monuments of those times. . . .

" It was then that adventurers, immovable by threats,
prayers or pity, were sure to yield to the verses of a learned
man. Lorenzo de' Medici went to Naples, and by force of
argument persuaded Ferrante d'Aragona to put an end
to the war and·conclude an alliance with him. Alfonso
the Magnanimous, a prisoner of Filippo Maria Visconti, and
whom all believed dead, was instead honourably liberated
because he had the skill to convince that gloomy and cruel
tyrant that it would better serve his turn to have the
Aragonese at Naples than the followers of Anjou. . . . In
a revolution at Prato, got up by Bernardo Nardi, this
leader . . . had already thrown the halter round the neck
of the florentine Podestà when the latter's fine reasoning
persuaded him to spare his life. . . ."

Such stories and examples, whether all true or not, show,
as Villari says (since they were constantly repeated and
believed), the mental habits and tendencies of the period.

Again, where a captain or a tyrant could, he would
conquer by charm and grace as much as by arms. As a
snake would rearrange its sinuous colour-pattern every
morning, no doubt, if it were able to, so Cesare Borgia would
get himself up " to kill " in more senses than one. Being
often very intelligent, further, an italian pope or tyrant
would understand very well the wonderful political uses
of the arts—of architecture and the splendid adornment
of buildings. These were the sort of reasons that produced

the flowering of the renaissance, with all its splendours and graces. But most of these patrons of the arts would have cut the throat of a Raphael Madonna with, if possible, less compunction than that of a living adversary. So it is, and has always been, very unreasonable to feel surprise at the existence of these things side by side—the crimes and debauches of the pope and tyrant, and art's beauty and elegance, so naturally dependent on each other.

The thing that it should be far more difficult for us to-day to understand, the thing that separates *this* time from *that* so completely, is precisely the respect and worship, almost, of learning and the powers and graces of the mind, which the renaissance Italian showed. Perhaps that is why we do not understand the conjunction of a murderous and chaotic reality, which is much the same in all times, except a few fortunate interludes, and the ideal beauty of the products of the mind. It is because art and philosophy seem unreal to us that we cannot see how they could consort with a reality that is not so very unlike ours. For though to-day, as I have already said, people should have less difficulty in accepting without surprise the spectacle of renaissance society, they still express a traditional astonishment.

We are reminded of the Normans' love of eloquence and the social arts by the same description of enthusiasm exhibited in the renaissance bandit or man of action. Such enthusiasms to-day are practically unknown. You would not recommend yourself to a sovietic commisar by a display of literary talent or a seductive eloquence, quite the contrary ; you would arouse his hatred and suspicion, and he would have you under lock and key very rapidly. The contemporary magnifico or multimillionaire is, similarly, notorious rather for his furious dislike of any accomplishment different from his own—especially if it involves a hint of some disobliging superiority. From that point of view (and what an important one it is, it is difficult at present for us to estimate) no times could be so dissimilar as the present one and that of the italian renaissance. In the growing violence of our political chaos, and in the flourishing of criminal propensities—but not made in any way conspicuous and repulsive by association with the fine arts or fine manners—through that the contemporary European must find it easier to get some imaginative foothold in renaissance Italy than his father or grandfather would. That once achieved, his astonishment and disgust could then be wholly concentrated on the art and culture he found there; for with the crimes he must daily feel more at home.

CHAPTER VI

THE INDIVIDUAL HERO OR PRINCE, AND THE *OTTIMATI*, FOR MACHIAVELLI AND GUICCIARDINI

IT is not my intention here to consider in any detail the doctrine of Machiavelli : but enough must be said about it to make the nature of its influence understood. And first of all it must again be insisted on that in everything the renaissance Italians were first and foremost men of science ; and that their political, military and artistic life was a constant experimentation. The façade of their art is probably not so deep and permanent as it has looked to us in the past. It is very thin in places, compared with the productions of eastern art, having behind them a long matured, undisturbed tradition, all of one piece. The political science of Machiavelli was the first strictly *scientific* doctrine produced in Europe, the result of an inductive psychological method. It was the first political system to refuse to admit anything that it could not directly observe. It was the first to finally break with the universalism of theological thought : the first expression of the new nationalist thought, responding to the new conditions of the centralized, differentiated states of Europe, forming outside the imperial system.

It was then, first, scientific or experimental (for that was the specific character of the italian genius of the renaissance). Secondly, it was nationalist—it envisaged conditions released from the notion of a universal control (as that of the Roman Empire or the Roman Church). And there was a third factor peculiar to the archæological mind of the renaissance, and this at first appears to contradict the second characteristic : it was *roman* in spirit, and looked to Rome—but to the Rome of antiquity—for its inspiration.

As Villari points out at great length, there was an

important way in which Machiavelli differed from his contemporary Guicciardini : that was that although in a sense as strictly based on direct observation and what roughly can be called psychology as the other, he was besides that a great generalizer; and when he looked to Rome (as Tacitus had looked to the virtuous german tribes of his fancy) almost a political apriorist. He will say, for instance, dogmatically : " It is a general rule " ; or : " It should be regarded as a general rule " ; whereas Guicciardini would not indulge in any general affirmation of that sort. He is actually trying to found (although ostensibly only from observation) a *system*. Guicciardini is merely providing, by means of a mass of psychological observations, a possible political education for a class of administrators, never generalized or developed into laws.

\This experimental spirit, and resolve to appeal only to expediency, can be found even in Savonarola's ordering of the florentine state (illustrated in his *Del reggimento del governo della citta di Firenze*). And there is a further thing in the mere history of this subject that it is necessary to note—namely, the conception of a *mixed* government that was apparently shared by all the men of this time. " Substantially, the government desired by Guicciardini was nothing more than a machinery by which it was sought to balance different ambitions, and cause the advantages of a monarchy and an aristocracy and a democracy to exercise reciprocal action by means of a Gonfalonier, Senate, and Great Council."

Now the book of Machiavelli's round which the discussion has raged is *The Prince* : and that is addressed to a single ruler, and deals with the laws of experience that must govern the action of one man attempting to rule a modern state. For this rule by one man he regarded as a necessary first step in founding a new society. This was no doubt the effect of a devoted and literal discipleship of antiquity : the Lycurgus or similar figure, the solitary personal lawgiver, or eponymous hero, found in the traditional belief of nearly every people.

" . . . it should be adopted as a general rule, that, in

order to found and reconstitute a State it is necessary to be single-handed ; all must be the work and creation of one regulating mind, for without this no true unity can ever be attained, nor any stable state founded. Therefore a ruler desiring to be of service . . . must endeavour to hold sole authority ; nor will he ever be censured by wise men for taking extraordinary measures in order to constitute a kingdom or found a republic " (*Discorsi*).

Hence for Machiavelli the importance of the individual tyrant, and of providing an unerring and infallible system to enable all such persons to efficiently enslave and discipline any community they have chosen for that purpose.

Going to the source—the source also of his predilection—Machiavelli says : " Many will consider it a most pernicious example, that one who, like Romulus, was the founder of a civil community, should first have killed his own brother and then consented to the death of Titus Tatius Sabinus, his chosen companion." So with this savage fable, which, of course, he accepted, the murder of the Duke of Gandia was satisfactorily transformed into a virtuous action.

Serving sometimes one element in the *mixed* government of the contemporary paradigm, sometimes another, the question is often asked what Machiavelli's or Guicciardini's true feeling on the subject of prince, oligarch or people was. As to the third—the people—there is no room for doubt : in the passages from *The Prince* quoted in the last chapter it is evident what he thought of them. And Guicciardini is equally emphatic. The second, and middle, category—that of the aristocrat, of the *ottimati*—is not liked by Machiavelli, but is, on the other hand, favoured by Guicciardini. The favourite of Machiavelli is evidently the *individual hero*. It is to the prince that his roman soul gives all the intelligent passion of its predilection. Whatever, in the unfolding of his perfect system, Machiavelli may eventually arrive at, superseding the prince with *ottimati* and delivering them in their turn up to the revolutionary fury of the populace, it is the phase in which the prince is called upon to perform his difficult, lonely work of initiation that interests him most. The *ottimati* are, after all, representatives

of the people—they are in the first place the representatives of the Many delegated to encompass and check
the heroic power of the One. So he does not like the
ottimati, the policemen of his prince. He even perhaps
prefers the populace.

Though it is perfectly true that in the *Discorsi* Machiavelli completes his structure of mixed government, going
through the three phases that he regards as ordained
invariably to succeed each other in one form or another,
it is certain that it is not solicitude for the personal liberty
of the mass of the citizens of any state that caused him in
his retirement to write these wonderful books. It is the
hero, the prince, that roused him to this action.

CHAPTER VII

MACHIAVELLI, GEORGES SOREL AND NIETZSCHE

IF we wanted in our world to-day to find a parallel to Machiavelli, or someone who could be said to have developed his philosophy, Georges Sorel would be a better figure to take than Nietzsche : though in significance and power Nietzsche is, of course, incomparably better. But Sorel has two or three points of resemblance to Machiavelli that specially recommend him for comparison.

Both are rather spare in their utterance, and both insist on the roman model. Both are confused and fanatical in somewhat the same way, and both are advocates of the utmost violence. The agent principle for both was the only one. Both have no room in their minds for anything but their arid roman doctrine of " power " and force—in that, as in many other things, differing very much from Nietzsche.

" Even in his histories," Villari writes, " Machiavelli's men appear incapable of any ambition or passion save the political ; there is hardly any mention of letters, art, culture or religion." It is where Villari is comparing Machiavelli with the Greeks that he says this, showing how the author of *The Prince* was a true child of Rome in reality, his nature alive only to the suggestions of power and mechanical control.

" . . . whoever passes from Aristotle to Machiavelli is at once driven to recognize an enormous and substantial diversity in the fact that for the latter the political idea alone seems to have existence. Like the ancients, he sacrificed the individual to the State ; but in his opinion the State is indifferent to every activity save the political and military, and is solely engaged in guarding the security of its own existence and increasing its own strength. . . . Now all this is opposed to the vaster, more various, and

94

more philosophic ideas of the culture of the Greeks. . . . Hence the heroes of Machiavelli must be sought on the Capitol, for his ideal country was always Rome."

Whereas Machiavelli is chiefly notable for his advice to a tyrant, encouraging him to every violence and crime, the " end justifying the means," Sorel is, on the other hand, advising the proletariat in the same sense.

There is no doubt then that the prince, not the democracy, still less the *ottimati* or aristocrat (whom he regarded as merely the best equipped, most powerful and adroit of the herd) was the hero of Machiavelli. And the roman was for him the heroic *race*. His ideal hero would thus be an individual, not a type; and, to be quite perfect, of roman blood (republicanism not insisted on, relentless *virtù* stressed) with roman political and military power as his supreme objective, as such power indeed seemed to Machiavelli the *summum bonum* of life on earth.

In assembling these very general elements of the Machiavelli figure the nature of its inconsistencies have not been particularly stressed—the more we attempted to finish the sketch, the more pronounced these would appear. They are principally due to the fact that Machiavelli was a man of the past as well, his foundations were deeper than was the case with Guicciardini (so much more consistently " a man of his time "). The conjunction of the *virtue* of antiquity, the opportunism and push of the small interloping *condottiere* princes, the new science and the old humanism, was effected only with a good deal of straining.

Georges Sorel I have put forward as probably the most caricaturally inconsistent figure that any " time of transition " has ever produced. As you think of him you see an olympian thorax and a pair of child's-size legs. With the aristocratic *virtù* of Cato he attacks the roman power of world-capital, and in the name of phalansterian brotherhood would turn the mechanic into a gladiator, fiercely pointing to Napoleon as the ideal, fiercely pricking his ears up as though he heard the drums of the old guard rolling on the approach of a man-god. Hauling up the *petit bourgeois* by the scruff of the neck, he asks him sternly why he is not a "blond beast," and sketches the gesture of slitting his throat. Feeling the road-mender's muscles with approval, he says: "these are meant for fighting and slaying; it was for that that road-mending was invented. Did you not know that men eat in order to fight? Follow me." There is as much phlebotomy in his doctrine as in that of Machiavelli: but he proposes that the operation should be performed in broad daylight and on a grandiose scale, in keeping with the *size* of the third estate—with which he consoles himself for its lack of distinction; whereas Machiavelli insists on the destruction of individuals rather than whole classes. Machiavelli did not have to bridge such chasms as Sorel found himself surrounded by: but nevertheless he would find two thousand years often enough between one emotion and the next.

M. Benoist—whose very interesting little book I shall shortly quote from—and most machiavellians, consider that the great mistake made by the critics of Machiavelli has consisted in the simple action of joining together once more what Machiavelli had carefully separated, the human and the inhuman, the whole man and that "a-moral" portion of him which is alone proper for any effective political operation. This appears to me to be confusing the issue, and attributing to Machiavelli at once too little and too much.

Machiavelli's hero, in the first place, was a physical hero, but a completely equipped one, clothed from head to foot in defensive armour of the latest possible pattern, and hedged round with stratagems. Every resource of the intellect was supposed to be his, which was assumed to be entirely docile to this mechanical destiny of waiting, hand and foot (under conditions of trying servitude), on physical force, and such intellectual satisfaction as can be derived from its exercise, at other people's expense.

What M. Benoist would say would be: "You are making Machiavelli say things he never said. He never said it was admirable or desirable to live in a nightmare of murder, disloyalty, lying and imposture of every sort. What he did say was that unless you did this you could

not govern men, because human nature, in its abjectness
and corruption, exacted that treatment from those born to
be human leaders. He cleared away everything but what
would succeed, and found that the only *safe* road was that
followed by Cesare Borgia."

This statement, however it is put, always implies that
Machiavelli was able to imagine other modes of life, equally
desirable, than that of political success: and it does not
seem that the writings of Machiavelli can bear that out at all.
On the contrary, it seems evident that he could imagine
nothing but a *political* life, nothing seemed worth while
to him but the acquisition and exercise of authority over
other men: and he had an overmastering admiration for
the man who was most eminent and successful in the life
imposed by those particular impulses. It was because he
could not imagine anyone sincerely wanting anything else
but such dominion that his doctrine possessed such wonderful
force and simplicity.

Before concluding this brief examination of Machiavelli,
it will be of assistance to consider a figure, occurring at a
much later date, who was a kind of super-machiavellian
prince—that is, Frederick the Great.

CHAPTER VIII

FREDERICK THE GREAT

THE setting was so different that it is perhaps idle to compare Frederick the Great with Cesare Borgia. He was without the latter's nervous frenzy ; his sadism dispersed itself with a northern and, so far, modern indirectness ; and his position was to start with more enviable and secure. His military instincts had the support of a powerful and obedient machine, in his well-drilled subjects. But there were points in which he was like a Borgia certainly ; more like Alexander the Sixth than his son, perhaps.

Many of the stories told about him recall the figure of the father Karamazov. He was very fond of flattery, but was exacting as to its quality. For example, when an eloquent person in the course of a harangue in which Frederick's kingly virtues were being enumerated, sure of his effect, enlarged unctuously on the deep love of the Berliners for their great sovereign, Frederick suddenly started back, banging his hat down dramatically on his head, and commenced declaiming :

" Croyez-moi les humains que j'ai trop su connaître
 Meritent peu, monsieur, qu'on daigne être leur maître."

This sensitiveness where bad and clumsy flattery was concerned—as in this case where a stupid satisfaction was imputed to him on the score of his people's "love"—which made him such a terrible master, led to many scenes reminiscent of the pages of the Brothers Karamazov. His solitary life, in which all the business of the country was transacted by himself and his famous groom in the early morning, his relations with his servants and delight to humiliate his equals or the members of his court, contribute to this.

FREDERICK THE GREAT

When blamed for his unseemly familiarity with his *heiduques* and servants, with whom he lived apart from his court, he would say : " Noah is their grandfather as much as he is mine; it is confidingness, and not familiarity, which has its drawbacks." It is just to compare him to a *condottiere,* of an extremely *raffiné* variety : and he was verbally a considerable artist, " using language like a dagger." His repartees alone place him very high in the social scale.

There are many " ragging " scenes that bear the same mark of a sort of *bengel*-like cruelty, that make him the father of the *corps-student,* as he was the brother of papa Karamazov. His butt, Captain Guichard, for instance, he loads with a grenadier's equipment, and compels to stand for a long time in a humiliating attitude, while he girds at him. This was because that officer had observed that a roman legionary carried more than a prussian grenadier. " We are shortly going to make some very long marches —much longer than the Romans ever made. Don't you think that our feats will surpass those of the Romans : or do you still think that the inferior weight of our equipment forbids us to institute such a comparison ? " And so on to the same effect. He had a german relish for such jokes, no one who approached him was exempt from spending part of the time in the rôle of butt for this privileged clown. The higher their position, the more they would arouse the clown in Frederick.

To a prince whom he knew had never been near a battle-field he would talk about his victories, and to a lady who had been guilty of indiscretions he would converse about her bastard children. All this was at all times heavily sugared. He was never so considerate and affable as when he was about to deliver one of his attacks. " No one could be more caressing than Frederick when he wanted to be, more adroit, more amiable. He was the most seductive of all sirens." His love of deceit was comparable to that of Pope Alexander VI., and his love of scandal and horseplay to papa Karamazov's. He preferred the company of servants and soldiers : his overmastering pride arranged his life for him in that way. With his social equals he was not only very much on his guard, but constantly in a mood of antagonism, never free of the itch to humiliate them. He is one of the purest specimens of which we have any record of the kingly type. He was in short in a very high degree the king-hero with which Shakespeare's dramatic work had so much to do. He was the ideal representative of the private soldier, the ostler, the footman, vowed to a natural enmity where the *ottimati* and mandarin of the feminine social world were concerned.

Frederick's ugliest characteristic was his extreme stinginess. But even that can be somewhat discounted as part of his war on the courtier, the upper-servant, the convention-ridden *rico hombre* or bourgeois, with all the—for him—maddening unreality and fuss of the essentially feminine world of the court and of society. In the same way his duplicity can be regarded rather as a weapon with which to meet the ineradicable falsity of the world, than as that sort of technician's love for the cleverest tricks of the trade —like the enthusiasms of a three-card-trick man—which characterized Alexander.

But there still remains an inveterate meanness. And to that must be added, as the drawback of a virtue, perhaps, a jealousy for any form of power but his own. He could never have been a patron of a great artist, as many renaissance grandees succeeded—with great difficulty usually and by overcoming all their natural instincts—in being. Such a king reigning in another and, his intelligence would tell him, probably a greater world than his, as Voltaire was, could never have been kept near him for long. His pride could not tolerate an intelligence greater than his own. So there must be no art, philosophy or science in his business, military and political world. So, by another road, he reaches the same bare, politically obsessed ideal as Machiavelli. It is the same cheerless and demented pursuit of power, leading, like science, when isolated, to a world of the bleakest mechanical abstraction.

So the courtier with such a master as Frederick was not to be envied : though the artist or artisan, unfortunately, shared the same fate. No one but the gladiator or the lackey, vowed to the hardest, most mechanical and abject life, could exist in the neighbourhood of this tyrant of genius.

" Frederick was a suspicious, disdainful and malevolent tyrant. He had the taste . . . for ill-natured pleasantries, which he translated into action. His vanity, as well as his ill-nature, enjoyed the spectacle of the confusion and mortification of those chosen as victims for his bitter wit. It was impossible to know how to take him : it was the most baffling of problems. If you appeared embarrassed in his presence, you were not obeying his orders, and you spoilt his pleasure. If, on the other hand, his companions permitted themselves the familiarity of intimates, the king never failed to punish their presumption by some cruel humiliation. . . . He regarded those who showed spirit as insolent and ungrateful : and those who were submissive as dogs designed to receive with the same patience pats on the heads and kicks elsewhere. It is difficult to imagine any motive, short of the most raging hunger, adequate to persuade any man to support the misery of being a courtier of this great king."

Displeasing as this picture must be, yet it should not be accepted, however substantially true, quite in the spirit in which it is presented to us here. Frederick was a very alive, resourceful and original man, and the average courtier is, of all men, he with regard to whom we can most easily spare our sympathy. If the king did not, with his penetrating and abstracted eye, discriminate much between a groom of the bedchamber and a groom of the stables, a lady in waiting and a waitress, if these distinctions constantly provoked his impatience, and if in the long run they were all treated equally as servants (with a bias in favour of the lower, less pretentious, ranks), that was because he was a very exceptional and high type of king, and a great ornament to his destiny. He was not a philosopher, but a king, the supreme political species of the individual human kind. And all the greatest kings have recognized in their courtiers the enemies of their kind, and behaved accordingly.

In spite of the admiration that every reasonable man

must feel for this very great monarch, it is still essential to define the limits of that admiration; and not convert it, as Machiavelli did (against the true principle of his adherence to the scientific spirit), into a *universal* admiration. As a king, Frederick the Great was almost perfect. But his was a functional perfection, seconded by a very rich and curious personality.

His great interest for us, however, at this point of our argument, is that he is a pure Machiavel, half-way between the renaissance protoplast made in italian clay (and by way of being a *pastiche* of the antique) and the Machiavel of the present day.

In the evolution of the machiavellian type under modern conditions Frederick the Great furnishes in a sense the furthest perfection that the type has yet attained. And he started most characteristically by writing a book against Machiavelli, in which he expressed his unlimited disgust and horror at this poisonous tract shamelessly extolling "rapacity, perfidy, arbitrary government, unjust wars." These are the things, of course, for which subsequently Frederick became famous: for his greatness rests on the fact that he was warlike, treacherous, tyrannic, and extremely stingy at the same time as extremely ostentatious; building a palace, but refusing to have any ministers because he did not wish to have to pay their salaries, and conducting all the work of government himself with the help of a groom, who read all his letters in the small hours of the morning, and brought what he considered it necessary Frederick should see at seven o'clock in a big bundle under his arm.

There is no more curious fact in history than this warlike despot beginning his career with such a book as his *Anti-Machiavel.* Voltaire expressed the belief at a later date that it was written in good faith, that Frederick was not intelligent enough for it to have been otherwise. In his *Memoirs* we read as follows:

"The King of Prussia, some time before the death of his father, took it into his head to write a book against the principles of Machiavelli. If Machiavelli had had a prince for disciple, the first thing he would have recommended him to do would have been to write a book against machiavellism" !

This is such an extremely obvious truth that, seeing what Frederick's subsequent career was like, it is very difficult to believe that his book against Machiavelli did not indeed prove that he had become perhaps that philosopher's most brilliant disciple. Macaulay also draws attention to this very obvious conclusion, that at least it was strange that this king should have written a refutation of Machiavelli while he was himself an illustrious practitioner of all the machiavellisms he inveighed against.

We have already said that on the appearance of Machiavelli's *Prince* every " responsible government " felt itself suddenly unmasked : that the very principle of authority, the laws by which one sort of man governs another, it seemed, could never look the world in the face again without a self-conscious squint. Frederick calls Machiavel " l'ennemi de l'humanité et le calomniateur des princes." It is as the " calumniator of princes," or as the individual who has unmasked them, in other words, that he attacks him.

The idea first came to him on reading some remarks of Voltaire that he regarded as too favourable to Machiavelli. He writes to Voltaire at once :

" Whoever teaches men to break their word, to oppress, to be unjust, even if he were a man remarkable for his intellectual attainments, should never be allowed to occupy the place reserved strictly for those of praiseworthy and virtuous achievements." To Voltaire he says : " You are too much *honnête homme* to wish to advertise the scandalous reputation of a contemptible fellow like that ; but I am satisfied that it was only as man of genius that you were envisaging Machiavelli."

Voltaire encouraged Frederick to write his refutation of Machiavelli : and he got to the heart of the matter from every point of view when he said about *The Prince* that it was " a book for long dear to the little princelings engaged in squabbles over small ill-governed states, but whose usefulness is past in a time when great armed powers suppress these insignificant ambitions."

So encouraging his princely patron to repudiate, with scorn, this small scurrilous textbook of power for the use of petty pretenders to power (considered beside such a redoubtable engine of war and acquisitiveness as Prussia could be converted into) he says:

"À quoi peut-on donc parvenir par cette politique affreuse? An malheur des autres et au sien même. Voilà vérités qui sont le catéchisme de votre belle âme" (Voltaire).

So the *Catéchisme de sa belle âme* is written by Frederick; and in it Machiavelli is very roughly handled. The philosopher would have enjoyed every line of it: and had he been alive would no doubt have helped Frederick to write it with much more interest than Voltaire showed: though, as Benoist says, Voltaire's corrections are highly politic and very amusing to follow.

Through having discoursed on moderation, peace, liberty, the happiness a good man finds in the happiness of others, Frederick had, says Macaulay, taken everybody in, especially those people who ought to have known better than to listen to such things. When his reign began some prophesied one thing, some another: some thought they were about to possess a *Télémaque à la mode de Fénelon*: others predicted a period recalling that of the Medicis, in which the arts and the sciences would flourish. *No one* suspected that "a tyrant, gifted with extraordinary talent for war and for politics, of a still more astonishing perseverance, without fear, without faith and without pity, had just ascended the throne."

He acquitted himself in the sequel in a manner that perhaps Machiavelli would scarcely have understood, but which appears faultless in the light of the machiavellian doctrines. Launching one terrible war after another, he never ceased to inveigh against his unlucky star that forced him into these conflicts, which were odious to his pacific nature, he would affirm. He never for a moment dropped his mask of negligent detachment from such events, or at least he never allowed it to reveal the features and expression of the bird of prey. And he was spared, by the happy circumstances of the time and place, the necessity of poisoning people; and nothing but his actions, on a great impersonal scale, and with masses of slaughtered soldiers, towns and villages destroyed and so forth (things so big that no one ever, in any period, suspects that a *person* or persons can be responsible for them, unless his responsibility is theatrically advertised as in the case of Attila) could ever have enlightened anyone on the subject of the true significance of this hero. Similarly he combined an invariable meanness with airs of liberality : social malignity with great politeness and the most accommodating affability.

So the Solomon of the North, the antonine Frederick, is the ideal of a greater Machiavelli. He is the last *Machiavel* in history no doubt that will ever be seen, or at least of which history will be allowed to preserve a true portrait.

CHAPTER IX

SOME CONSEQUENCES OF MACHIAVELLISM

IN the days of Voltaire and of Frederick the Great conditions had, of course, changed very much. The military art, invented by the free captain of the renaissance, and the political art of Machiavelli, had long been practised everywhere. The less direct, less philosophic, North European had got used to the new point of view ; people were thoroughly hardened, and these first manuals of the modern world were already archaic. The earnest philosophic children of the renaissance, and the scientific, disillusioned attitude they had inaugurated, were commonplaces. So the *naïveté* of these first discoverers was regarded as embarrassing. Machiavelli was already in the nature of an *enfant terrible*. Such a statement as his *Prince* was already a feature of the infancy of the scientific outlook : it was the *theory* only, which for long had been perfected and developed in practice. But it is the only clear theoretic statement we have. And from that point of view it is as valuable as ever, historically and philosophically.

In the few passages quoted in an earlier chapter we read : " In the world there are only the vulgar "—" this is to be asserted of men in general, that they are ungrateful, fickle, false, cowards, covetous "—so we saw Machiavelli's political wisdom building up its lawless necessities. In dealing with this contemptible cattle, if it is your will to deal with them, you must show no mercy, keep no faith, be neither humane nor just (although pretending to religion—there is " nothing more necessary " than " this last quality "). In this way you *may*—though " in politics nothing is certain "—succeed in—What ?

This *What ?* it never seems to have occurred to him to examine, or even to question (seeing the cost) its desirability.

CONSEQUENCES OF MACHIAVELLISM

Machiavelli, like Nietzsche, was the servant of the super-man: in his case of a particular superman—namely, Cesare Borgia. And the superman, as that term has been most generally used, is the child with rather more daring than the other children, who wants all the things that the other children want, but who has enough cunning to see through the fraud in time, and determines, by breaking the rules of the game on the one hand, and by utilizing them on the other, to get all the things that any other common little child ardently desires, smoking hot, by going one better than the skilled average.

In the passages from *The Prince* I have quoted there is nothing to contradict. It is the same black material of social truth to which hundreds of other philosophers have subscribed. Shakespeare, in every corner of his plays, and in the conception of all his characters, subscribes to it. There is no human being for whom others are not as much potential enemies as they were for Machiavelli's despot. Those are the conditions of conquest, of success in business or in social life.

We have in *The Prince* the best ABC of power ever compiled with a view especially to obtaining political and despotic power: the steps that you must take as a *sine qua non* of success and subjugation. And it is accompanied with an accurate general description of the creatures that it will be your privilege to subjugate. And *what then*? Well, you will ride about on an immense white horse like the young d'Annunzio, or an elephant: you will live in a palace the size of an elephant, you will have more slaves than anybody else: or if not that, *What*? But, of course, the end is a pretence, success even is a fiction, since nothing accomplished and terminated is worth considering. It is not the end, it is the doing it, that is the reward of these as of all other activities. The excitement of murdering ten of your most malicious friends, or six who fatigue you most with their stupidity, drowning them all in one bath, plunging them all into one well or pit, cementing them all up into one wall; all the contriving and bustling, the breathless, coloured life, the fierce danger, the satisfaction in deceiving

THE LION AND THE FOX

as Alexander VI. was able to do, and so on : that is the object of this at first sight strange life.

I think we have sufficiently examined Machiavelli, and his great work of political initiation. I will now turn to the results in the english nature, and its reflection in english dramatic art, of the italian renaissance, and the intellectual ascendancy of Italy at the beginning of our epoch. Its more distant results it would be a separate task to define, in its deep effect on the destiny of Europe and America.

Shakespeare's countrymen have generally looked at the fierceness and darkness of the productions of the elizabethan stage without understanding. Perhaps they may have accounted for it as a reflection of the strange habits of savage ancestors : it may also have seemed a certain advertisement for the truly passionate nature of the Englishman, masked by his calm ; rather as a modern Scandinavian might gaze at the incestuous myths of Signy and Sigmund with a certain proud freudian relish.

All educated english people know what Shelley, Keats and Byron—the figures in a little elizabethan revival a hundred years ago—were like. And Swinburne, closely followed by the Nineties—of which he was largely the inspirer—was another little revival. Now in the light of our discussions above (and before we go in greater detail into the elizabethan documents) do not these two later bursts take on a new complexion ? And cannot we say that we have found a habit of the english mind at work, a national *tic—a habit of horrified and shocked "naughtiness" and perversity* ? For we at once find all the ingredients in Byron and Shelley that Vernon Lee finds in her elizabethan forbears. Byron is the most accomplished type of braggart in the domain of sexual love, blood-curdlingly incestuous, wildly donjuanesque. Europe, of course, was his stage, on which he organized the " pageant of his bleeding heart " —throwing in italian courtesans and countesses (degenerate alas in the matter of poison) and arabellaesque half-sisters. Shelley, a " beautiful angel " beyond any question, was politically a child (as indeed you would expect an angel to be) repeating excitedly and naïvely its revolutionary lessons.

CONSEQUENCES OF MACHIAVELLISM

What splendid fun "revolution" was!—how thrilling!—and what opportunities it gave for lyrical humanitarian afflatus! And Shelley went straight, with a fascinated horror, to the *incestuous*, to the italian, theme, as the elizabethans had two centuries before him. For all these people, too, there was still something to be sucked out of this decayed storehouse of intellectual life. They all went to live in the land of the renaissance: and after the napoleonic wars considerable anglo-italian colonies were established in Florence, Rome and Naples. Because, owing to political disuse and decay, and the profits of antiquarian exploitation, Italy had remained physically much the same as in the sixteenth century, the elizabethan mood was easy for the Englishman, in the early nineteenth century, to recapture. With Marinetti and then fascist Italy, presumably that is at an end.

Swinburne was much better informed than his early victorian playmates, but he had in the first place the same obsession about "revolution"—Mazzini's Italy in place of Missolonghi; and also, of course, about vice—thrilling, delicious, exquisite *wickedness*. His *Poems and Ballads* were a schoolboy's learned essays in the romance of debauchery —wicked roman empresses, diabolism, sapphism, and the rest. Then came Oscar Wilde; and he claimed a european stage, once more, for his anglo-saxon "devilries." He would paint the town red from the bottom upwards; on the pederastic ticket he would enter Olympus, and if possible make love to Apollo himself. His prison and martyrdom, and Europe's reprobation of that action on the part of the english authorities—the thrusting of a man of genius into jail—to satisfy puritanic malice and native english dislike of "genius" was an immense advertisement for the particular vice in which Wilde specialized. And Italy to-day presents the arresting spectacle of an organized horde of *exoleti* and aged inverted romantics, largely german and anglo-saxon, perpetuating the Nineties in the very homeland of the Cencis and Borgias. They arrive in thousands in Venice in September, and are referred to in consequence by the Venetians as *Settembrini*: and from there they

THE LION AND THE FOX

migrate suddenly farther south. At last the promised land of debauch has been reached!—where renaissance art, with its beautiful italian names, can lend an ineffable atmosphere of culture to the exotic phases of the homosexual romance.

Wilde is the most wonderful illustration of the puritan elizabethan fascination for crime and sexual perversity. (In Wilde's case, only, incest is disregarded; but he may have felt that that had been sufficiently " covered " by his illustrious predecessors; whereas homosexuality had been rather neglected.) For in him we get, naïvely displayed, the whole armoury of puritanic inversion, delighted horror at " wickedness " and forbidden fruits, *in excelsis*. His *Pen, Pencil and Poison* is a sort of philosophy for a " gentleman " of the childish criminal cult that may really be traceable *to a fright England received in her intellectual infancy*, from Machiavelli's Italy.

Aubrey Beardsley is another good example of the same obsession about the perverse and diabolical. His diablesses characteristically enough issued from the rossettian virgins of Burne-Jones—unnatural vice comes straight out of unnatural and chlorotic virtue. Arthur Symons again exemplifies this peculiar weakmindedness. There is little doubt that the latest organized manifestation of the english mind in art—that of the Nineties of the last century—was as incurably gothic, diabolic and mediæval as it was at the time of Elizabeth; or as, at the beginning of the last century, with the Cencis and Don Juans.

CHAPTER X

A LADY'S RESPONSE TO MACHIAVELLI

WE are provided in the work of a lady (the *Euphorion* of Vernon Lee) with the best indication, perhaps, of the attitude of the anglo-italian resident of the more correct type to the lingering renaissance they have settled amongst. To read her pages is like watching a person of some intelligence administering electric shocks to herself.

" Let us be generous," she says, " to those unfortunates " (that is, the Italians of the renaissance) " who were wicked that we might be enlightened." This is her tone throughout ; but this strange tone of almost drivelling righteousness makes what she says frequently very pointed. And her talent, her appetite for these things, and perhaps her domicile in Italy, enables her to give us almost what the more stupid and provincial of Elizabethans must have felt about the society revealed by Machiavelli. She is as naturally lyrical as Sismondi about the abuses and depravity of the age.

So she exclaims, " Let us be generous ! " and embarrassing as the obligation must have been to her she bravely accepted it in a truly christian spirit (inured as in the nature of things all christian thought must be, to the notion of other people's sacrifices). Making the best of a bad job, she reflects in a Pecksniff-cum-Pangloss-like spirit, of which Webster would not have been capable, on the beautiful appropriateness of these compensations, but still full at bottom of puritanic " horrors."

This writer has actually provided us with an entirely new elizabethan thrill. For in contemplating the men and women of this dark and terrible period of italian renaissance life, observed from afar by our infatuated dramatists who cast such heavy shadows on the elizabethan stage, she

discovers, with a delighted shudder, how simple, sweet and
" ordinary " they in reality are. It is more or less as
though a blessed and immaculate angel were seen to produce from under his quattrocento drapery a poisoned dagger
and plunge it into the heart of his mother—" The Young
Baglionis, Vitellis and Orsinis grouped round Signorellis
preaching Antichrist at Orvieto are the veriest assemblage
of harmless dandies, pretty and insipid ; we can scarcely
believe that these mild and beardless striplings, like girls
of sixteen, are the terrible umbrian brigands, *condottieri*—
Gianpaolos, Simonettis, Vitallezzis and Astorres."

Cesare Borgia, the arch-villain of the Europe of his time,
has in his portraits a grave, noble and sensitive head. In
fact the only famous italian prince who has a countenance
sufficiently villainous and repulsive to live up to the reputation of his time was a prince of Ferrara : and they were
notoriously mild and benevolent.

Here is the very essence of the elizabethan " horror,"
according to Vernon Lee. The terrible part about these
people was that they *did not know how wicked they were*.
The elizabethans—Englishmen—Webster, Marston, Tourneur—knew it all right ; but the Italians did not. There
was no " vicious determination to be wicked," no " feeling
of the fiend within them," as in Shakespeare's Richard.
Vittoria Accoramboni or Francesco Cenci, reading their
own tragedies, examining their own lifelike and horrible
portraits, by Webster and Shelley, would not have been able
to make head or tail of them, or understood what all the
fuss was about. They were, in short, she says, quite normal
people in a very devilish time indeed. The terrible perugian
Baglionis were extremely loved and admired by their fellow-
townsmen. She almost suggests that incest was an asset
with a popular prince, although Machiavelli omitted to
mention it.

" The wickedness of the renaissance " was not a superhuman fury of lust and cruelty, like Victor Hugo's Lucrezia
Borgia ; but an indifferent, a characterless creature like the
Lucrezia Borgia of history : passive to surrounding influences, blind to good and evil ; infamous in the infamous

A LADY'S RESPONSE TO MACHIAVELLI

Rome, among her father and brother's courtesans and cut-throats; grave and gracious in the grave and gracious Ferrara, among the platonic poets and pacific courtiers of the court of the Estensi. The reality is, in short, complete prose, like some everyday business perfidy or crookedness, or like the gestures of some harmless little politician, one of which may be the signing of a declaration of war that wipes out millions of lives. It is quite colourless, mild and even respectable.

But we have in the midst of our elizabethan drama an authentic black sheep, a very different sort of criminal; one who, an Englishman, knew quite well what he was doing, or ought to have known, and who can in every sense be held responsible! For him there is no excuse. This man really *became* an Italian, as it were, by dint of admiring the Italians and hearing about Italy. As she approaches this terrible exception in the midst of our simple, scandalized, right-minded drama, she lowers her voice. The word falls heavily from her lips—an accusing finger is pointed at a shrinking form, who probably imagined himself safe in the turbulent and difficultly deciphered past. It is FORD! He is the man! It is the " sweet and gentle Ford " who is the " only Englishman who gets near the true renaissance spirit ":

" Giovanni and Arabella make love as if they were Romeo and Juliet! " Giovanni and Arabella were brother and sister : and the terrible parallel to the springtime of normal joys, which their infatuation apes, is supposed to provide us with an elizabethan thrill. The writer's indignation grows as she examines this play more closely: she sees this oblique creature " handling the filthy without sense of its being unclean, to the extent—the incredible extent—of making Giovanni and Arabella swear on their mother's ashes eternal fidelity in incest ; horror of horrors, to which no Walpurgis-night abomination could ever approach, this taking as witness of the unutterable, not an obscene Beelzebub with abominable words and rites, but the very holiest of holies."

On the other hand: " They [the renaissance Italians]

rarely or never paint horrors or death or abominations. Their flagellated Christ, their arrow-riddled Sebastian, never writhe or howl with pain ; indeed they suffer none. Judith, in Mantegna's print, puts the head of Holofernes into her bag with the serenity of a muse ; and the head is quite clean, without loathsome drippings or torn depending strings of muscle ; unconvulsed, a sort of plaster cast. The tragedy of Christ, the tragedy of Judith . . . the whole tragic meaning was unknown to the light and cheerful contemporiares of Ariosto. . . ." There is a note of disappointment in these observations of Mrs Lee.

That the famous renaissance monsters should have had shamelessly delicate and well-shaped heads is shocking, but is natural enough. That the harmless Este prince should have a criminal and hang-dog look is again only natural : as without invoking the greek notion of the divinity of the customary and usual, in such a time as his, to be *good* would be equivalent to being *bad* in a milder time : and he in consequence, feeling the weight of public opinion against him, would perhaps scowl defiantly at the world. That in time of great luxury and taste the adolescent noble should be adroitly curled and beautifully dressed—Machiavelli tells us that they thought of nothing else—is to be expected. Really consummate poisoners do not look like ruffians if they can possibly help it, either. All that part of the argument is too simple-hearted to require comment. As to the bland utopia of art, that is another thrilling difficulty for Mrs Lee—what great art is not utopian ? A canon of japanese art forbade the use of shadows in a picture as being insignificant accompaniments of our chief physical reality. All the greatest art is inclined to refuse or to discipline into something less hot and fluid such shadows as are cast every day by the half-witted excesses of the puny frantic animal crossed in his appetites, and flying for a moment above life's surface in isolated uncontrol.

PART III

SHAKESPEARE AND THE KING
OR HERO

CHAPTER I

THE REASON OF THE CHOICE OF THE EMINENT FOR THE PURPOSES OF TRAGEDY

AT this point the necessary work of preparation for such a study of Shakespeare as I have undertaken is terminated, and we can address ourselves to the evidence provided by the text of the plays on the intricate questions raised in the foregoing portion of this essay. But before passing from the mind of Machiavelli to the mind of Shakespeare, and applying the apologuical lessons of *The Prince* to the figures of Shakespeare's princes, some general statement will be necessary as to the shakespearian conception of the function of tragedy, and the philosophic basis of his conception of the prince or king.

First of all Shakespeare's choice of the eminent—of princes and emperors—was in conformity with the traditional instinct for the *hubris* involved in "greatness." Crystallized in the homely saying, "Pride hath a fall," this instinct has for us its classic expression in the greek drama. The Greeks realized with great acuteness the obvious dangers and certain "pathos" of the insolent splendour of the summer of the year, followed by the wintry retribution descending on the puffed-up vegetation.

Of the need of "exalted persons" for the purposes of tragedy, Mr F. M. Cornford (*The Origin of Attic Comedy*) writes :

"Why does ancient tragedy require this heroic atmosphere? Why was it, in Aristotle's words, a representation of exalted persons (μίμησις σπουδαίων)? When the french critics of the seventeenth and eighteenth centuries interpret this phrase to mean that 'Tragedy represented the life of princes ; Comedy served to depict the actions of the people,' we are disposed to set them down as snobs or, at the best, as courtiers. But we may reflect that

THE LION AND THE FOX

Shakespeare, though he accepted contemporary views of the divinity that hedged a king, was neither a courtier nor a snob. The french critics were not entirely wrong, even as interpreters of Aristotle's meaning. The persons in greek tragedy are royal for a better reason than any secondary cause—such as Pisistratus' encouragement of the achaian epic of Athens. They are royal because at one time to be a king was to be half a god; and these divine princes can therefore tread the same stage with the higher gods, whose will directs the course of human life and is itself immediately overshadowed by the ultimate power of Destiny. . . . Tragedy does not seek to ape the manners or portray the characters of everyday society; its function is to represent the destiny of man, the turning wheel of Time and Fate. To accomplish this, it must roll away the parti-coloured screen, the motley surface of social custom, the fashions and accidents of the place and the hour, and open to our sight a vision of man's life and death, which the bravest can hardly endure to contemplate until it is redeemed by art."

So the *diversity* of character we meet in Shakespeare's slighter plays, where the comic predominates; and the family likeness, and even in many cases identity in the tone of voice or mannerisms—the same sarcasm and gigantic pleasantries, the same magnificent despair—is accounted for if this description of the tragic and comic spheres be accepted. The plot or action becomes everything: the protagonist is always the same mighty shell—the projection of the infinitely complex, deep and universal—therefore, compared to the small " character " of comedy, *featureless* —spirit of the poet. What then generally can it be said that Shakespeare understood by *Tragedy*: how did it come to mean exactly what it did to him, why did he direct it into the exact form he did, and not another form? Professor Bradley can help us here, he has given the best-known account, and a very good one, of this phenomenon. His definition of this tragedy is, " *a story of exceptional calamity leading to the death of a man in high estate.*"

These four things compose it: (1) exceptional misfortune,

(2) death, (3) it must be *one* man, (4) who must be highly placed.

The reason that the individual chosen as the victim of a shakespearian tragedy must be highly placed he explains as follows : " . . . the story of the prince, the triumvir, or the general, has a greatness and dignity of its own. His fate affects the welfare of a whole nation or empire ; and when he falls suddenly from the height of earthly greatness to the dust, his fall produces a sense of contrast, of the power-lessness of man, and of the omnipotence—perhaps the caprice—of Fortune or Fate, which no tale of private life can possibly rival." Professor Bradley invites us to compare the *Lear of the Steppes*, by Tourguéniev (the tale of the tragedy of a peasant), with Shakespeare's *King Lear* : " . . . by an intensification of the life which they share with others they are raised above them ; and the greatest are raised so far that, if we fully realize all that is implied in their words and actions, we become conscious that in real life we have known scarcely anyone resembling them. Some, like Hamlet and Cleopatra, have genius. Others, like Othello, Lear, Macbeth, Coriolanus, are built on the grand scale ; and desire, passion, or will attains in them a terrible force. In almost all we observe a marked onesidedness, a pride of position in some particular direction ; a total incapacity, in certain circumstances, of resisting the force which draws in this direction ; a fatal tendency to identify the whole being with one interest, object, passion, or habit of mind. This, it would seem, is, for Shakespeare, the fundamental tragic trait. . . ." *Cymbeline* or the *Winter's Tale* end happily, and are abortive tragedies, because " the principal characters fail to reach tragic dimensions."

Tales *de casibus illustrium virorum* is the mediæval formula for tragedy ; and obsession and disaster are two of its essentials, and for disaster you must have a pre-liminary situation, for your hero, of the greatest eminence, involving the maximum number of contingent lives and human interests in his downfall.

Shakespeare was the poet of kings, and to the pathos of this function he was peculiarly susceptible, and technically the *pathos* or death of a king or hero was a subject he treated constantly in the course of his trade. I will now examine a few of the peculiar features of this great mainstay of shakespearian tragedy, in order to make clearer what its relation must have been to the poet's affectivity.

CHAPTER II

THE FIGURE OF THE KING

THE figure of the king, and the position of the man occupying the office of supreme power in a community, not by election but for some other reason, is a curious one. His office is connected in our mind with the institution of the patriarch. His period is near to that of the patriarch and his semi-regal system. The apotheosis of the *family* and the apotheosis of the *king* seldom overlap ; for those two institutions disagree. The king's function is in character the natural enemy of the family. In the mediterranean world of classic antiquity, " democracy " was not of course what we mean by that term to-day, but rather a wholesale extension of the aristocratic principle. It essentially consisted of making a race into a caste. The democratic " freedom " of antiquity was a privileged freedom, at the expense of all the world. All foreigners were eligible for slavery, for they were all " barbarian " inferiors. They were in the same category as an ox or pig. It is often noted, as though it were a blot on the early democracies of Greece and Italy, that slavery flourished " side by side " with the democratic form of government. But in fact it seems that slavery was an essential factor in the old idea of democracy. And slavery as it then existed was seemingly less burdensome than much industrial slavery of modern times : nor was it technically more onerous or severe than the family slavery to which everyone had to submit in many early communities.

But the " democracy " of antiquity would also contain the notion, of course, of the *many* against the *one* ; and its effective evolution would have its origin in the determination of the many (but *not too many*) not to become subject to anyone. It was in short a " freedom " balanced *between* the Many and the One ; as far as possible, in conformity with the numerical fancies of the greek mind, exactly half-way. To combine against the One and curtail his power, when he became too strong or too popular, and looked like threatening their liberties, on the one hand; and on the other to form barriers against the human sea of general foreignness, was their idea.

This antique " democracy " was the same sort of very exclusive political game, then, that was being played amongst a chosen few, productive in english history of Magna Charta. "It is impossible to gaze without reverence," says Green, " on the earliest monument of english freedom which we can see with our own eyes and touch with our own hands (in the British Museum): the great Charter to which from age to age patriots have looked back as the basis of english liberty." Indeed, from age to age the aristocratic historian has pointed to this Charter, glowing and beaming in the direction of british liberty; and the king from age to age has been not only the scapegoat and villain, but the screen for oligarchal exploitation. Everyone is now aware, of course, that this Charter had nothing to do with the liberties of " Englishmen," but that of feudal magnates whose " liberty " was of the same order as that whose death Cato did not survive, and which did not, Tacitus asserted, survive the death of Cato.

So the king in these early societies played the game of the One and the Many with a small chosen team, in a small chosen world. And the many on their side were not so very many, not so many as ever to be " the crowd," or the many-headed multitude: but enough to reproduce the general contrast of *numbers* to *singularity*. Everything—radicalism, conservatism, indignant protests against abuse of power, rebellion, severe censure of disobedience—was played on a narrow stage of privileged players. Later the rich burgess was admitted to the game. But he was even less " democratic," in the fictitious, sentimental sense in which that term is used to-day, than the earlier company, up into whose exclusive political sports or farces he had climbed. The poor man, the serf, the helot, was an outcast. He was a *barbarian*—only in class, not race; but more absolutely barbarous than a distinguished alien. He was as much a member of the outside and uncivilized world.

The *king*, however—he too was an outcast of a sort. What he represented was the eternal unit or personal ego ; a strange, unchecked, dangerous element in life (as indeed he usually proved himself). And from the moment he mounted on his solitary throne he was the object of all the jealous solicitude and disguised hatred of his subjects. He has always been the screen behind which the nobles sheltered, and on whose head the general tyranny must eventually be visited. Behind his lonely, spectacularly egotistic, eminent figure a thousand equally intense, cosier, privileged egotisms could subsist.

How near this figure is to the poor man is in a sense psychologically demonstrated in the commerce of Frederick with his *heiduques* and grooms : and it can be more abstractly demonstrated by considering a little closely one of the successors of the monarch, the modern " proletariat." The Proletariat—that fierce, pitiable, harassed abstraction —is in the same way a screen, but a far wider, better-built and more effective one. It can screen even more egotisms than can a king, and mask an even more powerful oligarchy than can coexist with a monarch.

The king is an especially interesting figure in feudal Europe—and it is of course about that figure as it has run its course with us that we are best acquainted. But indeed the king must always be one of the strangest of beings. A sham god : a licensed egotist : the emblem of profound inequalities : the ideally free man. The " pathos of kings " is evident enough : though most kings (although all " murdered ") were busy trying, as is only human, to evade their " pathos ": that is what was so " pathetic." But apart from their " pathos," their figure is full of the strangest interest. They are the emblem of something more important than their " pathos " or themselves : for like degenerate bullfighters, when passed in review—as it was Shakespeare's duty, as dramatic historian, to pass them in review, or as Gibbon does in his *Decline and Fall*—they are a poor and not very prepossessing crowd. As you read

of a mediæval king—in England, France, Aragon, Castille—
you see ideally this bold self-opinionated little speck defending itself against a circle of hostile forces. It is constantly
surrounded and threatened by an armed ring of great
nobles who browbeat and threaten it, and then kiss its
little foot or its hand. It squeaks angrily in reply : and lies
back to be kissed. In Castille these grandees even, or *ricos
hombres* as they were universally named in spanish countries,
had, as one of their most inalienable privileges, the right to
publicly renounce allegiance to it. In Aragon, even, the
strangest and most whimsically insulting obligation was
thrown on this solitary sovereign figure : when one of its
great vassals quarrelled with anyone, and decided to resort
to the noble's privilege of private war—it had to "mind"
the families and estates of the vassal while he was engaged
in these absorbing enterprises : even, presumably, if they
happened to be conducted against his own person.

The *rico hombre*, or noble, on the other hand, although a
sort of king himself, and the object, on a smaller scale, of
the same confusing attentions, is usually in history—at least
when on the same canvas with the king—one of a group.
He is not the same lonely personality. He has the king
between himself and God : whereas the king, at the pin-
nacle of the social pyramid, is alone with God in the midst
of the cloud of majesty that hedges a king—like Moses
on the mountain. The privileges of the feudal noble were
sometimes very great, enhanced by all the obligations of
chivalry. In Aragon, for instance, he appointed the judges
on his domain ; exercised over his vassals absolute criminal
jurisdiction ; was exempt from taxation, likewise was in-
eligible for corporal or capital punishment ; nor could he
be imprisoned. Further, as stated above, he had the right
to make war on the king when he wanted to, and it was
his acknowledged right to take service with a neighbouring
king against his own if he found that easier than fighting
him single-handed or with some fellow-barons. The Laras
of Castille " had a great relish for rebellion," and the Castros
were " much in the habit of going over to the Moors."

But the rôle of the king—or in a smaller way of the lord

of a demesne—in the psychology of subject-men was a different one to the head-man in a system of patriarchal agnate evolution. The feudal european king was essentially not a patriarch, but a stranger and an *enemy*. The king and his nobles were usually of another race to the subject, their mastery beginning in physical conquest. Their lordship could be grafted on to a fully working patriarchal or communistic unit. In Maine's *Ancient Law* the Russians are instanced in this connexion: "The Russian villages are not fortuitous assemblages of men, nor are they unions founded on contract; they are naturally organized communities like those of India. It is true that these villages are always in theory the patrimony of some noble proprietor, and the peasants have within historical times been converted into the predial, and to a great extent into the personal, serfs of the seignior. But the pressure of this superior ownership has never crushed the ancient organization of the village. . . ." In England the village life of the *gebur* and *cottier* passed over to some norman lord, intact, in the eleventh century.

These russian or anglo-saxon serfs had their *individual* stranger (a small personal god) quartered on them, giving a personal form to all the anonymous outer power of the universe, against which it was impossible to fight, but against which—on usurious terms and in exchange for service and taxes or, if a king's man, *tallage*—he agreed to protect them. He was their *enemy*, a representative of the outer hostile world, between whom and themselves the terms of propitiation and sacrifice had been systematized. It was a pagan, human arrangement, and naturally with the Reformation it disappeared.

Professor Leaf (*Homer and History*) shows the uprooted, migrating race receding from their pantheon (the apparatus of a settled life) and becoming "gods" themselves. They arrive ultimately in the country they are to govern *impersonating* to some extent the gods of their own pantheon. But they impose it on the subject inhabitants as a living system, in which *they* participate. "The Achaian regards his gods nominally with the greatest reverence, practically, with a detachment which covers an almost sceptical independence. On occasion he will speak of them with unsuitable levity. . . . The Achaian is in this respect, one may almost say, a typical man of the world. His attitude is the outcome of his experience . . . he has learnt completely the futility of the primitive magic : he has come to trust in his right arm, and to mock at the old magic, rites and dances and ' medicine '—the achaian outlook on the world is essentially human, emancipated and modern."

This is Professor Chadwick's "Heroic Age"; the scepticism and brutality of the actors in the great ages of migratory readjustment—of new birth by migration, the habits of people on the wing. The gods become heroes—the migratory conquerors themselves, in short. And as they are gods and heroes for themselves, so are they for some time, till seen through or assimilated, to their new subject population.

" The teutonic ' Volkerwanderung ' brought about, like the achaian, the destruction of the older group-system, and the substitution for it of a religion based on *gods in the likeness of men*, who are essentially what I have called epiphenomena in the government of the world."

So the irreligion of the later Greeks is accounted for by the fact that the agnostic conquerors imposed on the pelasgian population the official olympian system. But as they did not believe in it themselves, their new subjects did not either. Yet this huge northern theological ornament in a sense smothered the cults still held to, along with it, by the subjugated race.

The Pelasgians have no names for their gods, says Herodotus : but they get a name when Dionysos is imported from Thrace :

" The primitive powers or daimons were in their essence anonymous. The worshipper was at first, it would seem, the same as the worshipped, and the magic dance or other rite meant that the dancer was dancing his daimon, and was thereby identified with him. . . . But a time came when the impulse arose to give names to these vague nature powers. It may have arisen from the gradual evolution of the individual consciousness out of the group-consciousness" (Leaf, *Homer and History*).

Dionysos got only grudging admission to the olympian circle, where he was always " treated as a parvenu." However he fitted in with, gave a name to, and reinforced the field-magic and symbolic dances of the subject population. So he was a rustic and democratic god.

Many of the homeric heroes are divinized and become the object of a cult, however. The conquering race bestows its names, the names of its popular leaders, on the nameless functional gods of the conquered. The conquerors are a *race of gods* : they all have *names* (one of the aristocrat's names for a serf is " nameless one ") : death divinizes all of them. (It was at that point—the common meeting-place of *ancestor-worship*—that the two religious systems of the Achaians and the Pelasgians would have the best chance of coalescing.)

It is not meant that the above picture of the conquering race in early Greece should be associated literally with the destiny of the norman conquerors of England. William the Conqueror was a french noble and did not give himself out to be the son of a scandinavian god. Indeed it is supposed that when the Normans arrived in England they had forgotten even what their name signified, and regarded themselves as Frenchmen. But any conquering race must possess certain *débouchés* into the realms of divinity. Their power and success and martial superiority, joined to their alien speech and ways, appeals to the imagination of the conquered.

In the early chaos of mediæval France a baron would ride up to a township and, satisfied of its possibilities as regards position (at a cross-road or ford), would announce that he was going to be its protector in future, build his fort, and farm the tolls and revenues associated with his function of military policeman and magistrate. Whether by such means as this or as part of a wholesale event like the norman conquest of England, each little fold of sheep had its tame local Lion, which lay down with them, more or less, and acted as an expensive watch-dog. This lion—

king or lord—represented the primitive backgrounds of life. He also represented the male element: the female was represented by service and husbandry. He was idle, fierce, wandering and mouching about a good deal of the time: the serf and the female were rooted to the soil, theoretically. (The theory of the female origin of agriculture arose in such contrasts as this.) Ideally then the king or lord was a lonely, parasitic stranger. The superstitious dread that the primitive man has always felt for a stranger, endowing him with supernatural attributes, would at first act in favour of this cyclopian figure imposed on his settled life. As, however, hatred and dread are the principal components of the love that is offered to a divinity, it is easy to see how the king could be invested in feudal times by his poor subjects with distant and non-human attributes which he did not possess, certainly, for his peers. Hemmed in with this " divinity " it is easy to see how the king, on his side, liked " his people " better than he liked his swarm of great feudatories—how, in short, the king and the poor man were " drawn together," and how it was possible, in a hostile world, for a considerable sympathy to exist between them. There are some kings who felt this situation very much—like St Louis, for instance, who, dressed in the plainest clothes, would go and sit under the trees in the Bois and do justice, in a way reminiscent of the english *hundred court* held on the waste beneath a tree. The people would also sometimes show a paternal care for their king—as when in the thirteenth century a castillian king was presented with a petition advising him to spend less on his food and dress, and to " bring his appetite within a more reasonable compass." This was a turning of the tables on monarchy, from which direction sumptuary injunctions usually came.

As a government by a tyrant or king is that form of government by which the maximum of living and personal rule is to be obtained, at least that much is to be said for it. An oligarchy is more anonymous: "a democracy" still more so. The more names and personalities there are associated with an act of government the less personal responsibility of course is established in it; and liberty is personal irresponsibility, depending wholly on the *responsibility* of somebody else. So of course the dangers for the many in a form of government pretending to be by them—for you have no redress against what you do yourself or are supposed to have done yourself—are as patent as the inconveniences of a capricious government by the average man. But the idea of monarchy always implied that the king was not an average man, and it was that, the religious *motif*, that brought in the danger.

The mediæval king was usually divided between stupid love of power and self-importance, and a desire to escape the lonely implications of kingship. In any case, these considerations define the nature of the rule of the west european king of the Middle Ages, arising in the more or less free germanic communities of the north. He is always surrounded by an armed ring of powerful subject-kings of the same race and class as himself, and by a much larger sea of a foreign multitude of subjects. Sometimes this dark outer zone sleeps, or stirs with reverence, or, periodically, dashes menacingly towards him. He was in the nature of an auntsally always, as we find him in shakespearean drama. He was, from the moment he entered the arena, the bull to be attacked and sacrificed if possible. He was a lonely animal, he charged about : only, as the game was desultory and leisurely, except for the rush of occasional onslaughts, he often died a " natural death." But when Richard II. says, in Shakespeare's play, *all* " murdered," he was expressing his instinctive sense of what the function of the king was intended to be by the savage and superstitious society in the midst of which he lived. The later kings became merely more and more ineffective beggars and blackmailers ; until, with the final eclipse of the Stuarts, they ceased to be kings at all in the dramatic sense described above.

CHAPTER III

THE RÔLE OF THE JESTER, OR " VITUPERATOR," AND THE DIVINITY " HEDGING " A KING

LEAVING the lonely king where he vanishes from history in Europe as a full-blooded figure we will turn for a moment to some other, alien, manifestation of the same function, and see the inseparable gibing shadow, which is a usual accompaniment of the royal office, in a more picturesque form than is provided by the jester of a european prince. In the centre of the canvas in most of Shakespeare's plays we find the king or prince, and his peers ; and among them there is a man who is there, with some discretion, it is true, to slander and ridicule them. Even private persons have their " clown," or sort of comic conscience—like Olivia in *Twelfth Night*. Over against the fortunate central person is always another figure, or impulse, that contradicts his power and happiness. This propitiatory figure is a sort of periapt or *paratonnerre* : his function is to forestall adversity, and guarantee (should the dark powers look at the small human figure of authority with jealous eyes) that the *hubris* is not there, or that there is a factor of disillusion always present to prevent too dangerous and overweening an insolence. The jester is thus there *for luck*.

We can match this situation—showing it as a well-established arrangement—if we go to Africa for the purpose. The thonga kings had attached to them, as a part of their royal state, an official Thersites.

" In each of these diminutive realms there reigns an hereditary monarch. . . . His office is invested with an atmosphere of sacredness ; his name is taboo except in oaths ; he takes precedence in the rights of the first-fruits . . . and above all he is in possession of a powerful charm that magically ensures the inviolability of the country.

THE DIVINITY "HEDGING" A KING

The king exacts tribute in kind; he receives a basket of food from each kraal at harvest time and part of the game animals killed in the chase. His subjects must till the royal fields, clean his public square, build and repair his huts. Finally he appropriates a large portion of the fines imposed by him in court; for legislative, judicial and executive functions are merged in his person, and from his judgment there is no appeal."

So the thonga king possesses many points of comparison with the mediæval king or grandee in Europe.

But "although the king thus enjoys great prerogatives and wields considerable authority, he cannot be described as an absolute autocrat. If his actions run counter to received standards of propriety he is severely criticized by the people, and may even be deposed.

"There is little ostentation about thonga kings as compared with other african rulers. They do not differ in their attire from the subjects, sometimes occupy kraals no larger than those of commoners, and may indulge in ' so modest an occupation ' as scaring sparrows from a plantation."

So compared to the traditional splendour of oriental kings, and the state of many african ones, the thonga king has a western feudal simplicity. But his clown and another functionary outdo the freedom of Shakespeare's comic shadow to the kingship: ". . . The herald enjoys a peculiar official status. His duty it is to appear before the king's door every morning and to exalt the exploits of the ruler's ancestors, which is followed by vigorous disparagement of the present incumbent. Eloquence seems to be the sole qualification for this office, and what is its nature here may be gathered from a few characteristic sentences in a long rhapsody by a distinguished herald:

" Muhlaba Shiluvene [the king's father], you are like the rhinoceros who seizes a man, bites him through and through, rolls him over and cuts him in two ! You are like the crocodile which lives in water ; it bites a man ! You are like its claws ; it seizes a man by his arms and legs, it drags him into the deep pool to eat him at sunset ; it watches over the entrance to prevent other crocodiles from taking its prey. . . .

"Why do you govern them so mildly? Look at them with terrible eyes? You are a coward! . . . Act with bravery and defend yourself!"

At least equally remarkable is another licensed character, the "public vituperator," or court jester, who may hurl the most offensive insults at anyone in the country, from the king down. He may wantonly accuse his contemporaries of incest and snatch food from the hands of the king himself" (Lowie, *Primitive Society*).

So the thonga king is supplied by custom with a scurrilous chorus of the sort Shakespeare supplied the achaian heroes with in the person of Thersites.

How the comic servant of the *commédia dell' arte* harlequin, and every famous comic incarnation, down to Chaplin's "Charlie," have at the root of their function a considerable identity with that of the greatest tragic poet it would be interesting to show. The *thieving* of the comic servant, for instance, appeals to the same emotions as the *killing* of Coriolanus. One is taking some of the wealth away from the hated "boss," the other is destroying the semi-divine hero. But that is not all that is happening in the second case, of course; and there is every shade and variety of poetic justice, and an unlimited number of modifying factors, in both instances.

It would be interesting to examine a little the extraordinary machinery employed to effect the isolation of the individual called to this destiny of supreme authority. The accounts of chinese ceremoniousness (such as can be found, for instance, in Müller's series of the Sacred Books of the East) certainly have not been approached by any european society. The Valois paid great attention, however, to the mechanism of state, notably Henry III., who devoted a great deal of thought to "hedging" himself with the requisite divinity. But generally speaking the european has shown himself much less sensitive in these arrangements than the oriental. He hardly had time, perhaps, to get very far in that direction.

THE DIVINITY "HEDGING" A KING

The european has never been an absolute ruler in the way asiatic and african rulers have been. No feudal king ever reached the elaboration of even, for instance, the former kings of Dakomi. Here is an extract from an account of the extraordinary completeness of the ceremonial power of a small savage ruler, less civilized even than an early european king:

". . . in theory at least everything in Dakomi belongs to the king, and if any man has anything in his possession, it is only because the king tolerates it for the time being. This theory is pushed so far that parents are held to have no right or claim to their children, who, like everything else, belong to the king and are retained by the parents only at the king's pleasure.

"The person of the king is sacred, and if he drink in public, everyone must turn the head so as not to see him, while some of the court women hold up a cloth before him as a screen. He never eats in public, and the people affect to believe that he neither eats nor sleeps. It is criminal to say the contrary. In the royal presence the chiefs even of the highest rank are obliged to prostrate themselves like the meanest subject" (A. B. Ellis, *The Ewe-speaking Peoples of the Slave Coast*).

The refrain of Monsieur, in *Bussy d'Ambois*, "Anything but killing the king," is a mockery of a superstition of the sort described above. Even Bussy's children would, "like everything else, belong to the king." The word *king* is played on to ridicule this infatuation. In Dakomi an eighteenth-century king named Bossa carried the principle of kingship so far that, on succeeding to "the stool," he had every man and male child named Bossa put to death, so that no one should bear the same name as himself.

It is necessary, in order to realize the full potency of the tragic art of the stage in any country, to allow fully for these extraordinary conditions, which have no parallel to-day, and are perhaps not easy for the contemporary man to grasp. To see this semi-divine person, even in effigy and in play, exposed to the vulgarest misfortune, disgraced, humiliated and killed, must have been in most times an extraordinary sensation. This man masquerading as a god was suddenly confronted with powers superior to himself: the delight in the spectacle of this confrontation was one of the great assets of tragedy. If we do not accustom ourselves to the idea of the psychological strength of the " hedge " of divinity behind which the king lived we shall not understand the object of these dramatic spectacles, and their great appeal.

CHAPTER IV

SINGULARITY AND RESPONSIBILITY

THE function of the king is curiously bound up with the idea of sacrifice. Overwhelming evidence to this effect is provided by Sir James Frazer in his wonderful series of books, *The Golden Bough*. With regard to payment for his strange semi-divine eminence men have at all times been, when that was possible, very exacting. "Uneasy lies the head that wears a crown," and such homely observations, respond to a fact that no observer of the state of kings, such as Shakespeare was, could miss.

But of course this behaviour, so characteristic of all men where the function of political leadership is concerned, extends to everything having claim to eminence. To-day we are especially well placed to observe this : for in the universal organized revolt against authority it is not only the head of a state or the head of a family—the king (on account of political privilege), the man (on account of sex privilege), the employer (on account of his monopoly of wealth)—but, with an ingenious thoroughness, every form of even the most modest eminence, that is attacked. Indeed the centre of attack is rapidly shifting from the really eminent (who are considered as already destroyed) to the *petit bourgeois* mass of the smally privileged. The revolutionary waves, again, have long extended the scope of their action, and have found fresh "kings" or leaders in every province of life. It is in the course of this universal king-hunt, naturally, that the revolutionary crowd arrives, sooner or later, beneath the statue of William Shakespeare. The poet, a forefinger pressed upon his temple, gazes pensively at the assemblage, his short fat calves crossed ; one toe pressing his pedestal, as one finger presses his temple. The revolutionary crowd exults. This is evidently a king of some sort ! It is not a moment to be on a pedestal, **as** the monumental Shakespeare must already have had many occasions, of late, of observing.

But without the scientific organization of revolution, as effective as a vacuum-cleaner, men have always had this much wider instinct for the divine—that is, of course, the instinct to destroy it, isolate it, or corrupt it to their uses. In a time when there is no accredited divinity, or " divine right," left, it is in a sense easier to observe the universal operation of this instinct. It is almost more impressive to see a great writer like Tolstoi banned in Russia on account of his gentleness, and humaneness, than to see a king banished by his people on account of his quite unreal " greatness," usually accompanied with a stupid ferocity.

So that dark competitive self, in the smallest organism, that makes it murderous, becomes organized into the type of *herd-war against the head*, where almost anything high, unusual and unassimilable is sighted. From the supreme christian illustration, the Lamb of God, to the smallest stock—personally held—of that *virtù*, the steadfastness and virility, so dear to Machiavelli, such concentrations of life within one organism arouse fear and hatred—as six men looking out of one man's face through his eyes would ; or provoke a sense of the unnatural—as six men's strength in a hero's arm might seem like the six arms of a god whirling on the side of one body.

The ostensible reasons for most acts of human sacrifice, partial or entire, are very numerous and contradictory. These questions always arise where an individual destiny is at stake. It is the person wrenched out of the organic context by the impulses of some divine ferment, and this being appearing suddenly free, that is the signal for those dispensations and adjustments, culminating in his pathos, when the circumstances are favourable. In the case of the hereditary king it is usually an artificial isolation of an otherwise quite orthodox and often very small personality. But, as though the separation were real, he has to suffer in his state because of its symbolism.

It must be remembered that human beings are congeries

SINGULARITY AND RESPONSIBILITY

of parasites subsisting on The Individual, subsisting on a very insufficient supply of Individuals, who are consequently overstaffed or overstocked to a dangerous degree. And anything representing the principle of individuality they attack. They are easily deceived, and often mistake the sign for the thing. On the back of every great human intelligence there are millions of contingent forms, which it propels and feeds. The relations subsisting between this lonely host and the organisms to whom he is appropriated is not very often marked by a warm mutual sympathy.

Men are always on the look-out for some *responsible* principle—inevitably, as we have already seen must be the case—on which to cast their troubles and perplexities. There is the greatest danger, in consequence, in claiming any relation with the supernatural, for any man; for if taken at his word he assumes all the responsibilities of a god—and they are many. People are only too willing to accept such a claim; there is nothing easier than to be " great," or to be accepted as a leader, or as a person possessing magical potentialities—as many people have discovered with some astonishment, especially in disordered times, and to their cost. But the vengeance exacted of a god is a different thing to what men expect in repayment from each other.

It is the difference, not the superiority, that is the offence or the challenge, or that involves the responsibility. Thus the *ottimati* or oligarchy are, for the mass of citizens, merely *the same only more so* : whereas the king or prince is essentially in a different category. He is the Person, the One, the responsible representative of others, and for men a very strange principle of power, qualitative instead of quantitative. The " secret drinker " is an illustration of this : he might drink twice as much if he did not do it alone. And to wish to *be* alone, or to drink alone, or to do anything else alone, is the first step to the supernatural : which, in its turn, is the first step to the stake or the crucifix.

For those who are not familiar with *The Golden Bough* I will quote a few passages which it is very necessary to be acquainted with for the full elucidation of this sort of question. That the researches of Frazer are interesting in the widest way is certain. For the institutions of the primitive herd approximate to something that can be found, in however degenerate a form, in any herd at all.

CHAPTER V

SHAKESPEARE AS EXECUTIONER

" BY no people," Frazer writes, " does the custom of sacrificing the human representative of a god appear to have been observed so commonly and with so much solemnity as by the Aztecs of ancient Mexico." And the Spaniards in the sixteenth century were astonished to find in this distant part of the world a ritual so reminiscent of the central fact of christianity, the sacrifice of a god.

This is the general description of what happened, told by the jesuit Acosta :

" They took a captive, such as they thought good ; and afore they did sacrifice him unto their idols, they gave him the name of the idol, to whom he should be sacrificed, and apparelled him with the same ornaments like their idol, saying, that he did represent the same idol. And during the time that this representation lasted, which was for a year in some parts, in others six months, and in others less, they reverenced and worshipped him in the same manner as the proper idol ; and in the meantime he did eat, drink and was merry. When he went through the streets, the people came forth to worship him ; and everyone brought him an alms, with children and sick folks, that he might cure them, and bless them, supposing him to do all things at his pleasure, only he was accompanied with ten or twelve men lest he should fly. And he (to the end he might be reverenced as he passed) sometimes sounded upon a small flute, that the people might prepare to worship him. The feast being come, and he grown fat, they killed him, opened him, and ate him, making a solemn sacrifice of him."

It is probable that the festival occurred during May ; and the resurrection rite—*i.e.* the enthroning of a new victim—was a feature of it.

" At this festival the great god died in the person of one

human representative and came to life again in the person of another, who was destined to enjoy the fatal honour of divinity for a year and to perish, like all his predecessors, at the end of it. The young man singled out for this high dignity was carefully chosen from among the captives on the ground of his personal beauty. He had to be of unblemished body, slim as a reed and straight as a pillar, neither too tall nor too short. If through high living he grew too fat, he was obliged to reduce himself by drinking salt water. And in order that he might behave in his lofty station with becoming grace and dignity he was carefully trained to comport himself like a gentleman of the first quality, to speak correctly and eloquently, to play the flute, to smoke cigars and to snuff at flowers with a dandified air. He was honourably lodged in the temple, where the nobles waited on him and paid him homage, bringing him meat and serving him like a prince. . . . When this bejewelled exquisite lounged through the streets playing on his flute, puffing at a cigar, and smelling at a nosegay, the people whom he met threw themselves on the earth before him and prayed to him with sighs and tears. . . . Women came forth with children in their arms and presented them to him, saluting him as a god. For ' he passed for our Lord God ; the people acknowledged him as the Lord. . . .' Twenty days before he was to die his costume was changed, and four damsels, delicately nurtured and bearing the names of four goddesses—the goddess of Flowers, the goddess of the Young Maize, the goddess of ' Our Mother among the Water,' and the goddess of Salt —were given him to be his brides, and with them he consorted. During the last five days, divine honours were showered on the destined victim."

Then at the appointed time he was sacrificed :

" Like the Mexican temples in general, it [the one at which the sacrifice was to occur] was built in the form of a pyramid ; and as the young man ascended the stairs he broke at every step one of the flutes on which he had played in the days of his glory. On reaching the summit he was seized and held down by the priests on his back upon a block of stone, while one of them cut open his breast, thrust his hand into the wound, and wrenching out his heart held it up in sacrifice to the sun. The body of the dead god was not, like the bodies of human victims, sent rolling down the steps of the temple, but was carried down to the foot, where the head was cut off and spitted on a pike. Such was the regular end of the man who personated the greatest god of the mexican pantheon " (Sir James Frazer, *The Scapegoat*).

The similarity of the notions in this aztec sacrifice and the sacramental death of Christ is obvious. It becomes more so when the resemblance between the rites of the Saturnalia in western Asia and the account of the crucifixion of Christ in the gospels are contrasted for us, as is done by Sir James Frazer:

"An eminent scholar has recently pointed out the remarkable resemblance between the treatment of Christ by the roman soldiers at Jerusalem and the treatment of the mock king of the Saturnalia by the roman soldiers at Durnstorum; and he would explain the similarity by supposing that the soldiers ridiculed the claims of Christ to a divine kingdom by arraying him in the familiar garb of old King Saturn. . . .

"But closely as the passion of Christ resembles the treatment of the mock king of the Saturnalia, it resembles still more closely the treatment of the mock king of the Sacaea. The description of the mockery by St Matthew is the fullest. It runs thus: 'Then released he Barabbas unto them: and when he had scourged Jesus, he delivered him to be crucified. Then the soldiers of the governor took Jesus into the common hall, and gathered unto him the whole band of soldiers. And they stripped him, and put on him a scarlet robe. And when they had platted a crown of thorns, they put it upon his head, and a reed in his right hand: and they bowed the knee before him, and mocked him, saying, Hail, King of the Jews! And they spit upon him, and took the reed, and smote him on the head. And after that they had mocked him, they took the robe off from him, and put his own raiment on him, and led him away to crucify him' (Matthew xxvii. 26-31). Compare with this the treatment of the mock king of the Sacaea, as it is described by Dio Chrysostom : ' They take one of the prisoners condemned to death and seat him upon the king's throne, and give him the king's raiment, and let him lord it and drink and run riot and use the king's concubines during these days, and no man prevents him from doing just what he likes. But afterwards they strip and scourge and crucify him. . . .'

" We have every reason to think that the jewish festival of Purim is a continuation, under a changed name, of the babylonian Sacaea, and that in celebrating it by the destruction of an effigy of Haman, the modern Jews have kept up a reminiscence of the ancient custom of crucifying or hanging a man in the character of a god at the festival. Is it not possible that at an earlier time they may, like the Babylonians themselves, have regularly compelled a condemned criminal to play the tragic part, and that Christ thus perished in the character of Haman ? "

So if no one offers himself as a leader, or represents himself as a god, men will choose the best specimen they can find and compel him to adopt this deadly rôle. But they have never had to look far for their victims : for either a slave, a thief or some fanatical teacher has always been found to answer to this human requirement in one form or another. With the actual, secularly established kings, however, they have on occasion had some difficulty. This form of victim has either tricked them or rebelled. Frazer (in *The Dying God*) gives a very amusing example of this latter type of defaulter :

" Many days' journey to the north-east of Abomey, the old capital of Dahomey, lies the kingdom of Eyeo. ' The Eyeos are governed by a king no less absolute than the king of Dahomey, yet subject to a regulation of state at once humiliating and extraordinary. When the people have conceived an opinion of his ill-government, which is sometimes insidiously infused into them by the artifice of his discontented ministers, they send a deputation to him with a present of parrots' eggs, as a mark of its authenticity, to represent to him that the burden of government must have so far fatigued him that they consider it full time for him to repose from his cares and indulge himself with a little sleep. He thanks his subjects for their attention to his ease, retires to his own apartment as if to sleep, and there gives direction to his women to strangle him. This is immediately executed, and his son quietly ascends the throne upon the usual terms of holding the reins of government no longer than whilst he merits the approbation of the people.' About the year 1774, a king of Eyeo, whom his ministers attempted to remove in the customary manner, positively refused to accept the proffered parrots' eggs at their hands, telling them that he had no mind to take a nap, but on the contrary was resolved to watch for the benefit of his subjects. The ministers, surprised and indignant at his recalcitrancy, raised a rebellion, but were defeated with great slaughter, and thus by his spirited conduct the king freed himself from the tyranny of his councillors and established a new precedent for the guidance of his successors" (*cf.* A. Dalzel, *History of Dahomey*).

But not many kings in face of such a situation have shown themselves so undocile as this. Most have lain down obediently and allowed themselves to be strangled.

In the case of the "dying god" in the examples cited above his death is in the nature of a purgation. "The accumulated misfortunes and sins of the whole people are sometimes laid upon the dying god, who is supposed to bear them away for ever, leaving the people innocent and happy. The notion that we can transfer our guilt and sufferings to some other being who will bear them for us is familiar to the savage mind."

But another expression of the same notion of vicariousness is the choosing of a hero or champion who represents the people, and supports, like a shield in front of them, fortune's hardest blows. It would in any case be a matter of highest interest to the people that this shield should be sound and not impaired by time and fortune. But in the case of the Eyeo king just described the conception of his function includes a universal influence over the fertility of the crops and herds. So his responsibility becomes manifold. Thus " the people of the Congo believed . . . that if their pontiff, the Chitomé, were to die a natural death the world would perish, and the earth, which he alone sustained by his power and merit, would be immediately annihilated. Accordingly, when he fell ill and seemed likely to die, the man who was destined to be his successor entered the pontiff's house with a rope or a club and strangled or clubbed him to death . . ."

The shilluk king, again (in *The White Nile*), was held in very great honour, chiefly because he is regarded as a reincarnation of Nyakang, the semi-divine hero who settled the tribe in their present territory. This king, the moment his wives began to complain that he was no longer bestowing as much attention on them as formerly, was executed. It was the conviction of these people that a decline in the virility of their king would cause the cattle to sicken, the crops to rot in the fields, and probably his subjects to be decimated with disease. So this king must have watched his wives' transports with an anxious eye.

But also he had, if called upon to do so, to enter the lists against any challenger that might present himself, claiming to be a more suitable man than himself for his divine office. So he had to be a very strong man indeed, always in the pink of condition.

That is all the space I can devote to the psychology of the eminent, and the element of sacrifice in tragedy. To those unfamiliar with Sir James Frazer's books the extracts I have chosen will give some idea of how these subjects are connected ; and the barbarous pictures recorded in the course of Frazer's investigations, such as those provided by the jesuit Acosta, show, transposed as it were into a logical setting, the rationale, or the hidden meaning, of the "tragic" impulse. The innocent-looking, compassionate representation of an agony and death, like that of Othello, with its catharsis by means of tears and pity, is thus, as

SHAKESPEARE AS EXECUTIONER

though in a dream, revealed as something else. It is a show of the same nature as a public execution. And the attraction of the story of the passion and agony on the Cross was naturally of the same order as that which took people to Tyburn ; and the tudor playwright competed with the spectacle of bears and dogs rolling in agony in the sand of the bear-pit. But these connexions are not very obscure, they suggest one another plainly enough. It is of course far more difficult to follow the connexion when you come down to our time, when the mixture of the sensations of vengeance, superstition, hatred, envy, worship, all bound up with the ancient animal cunning, of which the " tragic " and dramatic instinct is composed, have to dispense with the gushing of blood, the vinegar and the fainting god, every murderous instinct translated into, and compressed in, civilized reserve.

Shakespeare was in this sense a public executioner, a quiet and highly respectable man, as might be expected. His *impassibility* was the professional mask of the hangman. For dramatic effect the dramatist, like the hangman, must be *impassible*. His attitude to the many kings and heroes who were done to death by him was *not* conveyed —that is the idea of this contention—by the impassible, impressive, dramatic, " unmoved " mask of the executioner. But actually the mask was incessantly convulsed with the most painful unprofessional emotions ; and it was apt to be tear-stained and fixed in a bitter grimace as he left the scaffold.

PART IV
SHAKESPEARE AND THE AGENT-PRINCIPLE

CHAPTER I

SHAKESPEARE A FEMININE GÉNIUS

AT the beginning of the preceding section it was said that Shakespeare differed profoundly from such a theorist of "action" as Machiavelli: and was, indeed, for all the bustle and vitality of his heroic plots, rather a contemplator than an actor. His actual performances on the stage appear to have been insignificant: and that is in keeping with the view of him advanced here. It is from this fact that the "impersonality" theory derives its principal support. He was always representing *action* and great movements of passion, and yet there is a feeling that he did not participate in this action. For this belief I would substitute the view that he *did* participate, but that he participated on the side opposed to action. His observation would have endorsed all the pessimism of Machiavelli: but, unlike him, he was without that mechanical appetite for what he would regard as a useless and degrading performance of a series of—however logically perfect—tricks.

There is no intention here of representing Shakespeare as a philosopher, or as one of those great generalizing minds that fecundate the world from time to time with new and dazzling principles of truth. He should probably be regarded, rather, as a sort of feminine genius, if that notion can consort with the circumstance of the very great energy of his work and its muscular appearance. He was receptive; he was the type, almost, of "the artist" (though it is true that other poets have produced more perfect work than he): he was the *ideal spectator*, we could say. But he was not, in consequence, without personality: the spectator in question was very much moved; and I believe it can be shown that he reacted according to laws that are not at all difficult to distinguish if he is read attentively, with that in view—instead of the more usual habit of pretending he was a sphinx. Asynartetic all such art must be, and its absolute rhythm is statelier than that of life: but what *titanism*, to use Arnold's word, is always threatening the peace of its heroic measure!

The emotion caused by the spectacle of some event may be different from that experienced by a participant; indeed usually it is. It is also of a different kind. Not mingled with action, the sense of the event in the spectator is even of a different character. Further, provided with that sense, and that sense only, it would be impossible to *act*. The audience sees one event, and the actor sees another. Action has one pair of eyes, contemplation another: or action has hardly any eyes at all—they are in any case very rudimentary.

But this was the situation also of the greek chorus: "There comes someone who relates, or definitely enacts, the actual death or 'pathos' of the hero, while the Chorus goes on as before expressing emotion about it. This emotion, it is easy to see, may be quite different from that felt by the Hero. . . . The dramatist may make his characters express all that they can properly feel; he may put into articulate dialogue all that it will bear. But there still remains some residue which no one on the stage can personally feel and which can only express itself as music or yearnings of the body. This emotion finds its one instrument in the Chorus" (Professor Gilbert Murray, *Euripides and his Age.*)

As the comic and tragic, so the looker-on and the actor—the spectator, the chorus, the doer and the god—were all mixed in Shakespeare.

Sir J. Robertson's account of the early Shakespeare—prior to the alleged "psychic transformation" occurring between the period of the comedies and the production of *Hamlet*—cannot be neglected. Here are some passages conveying the gist of it: "We are dealing with a temperament or mentality," Sir J. Robertson says, "not at all obviously original or masterly, not at all conspicuous at the outset for intellectual depth or seriousness, not at all obtrusive of its 'mission'; but exhibiting simply a gift for acting, an abundant faculty of rhythmical speech, and a power of minute observation joined with a thoroughly practical or commercial handling of the problem of life, in a calling not usually adopted by a commercially minded man. What emerges for us therefore is the conception of a very plastic intelligence, a good deal led and swayed by immediate circumstances . . . not much cultured, not profound, not deeply passionate; not particularly reflective though copious in utterance; a personality which, of itself, if under no pressure of pecuniary need, would not be likely to give the world any serious sign of mental capacity whatever.

"The fresh conditions of deeply moving experience or deep intellectual stimulus must therefore be invoked to account for the Shakespeare of the great tragedies and tragi-comedies."

This estimate is largely based on *Venus and Adonis* and *The Rape of Lucrece*. There is "no innate burden of thought, bound to be delivered"; there is "only the wonderful sensitive plate or responsive faculty."

Before this passage Sir J. Robertson has explained how necessary he believes it to be for an understanding of Shakespeare to dispose of the criticism of the earlier shakespearian commentators. A mastery of the *apparatus criticus* would be required before you were qualified to form an opinion on the interesting question of Shakespeare's transformations raised by this critic. Such questions as to whether the phrase "rough-hew them how we will," and the same wording ("rough-hew"), in the same context of thought, in Florio's *Montaigne*, is a proof of borrowing; whether the resemblance of Clytemnestra and Lady Macbeth, of Alcestis and Katharina (in the *Shrew*), and much identity of thought scattered through the plays, proves that he was in reality penetrated with early greek thought (as Mr Collins says was the case), or whether this was merely accidental borrowing from Sophocles, or whether he was thinking for himself; such questions must be kept for the specialist. Where we can be of use to the specialist, perhaps, is by bringing, largely by contact with the plays, as an innocent student, direct registrations that might from the region of experience bring confirmation of what the specialist may claim to have found in analysis and research. It must also not be lost sight of that what the specialist discovers (among all the things there are to discover) have usually first existed as intuitions in the field of experience : from which field he has passed, full of purpose and usually formulating his theories as he goes, into the laboratory. He also has a habit, armed cap-à-pie with the spoils of the laboratory, of returning into the experiential field once more, where it is that we usually find him.

Whether we are prepared to follow Sir J. Robertson or not in his estimate of Shakespeare, it is certain that the character of his genius was *responsive* and not *active* : he was not a philosopher himself at all, so much as a very great and accommodating artist—accommodating himself, with great suppleness, but not slavishly or without bitter comment, to the life, art and ideas around him. He was not inclined to any very strong expression of belief. Although within that receptive frame he displays very much more passion and prejudice than is generally allowed, nevertheless, that the framework was opportunist, accommodating, and in that sense " unoriginal " is evident. And it is in this sense that he was " impersonal "—a particularly glorious parasite on everything. But of all parasites that have ever breathed on a human back he was the most fastidious, most critical of his bloody supper, possessed the greatest moderation and rectitude, and an infallible taste.

CHAPTER II

SHAKESPEARE'S INFATUATION FOR ANTONY

A POINT that it may sound fantastic (if not in some way unsuitable) to make, it yet seems impossible to do without in dealing so thoroughly as this with Shakespeare. I refer to his sex organization, and to the fact that there is great reason to suppose that, like many of his contemporaries, his sentimentality was directed towards other men and not towards women. He would seem to have been what—using the word familiar to students of the habits of many primitive uranian tribes—I have elsewhere referred to as a transformed or *shamanized* man. To-day, luckily, this question has been reduced to a matter of taste, and no reproach is involved in suggesting that an individual is predisposed to this form of physical self-expression.

To have his " normal " woman-love castrated, and to be turned into a female at an early age, must have a considerable effect on the mentality of a man. Or to be born sexually aggressive but so constituted that the usual female dish provided by nature is turned away from with disgust, must also leave its little mark on the mind. The extent to which these activities, or inactivities, colour the whole life of the creature, and give all his thoughts a very special texture and tint, I discuss elsewhere. But at least it can be assumed at once that it will have a decisive influence on an individual's outlook. Anyone dealing, as Shakespeare was, with the finest shades of character, constantly representing military events, in which women take no part, or on the other hand the intrigues in which they delight, would gain and lose something if he came to all this from the midst of the normal experiences of life ; or if his wits and senses had been sharpened and specialized in the school of Sodom, long adapted to more esoteric courses. That this latter really describes his position appears to me to be proved by the *Sonnets* : and much of the mysterious perfection of his plays would be accounted for on the same ground—or rather some of those perfections that otherwise might seem difficult to explain as the work of the rough actor.

Whether Homer was written by a woman or not, I think that Shakespeare was—to the extent at least to which I am referring. Generation after generation has marvelled at the truth and delicacy of "Shakespeare's women." Although this has been overdone it certainly is a feature of his plays that where the women appear they are not men dressed up, but really women, although very simple and obedient ones. The men actors that took their parts, even, would have to be delicate impersonators. But this understanding of the female nature, so characteristic of the "unmanly," and it is true anti-womanly, brotherhood of Sodom would tally with what we are supposing.

In Shakespeare's attitude, again, to his heroines, there seems much evidence pointing the same way : and I think even stronger evidence in his attitude to the warlike demi-gods, one aspect of the certain duplicity of his attitude to them. Of course these traits by themselves might merely signify that he had been endowed with a very wide and un-partisan nature : but both these features of his mind are marked in a way suggesting strongly the female nature. In many cases it coincides with the other political duplicity of his period that otherwise we have been examining. But sometimes it cannot be explained so readily by that as by this other impulse.

In *Antony and Cleopatra*, for example, it is evident that the author of the play, if in love with anybody, is in love with Antony. And his attitude generally to his "strong men" is one of romantic devotion, that does not, as we have seen, tally with his attitude in colder moments, and cannot be entirely covered by the blank-verse form, of course. The mysterious and unreasonable *change* occurring in the character of Cleopatra, at the end, culminating in her death (although it is explained by her fear of being taken to Rome and put on exhibition), is a female self-immolation to the man-god of whom she has made a cult.

SHAKESPEARE AND ANTONY

Antony grows and grows as he approaches his *pathos*.
Such a dazzling and gallant giant cannot be allowed to
sink and die *forgotten*. " I am dying, Egypt, dying " : as
the greatness oozes melodiously out of the divine victim the
fascination of his demise draws other sacrifices with it.

When he dies Cleopatra exclaims :

> " O, see, my women,
> The crown o' the earth doth melt :—My lord !—
> O, wither'd is the garland of the war,
> The soldier's pole is fallen : young boys and girls
> Are level now with men ; the odds is gone,
> And there is nothing left remarkable
> Beneath the visiting moon."

So with words like those of a hebrew lament over the
fallen, in terms of exaggerated worship and flattery, the god
Antony's death is received. The " serpent of old Nile," in
the act of female adoration, follows her master.

All Shakespeare's *sympathy* is with Antony : he is be-
trayed and disgraced " all for love." But it is the nature
and destiny of this particular giant to be slain by love-of-
women—he is handed to Shakespeare by the muses with
this fate labelled on him—and Shakespeare loves him none
the worse for that. (Although he does not like women, he
likes their business, and is a great specialist in the passion
of *love*.) A giant has to die pathetically, somehow or other,
and he might as well succumb in this way as the next.
But the woman entrusted with the sacrifice receives none
of the poet's bounty till we come to the part where she, in
turn, has to die. Indeed once Antony is dead, Cleopatra,
collecting herself to follow him, receives in some mysterious
way an overflow from his departed spirit :

> " Give me my robe, put on my crown ; I have
> Immortal longings in me : now no more
> The juice of Egypt's grape shall moist this lip :
> . . . Methinks I hear
> Antony call ; I see him rouse himself
> To praise my noble act . . .

THE LION AND THE FOX

Husband, I come :
Now to that name my courage prove my title !
I am fire, and air ; my other elements
I give to baser life. So, have you done ?
Come then, and take the last warmth of my lips."

These sunset speeches are really the afterglow of Antony;
it is the last warmth of *him* that we are invited to taste.
Cleopatra is already half out of life in the midst of the
insuck caused by the foundering divinity. It is a part of
him, swelling with his posthumous voice, that is bidding
us adieu.

As to the general attitude to the " hero," and especially
the warrior ; that is investigated at considerable length
immediately, and I need only refer you to that, and suggest
that you supplement the political motive that evidently
controls some part of that with these erotic and more
intimate conclusions. As to direct evidence of what is here
—and has often been—surmised, the best is to be found of
course in the twentieth sonnet : which is testimony very
difficult to contradict :

" A woman's face, with Nature's own hand painted,
   Hast thou, the master-mistress of my passion ;
   A woman's gentle heart, but not acquainted
   With shifting change, as is false woman's fashion ;
   An eye more bright than theirs, less false in rolling,
   Gilding the object whereupon it gazeth ;
   A man in hue, all hues in his controlling,
   Which steals men's eyes, and women's souls amazeth.
   And for a woman wert thou first created ;
   Till Nature, as she wrought thee, fell a-doting,
   And by addition me of thee defeated,
   By adding one thing to my purpose nothing.
      But since she prick'd thee out for woman's pleasure,
      Mine be thy love, and thy love's use their treasure."

In such a matter more definite evidence (short of public
scandal—as in the case of Wilde) would in the nature of
things not probably be available. With Marlowe the accusa-

tions of Baines (as investigated by Boas) seem to make it probable that Marlowe was homosexual, like so many other figures in the renaissance world, whose sacred books, suddenly unearthed, were the works of greek antiquity. The treatment of Gaveston (the " night-grown mushroom " of the reign of Edward the Second) implies anything but distaste for the destiny of " a minion." Where the queen and Gaveston squabble over the king, Gaveston is apt to get the better of the argument :

> " *K. Edw.* Away, then ! touch me not.—Come, Gaveston.
> *Q. Isab.* Villain, 'tis thou that robbest me of my lord.
> *Gav.* Madam, 'tis you that rob me of my lord ! "

The elder Mortimer is made to argue as follows (showing, incidentally, what must have been at the back of the minds of the renaissance men, with all their snobbishness about antiquity, and love of paradox). He is speaking to his nephew about the king :

> " Thou seest by nature he is mild and calm ;
>   And, seeing his mind so dotes on Gaveston,
>   Let him without controlment have his will. . . .
>   Great Alexander lov'd Hephæstion,
>   The conquering Hercules for Hylas wept,
>   And for Patrocles stern Achilles droop'd :
>   And not kings only, but the wisest men ;
>   The Roman Tully loved Octavius,
>   Grave Socrates wild Alcibiades."

That is the catalogue of the sanctions, for a man of the renaissance, of that particular " offence," and also their incitement to it : apart from the fact that their dislike of the respectabilities of their puritan brothers would be sufficient to urge them to every excess, if sexual paradox had not been of the nature of an historic duty—a sort of veneration for Socrates.

Then of course we have Gaveston's famous speech when he is imagining the parties and fêtes he will organize for the king :

" I must have wanton poets, pleasant wits,
   Musicians, that with touching of a string
   May draw the pliant king which way I please :
   Music and poetry is his delight ;
   Therefore I'll have Italian masks by night,
   Sweet speeches, comedies, and pleasing shows ;
   And in the day, when he shall walk abroad,
   Like sylvan nymphs my pages shall be clad ;
   My men, like satyrs grazing on the lawns,
   Shall with their goat-feet dance the antic-hay ;
   Sometime a lovely boy in Dian's shape,
   With hair that gilds the water as it glides,
   Crownets of pearl about his naked arms,
   And in his sportful hands an olive-tree,
   To hide those parts which men delight to see,
   Shall bathe him in a spring ; and there, hard by,
   One like Actæon, peeping through the grove,
   Shall by the angry goddess be transformed,
   And running in the likeness of an hart,
   By yelping hounds pulled down, shall seem to die."

There is no need to insist on these passages : they are
well known, and they seem to show that Marlowe was not
a stranger to the delights he defended. *Edward the Second*
is also the play (like Gogol's *Mantle*, from out of whose
fertile folds all russian literature is said to have issued) out
of which all Shakespeare's historical drama came.

I propose, then, to consider Shakespeare's attitude to
the world somewhat as that of a woman—rather more that
of a woman than of a man.

CHAPTER III

SHAKESPEARE'S WORK AS "A CRITICISM OF ACTION"

IN considering Machiavelli there was one aspect of his genius that was not insisted on, and which yet is of capital importance where we are directly contrasting this ferocious pessimistic theoretician with " sweet Will," with that greatest master of english literature who for preference is described as " sweet " or as " gentle " by those other masters nearest to him in time. All the great characteristics of Machiavelli's, as of Nietzsche's, thought are traceable to a passion for *action*. It was on the agent-principle, as it may be called, that these philosophies were built.

In Machiavelli we have heart and soul a Cesare Borgia —the writer was the intellectual equation of the statesman : as (in a less sharp and classical way) Stendhal was an expression of Napoleon. Could Machiavelli have chosen, he would have lived the life of Cesare Borgia. He was attached blindly to *action*—believed in it and nothing else, and would not for a moment have compared his *contemplation* of his terrible prince with the living prince that he contemplated. He was beholden to his enthusiasm for action for every syllable that he wrote. Stendhal, founding his style of writing avowedly on the napoleonic code, expressing in his typical hero, Sorel, the napoleonic personality, would also, if he could, have been some sort of Napoleon. But he was only partially dependent on a hero of action, of whom he was not at all times very sure. But *action*, in one obvious form or another, was also his god.

Shakespeare, " holding the mirror up to nature," evidently possessed no obsession of that sort, and at first sight would seem the exact opposite of these two apostles of action, or professors of energy. He was doubly their opposite inasmuch, we should say, as his typical hero, Hamlet, is the impersonification of non-action : is action's opposite.

All Shakespeare's work can be regarded as a criticism of action and of the agent-principle : though it is only in *Hamlet* that this mood becomes explicit, and as it were personal. This incomparable observer of the life around him " had his opinions " of what he saw, although he had no gesture of rebellion against individual phases of it, but innumerable gestures against life itself. And, if against life itself, then against action itself. It was the *universality* or impersonal all-inclusiveness of this rebellion that makes him a " universal " artist, as he is often called.

Whereas Machiavelli was the hypnotized advocate of a specific contemporary type of active life : and as Molière was—in a different way—its adversary and critic : Shakespeare was neither one nor the other. He was, if anything, the adversary of life itself (if to be the critic is to be the adversary, and that poetry is a criticism of life has been accepted as a good definition), and his works a beautifully impersonal outpouring of fury, bitter reflection, invective and complaint—complaint in the *Sonnets*, for instance ; fury in *Timon*, or his other tragedies and histories. Of that sort of action—and that was the only action for which he had not a contempt—Shakespeare was a tremendous adept. In the tragic experiences of all his characters he tragically participated : and they were much more mirrors held up to his tired and baffled mind than they were the mirrors of any nature that he objectively could know. *Tired with all these*, we find him, but there was something that attached him to them ; and which, if he had left them, he would also have had to have left.

All that can strictly be described as his philosophy is contained in Montaigne's *Essays*. There is the same curiosity and discouragement, wonderful flexibility of expression, passionate friendship for another man, humour and scepticism, in both. Both are the critics of action, but Shakespeare paradoxically criticizes it by showing you its adepts in *action*.

So how much did Shakespeare approve of the various

objects to which he held his famous "mirror" up, let us ask "once more." And, in order to show him as an impassive divinity, shall we reply that he neither approved nor disapproved, any more than a photographic plate, or a god?

What was his attitude to the violent *action* in the depicting of which he was such a great specialist? What was his private opinion of the many kings and heroes it was his task to fit out for their *pathos*, with blank verse of the highest quality? Did he feel that without their doings there would be no blank verse, and so did he have a warm corner in his heart for them? Or, in the course of writing the series of warlike histories for which he is famous, must not a man of such a brilliant and free intelligence have arrived at Gibbon's conclusion—that history is a record of mankind's follies?

Shakespeare spent his life, as a poet, in the company of tyrants, soldiers and the pomp of courts, and seems to have been very much at home with all this feudal machinery. The fact that he dealt so exclusively in such compromising material has prejudiced opinion against his poetry in many quarters. (This is apart from the fact that he has been called the "king of poets" too often for some hostility not to have been aroused against him, on his own personal score.)

The view adopted here is that there is a great deal of evidence in Shakespeare's plays that he had the poorest opinion both of the action and the actors that he spent his life writing about.

It is on the face of it unlikely that the man who wrote, or who declaimed, on the "insolence of office," "the spurns that patient merit of the unworthy takes," "the oppressor's wrong," and who had such a wonderful understanding of his kind, did not "see through" the august machinery to which his grand style lent a nobility that it certainly never can have possessed in the flesh. The most insignificant figures speak at a pitch of emotional tension, and with a felicity of expression, that is as far beyond them as it is possible to be. Every king and chieftain speaks as only a great poet could make him; and, to put it in another way, as only a great poet would. And there are no great poets, but only kings and princes, most often resembling Cesare Borgia more or less, throughout his many plays. He put into articulate dialogue very much more than it could bear, and into any vessel he entered with the music of his " mighty line," or Marlowe's if you like ; and immediately that vessel began uttering itself with the tongue of gods and angels. For not only Shakespeare's kingly largess where any relatively small character was concerned in the *matter* of what was said, but also the manner (namely, the grandeur of the blank verse), transferred them into an " aristocratic " region, where Pistol attempts but fails to follow them. As though with the cothurnus of the antique stage everyone was inflated to a superhuman stature.

So the grand music of blank verse was in itself enough to banish all question of emotional hierarchy. Prose can trip and caper at one moment, and behave like an organ the next : change from the notes of the spinet to the thunders of the hailstone-beaten beach : but blank verse has not this range. It transforms everyone that uses it into a member of a race of heroes. A serving-man speaking blank verse is of a different race to us, who speak prose. If employed constantly by a man of genius it leads inevitably in the end to a world peopled by Othellos, Antonys, Timons and Lears entirely, except for a few prose intruders, or for occasional lapses on their own part.

The phenomenon of the grand style is important in any discussion of Shakespeare's " politics "—which Coleridge assures us exhibited a " wonderfully philosophic impartiality." But making the drawer or serving-woman speak in prose and the court official in blank verse decides nothing about Shakespeare's political sentiments, any more than would the appearance in a play of a legal document in the pompous vernacular of the law, and a private letter in the intimate undress natural in that case.

" Shakespeare—who is nothing if not english, except that he is also universal—is never more english than in his preference for mufti on occasion. . . . And yet no one can wear his uniform with more dignity or assume it with such

A CRITICISM OF ACTION

lightning quickness : while no one can keep it longer fresh on duty " (Saintsbury, *Shakespeare and the Grand Style*). It was very much a dress—a court dress—for Shakespeare, except where it naturally is explained by the grandeur of the dramatic motive, apart from the official character of the personage speaking.

For a classical perfection, no doubt, this uniform magnificence of utterance added to the too indiscriminate suggestion of intellectual power in the various figures, bestowed over a great variety of characters, is a blemish. Dionysius of Halicarnassus writes (*De Compositione Verborum*, chap. iii., one of the best style-manuals of antiquity that have come down to us) : " I take it in fact to be always necessary, whenever ideas are expressed in proper and appropriate language, that no word should be more dignified than the nature of the ideas." The same rule would apply to personages of drama and what they express. Shakespeare for that sort of perfection was certainly too liberal with himself.

It is important, in analysing this *effect* produced by these two things—the grand style and the undisciplined prodigality of Shakespeare where the resources of his intellect are concerned—to separate them strictly. It is not the phenomenon of the grand style that will interest us in this connexion, but rather the latter peculiarity.

" As for Timon himself, his misfortunes make him a Shakespeare," Mr Saintsbury remarks. But not only Timon benefits in that way from his suffering : any sufficiently harassed principal of a piece of his enjoys the same privilege, with the impunity belonging to the creations of an incomparable artist. When the misfortune arrives, they automatically become Shakespeare. As a good example of this Richard II.'s well-known speech when he finds that he has lost his kingdom can be cited. This second Plantagenet, who up till then has shown in his harangues in the play no sign of especial intelligence, has been only crossly harsh and pompous by turns, lets drop a series of remarks that certainly no Plantagenet would ever have made, and in language to match their depth and ingenuity. Although so

generally familiar, I will quote it fully, to have the details
of what we are talking about before us.

"*K. Richard*. No matter where; of comfort no man speak:
Let's talk of graves, of worms and epitaphs;

.   .   .   .

Our lands, our lives, and all are Bolingbroke's,
And nothing we can call our own but death,
And that small model of the barren earth
Which serves as paste and cover to our bones.
For God's sake, let us sit upon the ground,
And tell sad stories of the death of kings :—
How some have been deposed ; some slain in war ;
Some haunted by the ghosts they have depos'd ;
Some poison'd by their wives ; some sleeping kill'd ;
All murder'd. . . .
[Death allows the king] . . . a breath, a little scene,
To monarchize, be fear'd, and kill with looks ;
Infusing him with self and vain conceit,—
As if this flesh, which walls about our life,
Were brass impregnable ; and, humour'd thus,
Comes at the last, and with a little pin
Bores through his castle-wall, and—farewell, king !
Cover your heads, and mock not flesh and blood
With solemn reverence ; throw away respect,
Tradition, form, and ceremonious duty ;
For you have but mistook me all this while."

This is evidently a sort of *parabasis* of the author, taking
his place within the dramatic skill of the protagonist at the
moment where the loftiest truth can naturally live, in an
atmosphere at length abnormally heated or depressed to
the required temperature for such an apparition through
these Acts of gathering tragedy. No chorus *outside* the
temporal progress and expressive life of the play itself could
be so effective ; and in every consecutive act of english
history there could not be a figure of the stature required
for such utterances as these. That is all : and it would be
absurd, seeing the haphazard growth of this drama from
vulgar forms, in a not very mature period or country,

produced as a distraction for kings, and the savage rabble of an elizabethan pit, to expect this to be otherwise.

If, as I think, this is the irruption of the mind of the author into the midst of the shallow events it was his task to depict: and if, as is the case, he always on these occasions delivers himself in the same terms of these events, with a monotony, indeed, that sweeps them all into *one* monotonous, eternally repeated event, which is *life* stripped of its typical variety and specific colouring : then what is said in these bitter meditative harangues can show us Shakespeare's mind.

Of the long line of kings that came under his hand for dramatic treatment, some had "been deposed," "some slain in war," " some haunted by the ghosts they had deposed " some had been " poisoned by their wives," " some sleeping killed " : but most if not all had come to a violent and stupid end, clamouring about their divine right and their kingly ways, defiant or idiotically remorseful. He probably did not think much more of these kings that passed through his hands than Gibbon did of his gallery of despots. The image of the " little pin " which bored through the life-wall so easily, and then " farewell king ! " was a reflection of the critical experiences of the poet, not of Richard Plantagenet : " *For you have but mistook me all this while !* " That great undressing of the dressed-up self in a simple phrase is Shakespeare's, and has a universal application beyond the royal disappointments of Richard II.

But for all his contempt for the individual being, it was not because he was a king, but because he was human, that Shakespeare would regard him as he did. Hence there is no occasion for surprise if Shakespeare did not adopt a militant attitude toward those privileges. He knew them too well to suppose that, dressed up differently, and forbidden to deliver themselves in blank verse, or deprived of the mechanism of royalty, they would change their skin. Nor was he innocent enough to suppose that he was living beneath a more oppressive system than the next, the next after that, or the one before it. So he accepted his kings : but with a much worse grace than is generally believed.

CHAPTER IV

THE WORLD OF ACTION AND THE WORLD OF TRAGEDY

"**O**UR thoughts are ours, their ends none of our own ": that is to say that in our thoughts, only, are we ourselves, in our actions we are the creatures of God or fate. " Their ends " are the issues or entrances of our thought, and these, says the speaker, are not our own. "It takes two to make a quarrel." But it takes two or more to make an action, it could equally well be said. Equally, that without a *one*, somewhere, no action could be made. Thought, however, is also an action : so we should, if we were playing at that game, have to divide these different sorts of action, perhaps into "private" and "public": pure and mixed, the action of the one, and the action of the many.

" The tragic world is a world of action, and action is the translation of thought into reality. We see men and women confidently attempting it. They strike into the existing order of things in pursuance of their ideas. But what they achieve is not wholly what they intended ; it is terribly unlike it. They understand nothing, we say to ourselves, of the world on which they operate. They fight blindly in the dark, and the power that works through them makes them the instrument of a design which is not theirs."

That Shakespeare's tragedy is *tragedy of action* is true. But according to Professor Bradley it is not that so very simply as might at first sight appear, because as " tragedy " it defeats its own ends, largely through the vital reality of the characters presented. They, as it were, surge out of the frame ; *they are too real and too alive for you to be able to feel that what in fact is happening to them is happening to them in the " real " world at all*. Where he is explaining the irony accompanying the death of Cordelia he seems to be trying to impart a religious optimism into the explanation, and to be engaged in disinfecting the irony. A truer explanation had he wanted it, and ensuing from his account of this certain sense of unreality in these plays, would have been that Shakespeare—and above all Shakespeare the professional actor, with something inevitably of the cynicism of the mountebank—did not take the deaths of his characters quite so seriously as Professor Bradley does, or as his audience would be expected to do. Sometimes, perhaps, a *sans gêne* is visible in his dispatching of even the most celebrated hero, or sweetest heroine.

"Shakespearian tragedy . . . assumes that the world, as it is presented, is the truth, though it also provokes feelings which imply that this world is not the whole truth, and therefore not the truth."

Professor Bradley writes, where he is discussing the feeling that he describes as one of *reconciliation* accompanying often the end of a Shakespeare tragedy :

"It is simply the feeling that what happens to such a being does not matter ; all that matters is what she [Cordelia] is. How this can be when, for anything the tragedy tells us, she has ceased to exist, we do not ask ; but the tragedy itself makes us feel that somehow it is so. . . . The force of the impression . . . depends on the very violence of the contrast between the outward and the inward, Cordelia's death and Cordelia's soul. The more unmotived, unmerited, senseless, monstrous, her fate, the more do we feel that it does not concern her. The extremity of the disproportion between prosperity and goodness first shocks us, and then flashes on us the conviction that our whole attitude in asking or expecting that goodness should be prosperous is wrong ; that, if only we could see things as they are, we should see that the outward is nothing and the inward is all."

It would be found, if great examples of satire were examined one by one, that satire aims its dart only at the fortunate. In the same way tragedy deals only with the fortunate. Boëthius' famous remark, "In every adversity the most unhappy kind of misfortune is to have been happy," can be recalled : that is the psychological spring of the tragic: without that there would be no life in the black, for it has none except what is reflected from the white. All tragedy is a *change*, necessarily, a movement. It is also a dying, and not a death.

Both tragedy and satire aim their blows at the fortunate. They are both occupied with *hubris*, whose representatives they execute. But whereas satire is essentially ethical, or it is difficult for it not to be, tragedy does not necessarily regard its victim with exultation, however much it shares in the general delight at his fall. But it does not even share this always. Such an executioner as Shakespeare often entered into the dying god—which as a poet he was able to do. And from the lips of how many of his expiring heroes did he not turn on their betrayers and curse them, as we should not have found the god or the hero doing? For as the representative of the crowd, of humanity, at the execution of the hero, he could hardly have always felt a dutiful enthusiasm for his "many-headed" master. So for the lonely, dying hero he is often the gentlest confessor, or the most furious advocate.

In referring to *Lear*, Professor Bradley says: "The whole story beats this indictment of prosperity into the brain." The Prosperous, Shakespeare liked as little as he liked "the gods" (Mr Bradley admits the Prosperous, but shies at "the gods"): "Lear's great speeches in his madness proclaim it like the curses of Timon on life and man. But here, as in *Timon*, the poor and humble are, almost without exception, sound and sweet at heart, faithful and pitiful."

The "poor and humble" get many more kicks than ha'pence from Shakespeare, and Professor Bradley's attempt to *christianize* Shakespeare is a blemish the whole time on his exposition. In fact he readily drops into the dialect of the pulpit, which is a great pity, as follows:

"Throughout this stupendous Third Act the good are seen growing better through suffering, and the bad worse through success. The warm castle is a room in hell, the storm-swept heath a sanctuary. The judgment of this world is a lie; its goods, which we covet, corrupt us; its ills, which break our bodies, set our souls free.

THE WORLD OF TRAGEDY

" ' Our means secure us, and our mere defects
Prove our commodities.'

" Let us renounce the world, hate it, and lose it gladly.
The only real thing in it is the soul, with its courage,
patience, devotion. And nothing outward can touch that."

This blemish (more serious of course in the orientation it
gives his criticism than in the tone, which is occasionally a
little disturbing) is all the more to be regretted as he appears
to have seen that it should be avoided. He has a passage
that seems very applicable to Lamb, for instance, and yet
he fails himself in that respect :

" Most people, even among those who know Shakespeare
well and come into real contact with his mind, are inclined
to isolate and exaggerate some one aspect of the tragic fact.
Some are so much influenced by their own habitual beliefs
that they impart them more or less into their interpretation
of every author who is ' sympathetic ' to them "—and later,
as regards the question as to the tragic world of Shakespeare,
and the ultimate power in it : " It will be agreed, however,
first, that this question must not be answered in ' religious '
language. . . . The elizabethan drama was almost wholly
secular ; and while Shakespeare was writing he practically
confined his view to the world of non-theological observation and thought, so that he represents it substantially in
one and the same way whether the period of the story is
pre-christian or christian. He looked at this ' secular '
world most intently and seriously . . . without regard to
anyone's hopes, fears or beliefs."

" The tragic world is a world of action, and action is the
translation of thought into reality. We see men and women
confidently attempting it. They strike into the existing
order of things in pursuance of their ideas. But what they
achieve is not wholly what they intended : it is terribly
unlike it." That is the core of the argument of the passages
I have just quoted from Professor Bradley : and that is a

THE LION AND THE FOX

generally acceptable statement. But in what, as a conscious reading of the world on the part of a great artist, would that result ? It would result in the attitude to *action* of every sort, and the great agents whose *pathos* he registered, which I have ascribed to Shakespeare. The " Hamlet problem," solved in that sense, becomes not a curious study of insanity, or a detached picture of one amongst many characters equally favoured by an impartial creator, but a philosophy, a system of predilections and beliefs, embodied in a character of fiction.

Hamlet was not a " hero," unless you can be a hero of non-action. But, in the nature of things, all the heroes of shakespearian tragedy, as of all other tragedy, were heroes who failed : their failure was what the tragedy was about. But you cannot imagine Machiavelli choosing to write about Cesare Borgia because he failed in his attempt to unify Italy, because he was banished and died in relative obscurity in a battle in Spain !

Machiavelli, like Stendhal (and all the enthusiasts for Napoleon, Rockefeller, Lord Northcliffe, etc., who have ensued), is the devotee of *success*. Tragedy, on the other hand, tells of nothing but *downfall*, and the powerlessness of men : it is the agony of the hero that is represented, either in glorification of the power of God and fate, or registering the success of the many over the one. The implication of those monotonous sacrifices is clearly non-heroic, and not engineered in favour of the titan ; and in that sense tragic art is in its essence democratic and religious, the enemy of human energy and success, or such a check on them as to be that, and the opponent of action. Nothing but light-heartedness, the insolent spectacle of eternal success, gaiety and grace, would characterize an art which was the expression of the purest despotism or securest aristocracy. The form of art whose function it is eternally to record the triumph of supernatural powers, or of necessity, over the great ones of the earth—as was that of the tragic drama in Greece—is obviously not inspired in the first place by a tyrant or king. The same applies to the tragedies and histories of Shakespeare.

CHAPTER V

SHAKESPEARE AS A SHOWMAN

WRITING of Marlowe, Swinburne says: "Flutes and lutes and harps and harpsichords we had heard before the organ-music of his verse astonished and entranced all ears not naturally sealed against the nobler tones of thought. And Shakespeare heard at once, and cast off shard by shard the crust of habit which fostered and sometimes fevered the jigging vein of his rhyming mother-wit, sweet and exquisite as it was."

Shakespeare was like a very supple, resourceful punch-and-judy showman: he would send his voice first up into the puppet that was the king, and then into the puppet that was the clown: it cannot even be said that he was not in some respects a gagger, like one of those officious clowns with whom as a playwright he had so much trouble: for he was quite capable of introducing into the puppets' mouths some of the things he happened at the moment to be feeling about the audience. And he was also capable of inattention; on which occasions Timon could speak like Hamlet, or Hamlet like Thersites, or even King Lear.

"To the public of the present day a play is merely an entertainment, and it was the same to the elizabethans. Shakespeare can say to his audience : ' Our true intent is all for your delight,' and we feel no particular shock in reading the words. The companies were just noblemen's servants ; and it was natural enough that if Lord Leicester's players did not amuse Lord Leicester's guests they should be sent away, and others hired. If they too proved dull, the patron would drop the play altogether and call for tumblers and dancing dogs " (Professor Gilbert Murray).

Professor Murray goes on to contrast this state of affairs with the religious character, and high ritualistic origins, of greek drama. And that again, as has been often pointed

171

out, has always to be remembered with these players:
Shakespeare and the rest were hired entertainers, and not
hierophants; they had to be supple and in some sense
vulgar: and were as much in search of that terrible *néant,*
" what the public wants " (only it was on the whole a little
better public), as is any journalist to-day. And it is no doubt
true that the artist, unless he is in some way godsman
instead of Lord Leicester's merely, or Lord Northcliffe's,
is coaxed or beaten off, and never allowed fully to possess,
the perfection of expression.

To a Shakespeare these sad compromises and shifts,
necessitated by the stupid and mean egotisms of his
audience (whose tastes or lack of taste it is his unpleasant
duty to learn by heart and have at his fingers' ends), can
hardly endear them to him. Professor Tatlock's requirements, for instance—suggestive of a cheerful, benevolent
domestic putting his foolish masters at their ease with a
manner presumably between that of a professionally beaming anglican divine and the characteristic old country
family-servant bred in the heart of the squirearchy—do
insinuate an absurdity which, if the accommodating idol
conceded it, would make him less worthy to be idolized. Nor
would his audiences of gentlemen and ladies appeal to him
much more than his pit. In fact, with their pretentious
arrogance, greater power to interfere with him, and with
the eternal cheap effrontery of the *enfant gâté,* they might
appeal to him at most times even less.

As a showman, his remarks would not, as is generally
supposed, be addressed to the more " rotten-breathed " of
his audience, the many-headed multitude, only. The crowd
of his more elegant clients were " many-headed " too. Their
breath probably did not smell especially sweet to the author
of *Timon.* What is Shakespeare supposed to have thought
of Lord Leicester's guests? He saw a good deal of them.
He must have thought a good deal in consequence.

What shall we suppose that Shakespeare thought about
that curious lady who gave her name to his period, Elizabeth? We know what he thought about women in general,
as he has not stinted, mirror though he may be, to inform

us of that. Perhaps his very typical virgin-queen would be excepted from the generalizations by this " kindly " servant of her destiny ? For we are told that he was a feudal poet : so that would make him a *feudal-mirror*, we with justice could call it (using the impersonal pronoun as well) : and so he would reflect, we must suppose, the supreme feudal effigy without equivocation.

But with ordinary alertness the student reading his plays will, I think, have frequent occasion to doubt if the more prosperous and self-satisfied of his audiences did not share with the humblest the contempt he lavished on the latter. And a king was nothing more than a prominently placed aunt-sally for the sport of his " mighty line."

PART V
THE COLOSSI OF THE THIRD PERIOD

CHAPTER I

SHAKESPEARE'S NIHILISM

THE form this essay has been given has been that of a hunt in the mind of Shakespeare, as exhibited in his plays, for the two symbolical animals, the lion and the fox, used by Machiavelli in the composition of his perfect human being. This resolves itself to some extent into a contrast between the temperament of Shakespeare and that of Machiavelli. It has involved us for some time in a consideration of the factors of race, country, period and so forth, respectively, of the one and of the other.

As regards this final phase of the investigation it can be said that, " the elements being so mixed " in him, no rounded and simple picture of Shakespeare is possible on these or any other lines. Yet this problem symbolized by the figure of the lion and fox is constantly present to the imagination of the poet, and recurs incessantly in his plays. *Othello* is where it is seen at its simplest : but it presents itself for revaluation at every turn.

Was Shakespeare a *machiavellist* himself ? Did he relish and countenance the duplicity and ruthlessness that he so often depicted ? Would he have inclined to be a machiavellian *anti-Machiavel* of the type of Frederick the Great of Prussia ? Or was he a rebellious or morally scandalized pupil of the " academy of manslaughter " in which every European of his time had more or less to graduate ?

Morgan, the moralistic eighteenth-century critic, regrets that Shakespeare did not reprove John of Lancaster for his treachery to the Archbishop of York. This is, of course, very absurd ; for it did not present itself to Shakespeare as " treachery " at all. Shakespeare is the only one of his contemporaries who seems to have been able to absorb the melodrama of italian life with equanimity. He was neither delighted, like Ford, nor horrified, like Webster. But he shared many of Machiavelli's characteristic conceptions, in the same way that he often thought like Montaigne. The incest theme, for example, he never touched. The freudian complex of his day (the " horror " incarnated by Count Cenci) left him intact and indifferent. The working of the puritan conscience at the spectacle of borgiaism is not exhibited by him.

" Brought face to face with these aberrations from the normal trend of human conduct, it was not with this indifference that the northern gothic mind reacted. Horrified and fascinated, it translated that horror and fascination into moral terms and infused into its Vittorias, Bosolas, Vindicis and the rest a superhuman struggle of the agonized soul with evil, absolutely unknown to the facile consciencelessness of the actual personages depicted. These overwrought tragedies . . . were only possible to the grim puritan inherent in the english nature . . ." (Vernon Lee).

It would not be true to say that these effects were not visible in Shakespeare's work ; but they were mastered by the great vitality that, with a coolness equal to their own, reproduced them.

If the question were put categorically in this form : " On whose side was Shakespeare in the conflict that played such an important part in his work, between the simple man and the Machiavel ? " it could not, of course, be answered : or we should have to answer, if at all : " On neither side." For it would not be natural for Shakespeare to intervene in the eternal dispute of good and evil, or in the battles of the animal kingdom, where the foxes and lions perpetually manœuvre. It is impossible to make a fox-hunter of him : and he showed no tendency to wish to be a lion. So the answer would have to be complex, as is the phenomenon we are handling. One thing however can be decided at once where Othello, at least, is concerned ; that with that first of his colossi (the series of titans of his third period, or the last phase of his career) he was not on the side of Othello's small destroyer. If most critics have tried to make of Iago a colossus, too, to match Othello, I do not think that Shakespeare ever did.

SHAKESPEARE'S NIHILISM

First of all, Shakespeare was no more the servant of the gods than he was of the populace. He was neither religious nor democratic, in any dogmatic sense, but philosophic. And so when he approached his hero in pursuance with his function of writer of tragedies, it was not with the frenzied intolerance either of a messenger of the gods or of a malignant emissary of the crowd. Noting his peaceable, humdrum manner of life—rather like those hangmen who when not engaged on their terrible trade are grocers or barbers in some small provincial town—it is certainly natural to wonder how it was that he ever adopted such a profession.

With the exception of Chapman, Shakespeare is the only "thinker" we meet with among the elizabethan dramatists. By this is meant, of course, that his work contained, apart from poetry, phantasy, rhetoric or observation of manners, a body of matter representing explicit processes of the intellect which would have furnished a moral philosopher like Montaigne with the natural material for his essays. But the quality of this thinking—as it can be surprised springing naturally in the midst of the consummate movements of his art—is, as must be the case with such a man, of startling force sometimes. And if it is not systematic, at least a recognizable physiognomy is there.

Shakespeare is quite conscious of the fact that he is not the servant of a god : nor is he a nihilist without knowing it. As an instance of this the death of Cordelia can be instanced : and an account of this incident quoted to show how this nihilism can be misinterpreted, in the course of a process of "whitewashing."

Professor Bradley draws attention to the "ironic collocation" in *Lear*, where you get the appearance of Cordelia's corpse on the heels of a supplication to "the gods."

"*Edmund.* He hath commission from my wife and me
To hang Cordelia in the prison, and
To lay the blame upon her own despair,
That she fordid herself.
    Albany. The gods defend her !
        [*Re-enter* LEAR *with* CORDELIA *dead in his arms.*]"

THE LION AND THE FOX

In this "irony" Mr Bradley sees the "moral" of the whole play. "The *gods*, it seems, do *not* show their approval," he writes, "by defending their own from adversity or death, or by giving them power of prosperity." He implies that in this irony there is no ultimate despair, but rather that it is to be referred to a christian optimism. That does not seem likely, although he uses this theory with success in some other instances of bitter endings. But the punctual arrival of Cordelia, brought in like a Christmas present, so *narquois* and so pat, cannot be anything but what it forces us at once to see it as : an expression of the poet's mockery at the vanity of human supplications, and notions of benevolent powers, of whom we are the cherished children. If we were looking for an "influence" to which to trace this ugly despair recurring so often in Shakespeare, we should be more likely to find it in the *Maximes—Traitant de la Religion*, which I have quoted, of Gentillet, than in the dogmas of christianity.

CHAPTER II

THE MANUFACTURE OF A SHAKESPEARIAN COLOSSUS

NOW at the opening of a more detailed examination of the plays I will record my view of the relations of Shakespeare with his colossi. It is ultimately in them, even, that we shall probably find the answer to the particular questions discussed in this essay. Monsters of grandeur and simplicity, the gigantic figures of Othello, Lear, Antony, Macbeth, Timon, Coriolanus, fill the period of Shakespeare's utmost maturity and power. They have a strong tribal likeness. If we want to know from what stuff they were made we have to go to *Tamburlaine* and there we find their great ancestor displaying himself like a Shakespeare colossus in undress. We find ourselves in the *chantiers* almost, and can observe the colossal in process of being built and articulated.

Cosroe asks Menaphon what Tamburlaine is like: he says :

> " But tell me, that hast seen him, Menaphon,
> What stature wields he, and what personage ? "

Menaphon's reply is the rough plan on which all the Shakespeare giants are based :

> " Of stature tall, and straightly fashioned
> Like his desire, lift upwards and divine ;
> So large of limbs, his joints so strongly knit,
> Such breadth of shoulders as might mainly bear
> Old Atlas' burden ; 'twixt his manly pitch,
> A pearl more worth than all the world is placed,
> Wherein by curious sovereignty of art
> Are fixed his piercing instruments of sight,
> Whose fiery circles bear encompassed

A heaven of heavenly bodies in their spheres,
That guides his steps and actions to the throne
Where honour sits invested royally ;
Pale of complexion, wrought in him with passion,
Thirsting with sovereignty and love of arms ;
His lofty brows in folds do figure death,
And in their smoothness amity and life ;
About them hangs a knot of amber hair,
Wrapped in curls, as fierce Achilles' was,
On which the breath of heaven delights to play,
Making it dance with wanton majesty ;
His arms and fingers long and sinewy,
Betokening valour and excess of strength ;—
In every part proportioned like the man
Should make the world subdued to Tamburlaine."

There is the building of the type, "thirsting with
sovereignty and love of arms," everything about him
"betokening valour and excess of strength," with nothing
but honour as his goal. Even the play containing the first
shakespearian colossus has many parallels in *Tamburlaine.*
Zenocrate, on whom the hero has fixed his affections, is
warned of what she will have to expect, and seems to feel
about it very much as Desdemona did. Agydas says to her :

"How can you fancy one that looks so fierce,
   Only disposed to martial stratagems ?
   Who, when he shall embrace you in his arms,
   Will tell how many thousand men he slew ;
   And, when you look for amorous discourse,
   Will rattle forth his facts of war and blood,
   Too harsh a subject for your dainty ears."

You can hear Zenocrate behaving much as Othello
describes Desdemona doing :

"She swore, in faith, 'twas strange, 'twas passing strange ;
'Twas pitiful, 'twas wondrous pitiful."

Iago expresses it in his way as follows, when he is re-
assuring one of his dupes : "Mark me with what violence

A SHAKESPEARIAN COLOSSUS

she first loved the Moor, but for bragging, and telling her fantastical lies [about ' how many thousand men ' he had slain] : and will she love him still for prating ? Let not thy discreet heart think it."

Shakespeare in his great historical cycle, and in this group of colossi with which he chose to crown his achievement, was always dealing in facts of war and blood, and more often than not in men whose lives were composed of that primitive material. And on account of their mere scale and aloofness, in that sense, from human experience, they tended to become still more primitive ; just as a man living by himself would return to a simple condition of life, more direct and animal. All his life Shakespeare worked among such figures, and spent all his time with them, and appeared outwardly to delight in their society. Indeed they were in a different category for him to the stereotyped king-figure we have already discussed, especially the english kings of his historical series. Yet their destiny was a similar one. But they were all of the distant, semi-divine and saga type : and Shakespeare could develop the genius of their heroic individualism as he pleased, without much interference from history.

The reason adopted here for the enthusiastic relations of Shakespeare with these heroes has already been given. If that assumption is correct, that would make the creation of these colossal figures by this *transformed* man particularly curious. But just as Shakespeare's attitude to the more ordinary king-figure is not usually marked by any special enthusiasm, so his attitude to the physical hero in general is by no means of that character that he accords to the hero of his choice, such as Othello or Antony.

CHAPTER III

THE " MAN OF THE WORLD "

SHAKESPEARE—the even, impartial spectator of life, quite undisturbed and without any personality —is often referred to in a flattering way (and to give an idea of the good impression this characterless character has made on the person speaking of him) as a " man of the world." By this, of course, is meant " one of us," a typical member of the minor, more fortunate, herd " in the know "—what Nietzsche brands in his admirable description of " the Cynic."

That he was in some profound way feminine we have already said. But, of the various figures that approximate to the feminine ideal, that of the " man of the world " he has no claim on, I think—any more than he has on that of the jesuit. But the most illustrious " men of the world " are almost invariably very unworldly : in short, they are anything but " men of the world," although " the world " has been their habitat. Machiavelli himself was no exception to this rule. Did he not, when accused of being the doctrinaire of every super-" worldly " duplicity, refer, with some point, to the great simplicity of his life, to his poverty and to the fact that as a result of his " worldly " adroitness he was unable to obtain employment under any florentine government ?

La Rochefoucauld can be taken as another excellent instance. In all his dealings with the world he displayed a minimum of address. Sainte-Beuve in his essay (introducing his *Maximes* in the *Édition Garnier*) writes :

" In his various rôles of soldier, politician, courtier, his heart was not in any of them ; there was always an essential element in his nature which did not participate, upsetting the balance. His nature, without his being aware of it, in all these enterprises had an *arrière-pensée* ; that *arrière-*

pensée was the process of reflection, and its demands, lying in wait for him once the action were past. All adventures finish with him, not like the *Fronde* in songs, but in maxims. . . ."

He regarded *action*, Sainte-Beuve says, as a pretext for thought, not a substitute for it. All that he saw in it was the material for reflection : so his heart was not in it, and he was not good at it. But another passage is even more to the point :

" A further slight indication, but a very singular one, reveals still better what was the real destiny of M. de la Rochefoucauld. For a man so used to society (*pour un homme de tant de monde*) he had, Retz tells us, an air of embarrassment and timidity in social life. Huet (in his *Mémoires*) describes him as so confused in public that, if he had had to speak on some set occasion before six or seven people, his heart would certainly have failed him. Dread of the solemn harangue always prevented him from belonging to the french academy. Nicole was the same. . . . Montesquieu says somewhere that if he had been forced to make his living as a professor he could not have done so. . . . The Maxims of de la Rochefoucauld are among those things that cannot be *taught* ; an audience of six is already too many. Only in a *tête-à-tête* could the author find the ideal condition to communicate them. For man in the mass, you must have a Jean-Jacques or a la Mennais."

One is reminded here, in the number six chosen as the figure for the group that is *déjà trop* for the communication of this philosophy, of Tourguéniev's remark when asked for what audience he wrote : " *For the six unknown.*" However, what is essential in the above passage is the evidence provided there of a very strange disability where " the world " was concerned, or in *action* of any sort, on the part of this typically " worldly " personage. Jean-Jacques was cited on the other side. But was not Rousseau, too, as inexpert, in his democratic way, as de la Rochefoucauld in his aristocratic ? Could any man have neglected the teaching of Machiavelli in the conduct of his life more thoroughly than Rousseau—except Machiavelli himself ?

It is even more the theoreticians of *action* than any other type of man of thought, it seems, however, who offer us first-rate examples of ineffectiveness, on the practical side, in their own lives and works. There is no better example of this than Stendhal, somewhat in the same position where Napoleon was concerned as Machiavelli *vis-à-vis* to Cesare Borgia. In the *Life of Henri Bruyard* (an account of his early adventures) you see this " professor of energy," as he called himself later on, spending literally years in waiting for the psychological moment to snatch a kiss from the young lady he envelops with his respectful attentions. He is, as a lover, the perfect Hamlet, entirely incapable of any resolution at all, so unable is he to act the lover's part. Flaubert's hero, in *L'Éducation Sentimentale*, is another variety of this type. " Que c'est triste, la jeunesse ! " the elderly countess, observing his irresolute devotions, at last exclaims. Julien Sorel, in *Le Rouge et le Noir*, after really superhuman efforts, succeeds in snatching a kiss or two ; and, eventually, more dead than alive, gets into bed with a woman, or is pulled in by her. And he is the great hero of *action* of the first " psychological novel " written by one of the first professors of *action* !—the forerunner of *Crime and Punishment* (in which Raskolnikov furnishes us with the curious spectacle of another of these sub-Napoleons in action).

What is the solution of these contradictions ? It seems to be that the qualities that make a man a successful theoretician are the opposite to those that make him a successful man of action : and that even if, as in the case of Machiavelli, he is a theoretician of *action*. The material of which the mirror destined to reflect action is made is at the other pole to the violent ferments providing the substance of *action*. Perhaps, as the *reflecting* mind is at all events living, it would be better to say that it must be both motionless and deep to reflect to the fullest advantage the conflict occurring in its world.

It is strange how many people consider themselves " men

of the world ": it is a very popular rôle. But it is the last thing, with its " knowingness," its smartly advertising cynicism, herd-reclamation, mechanical snobbery, that even the smallest poet or philosopher could ever be, though no doubt they might affect it.

Like the woman, or the jesuit, the *man of the world*, if we erect him into a figure, is one of abnegation. His is essentially a system of defence and not of attack. He is a man who is himself small and weak, but who has acquired, who lives in the midst of, a powerful defensive machinery. He is in this sense the champion of the mechanical, and the constant adversary of the individual. His strategy is not the daring, ambitious, strategy of machiavellism ; but a system of maxims that vary little from age to age in the freemasonry of " the world."

If the strategy of the world, however, has to be matched with its opposite (as many people wish, as we have said, to match Iago with Othello) it would not be the man of the world who would be chosen to be its champion, naturally enough ; for with many a " Thank-you ! " he would hurry deeper into his labyrinth if approached to play the part of a champion, even of the most unheroic strategy. The great figure of human heroism, of the world's adversary and opposite, in such a match, could be found, I should say, in its fullest flower in the works of Shakespeare : though in the nature of things, since tragedy is a butchery and not a duel with equal arms, the ideal adversary is not introduced.

The ANTONY of *Antony and Cleopatra*, or CORIOLANUS, TIMON, OTHELLO or LEAR ; all these great heroic children, who compass their *pathos* with such a pathetic magnificence, are the ideal saga types. The modernity of the language and the extreme subtlety of their creator make them more acceptable and more real to us than the great figures of what Professor Chadwick has called the " heroic age."

Shakespeare's tremendous heroes, then, answer to the requirements of the contest on the heroes' side. But their tragedy is that they are involved in a *real* action : whereas they come from, and naturally inhabit, an ideal world.

THE LION AND THE FOX

They are struck down always by the puniest weapons;
always by deceit, but quite ordinary deceit. The weapon
has to be weak : for in the pessimism of tragedy not only
have the great always to be vanquished ; but they have
always to be overcome by trivial opponents who substitute
a poor and vulgar thing for the great and whole thing that
they have destroyed. The point of the tragedy, like the ideal
basis of christianity, is the " strength of weakness," and the
corresponding "weakness of strength." "The first shall be
last and the last shall be first," then, or " He who humbleth
himself shall be exalted," etc., in a dramatic action. But it is
of course the exact opposite of christianity, inasmuch as the
pathos of the Great is what fills it, in place of, as in christianity, the *pathos* of the Little. There the comparison
ceases, because the *little* of christianity is not theoretically
the same as that of tragedy, nor is its *great* the same. The
Rich Man of christianity (who is its *great*) is never the hero
of tragedy : or if tragedy consents to use him it loses its
power over the mind : or its effect is greatest when its
victim is least identifiable with him. Owing to this fact, the
operation of tragedy resolves itself into something nearer
to the christian spirit than would at first appear. It is as
though the christian *little*, purified, exalted by the great
simplicity of its faith, and become *great*, were vanquished by
the christian *great* (the villain of the piece in that religion),
degraded also by the magic of faith, but not altered.

Iago is very near to the man of the world, but he is far too
" honest." He is a quite normal and commonplace worldly
person complicated by an honesty *à la* Machiavel. He is not
the unusual villain that he is often made out to be. With
a little more intensity and resolution, most of the individuals
composing any contemporary european " educated " society
would be very much like Iago. The tremendous intricacy of
Shakespeare's art is well known in this treatment of Iago.
The making of this villain Everyman is a supreme invention of genius. He is just the ordinary bluff, " honest "
man in the street, proud of his strategy, and the power
it gives him ; saying without any self-consciousness (pity
almost coming to join with his envy) :

THE "MAN OF THE WORLD"

"The Moor is of a free and open nature,
That thinks men honest that but seem to be so:
And will as tenderly be led by the nose
As asses are."

Iago is strictly the "man of the world," with so much purpose and energy added as is required to be the David to Othello's Goliath in a predestined tragedy, where the dice are palpably loaded in the interest of the small and crooked. So Iago is the *small* destroyer, the eternal Charlie Chaplin figure of human myth, the gods on his side, their instrument in their struggle with the hero. . . . He is the ideal *little man* with the sling and the stone. Othello is the ideal human galleon, twenty storeys high, with his head in the clouds, that the little can vanquish.

CHAPTER IV

OTHELLO AS THE TYPICAL COLOSSUS

OF all the colossi, Othello is the most characteristic, because he is the simplest, and he is seen in an unequal duel throughout with a perfect specimen of the appointed enemy of the giant—the representative of the race of men at war with the race of titans. The hero comes straight from a world where Machiavelli's black necessities—the obligation, for animal survival, for the lion to couple with the fox—are not known. He is absolutely defenceless : it is as though he were meeting one of his appointed enemies, disguised of course, as a friend, for the first time. He seems possessed of no instinct by which he might scent his antagonist, and so be put on his guard.

So, at the outset, I will present my version of Othello ; and anything that I have subsequently to say must be read in the light of this interpretation. For in Othello there is nothing equivocal, I think ; and the black figure of this child-man is one of the poles of Shakespeare's sensation.

Who that has read Othello's closing speech can question Shakespeare's intentions here at least ? The overwhelming truth and beauty is the clearest expression of the favour of Shakespeare's heart and mind. Nothing that could ever be said would make us misunderstand what its author meant by it. Of all his ideal giants this unhappiest, blackest, most " perplexed " child was the one of Shakespeare's predilection.

The great spectacular "pugnacious" male ideal is represented perfectly by Othello; who was led out to the slaughter on the elizabethan stage just as the bull is thrust into the spanish bull-ring. Iago, the *taurobolus* of this sacrificial bull, the little David of this Goliath, or the little feat-gilded *espada*, is for Shakespeare nothing but Everyman, the Judas of the world, the representative of the crowds around the crucifix, or of the ferocious crowds at the *corrida*, or of the still more abject roman crowds at the mortuary games. Othello is of the race of Christs, or of the race of " bulls " ; he is the hero with all the magnificent helplessness of the animal, or all the beauty and ultimate resignation of the god. From the moment he arrives on the scene of his execution, or when his execution is being prepared, he speaks with an unmatched grandeur and beauty. To the troop that is come to look for him, armed and snarling, he says : " Put up your bright swords or the dew will rust them ! " And when at last he has been brought to bay he dies by that significant contrivance of remembering how he had defended the state when it was traduced, and in reviving this distant blow for his own demise. The great words roll on in your ears as the curtain falls :

> " And say besides, that in Aleppo once. . . ."

Iago is made to say :

> " The Moor, howbeit that I endure him not,
> Is of a constant, loving, noble nature."

But we do not need this testimony to feel, in all our dealings with this simplest and grandest of his creations, that we are meant to be in the presence of an absolute purity of human guilelessness, a generosity as grand and unaffected, although quick and, " being wrought, Perplexed in the extreme," as deep as that of his divine inventor.

There is no utterance in the whole of Shakespeare's plays that reveals the nobleness of his genius and of its intentions in the same way as the speech with which Othello closes :

> " Soft you ; a word or two before you go.
> I have done the state some service, and they know it.
> No more of that. I pray you, in your letters,
> When you shall these unlucky deeds relate,
> Speak of me as I am ; nothing extenuate,
> Nor set down aught in malice : then, must you speak
> Of one that loved, not wisely, but too well ;
> Of one not easily jealous, but, being wrought,

Perplex'd in the extreme ; of one, whose hand,
Like the base Indian, threw a pearl away,
Richer than all his tribe ; of one, whose subdued eyes,

. . . .

Drop tears as fast as the Arabian trees
Their medicinal gum. Set you down this ;
And say, besides, that in Aleppo once,
Where a malignant and a turban'd Turk
Beat a Venetian, and traduced the state,
I took by the throat the circumcisèd dog,
And smote him—thus."

And it is the speech of a military hero, as simple-hearted
as Hotspur. The tremendous and childlike pathos of this
simple creature, broken by intrigue so easily and completely, is one of the most significant things for the comprehension of Shakespeare's true thought. For why should
so much havoc ensue from the crude " management " of a
very ordinary intriguer ? It is no great devil that is pitted
against him : and so much faultless affection is destroyed
with such a mechanical facility. He is a toy in the hands
of a person so much less real than himself ; in every sense,
human and divine, so immeasurably inferior.

" And say besides, that in Aleppo once."

This unhappy child, caught in the fatal machinery of
" shakespearian tragedy," just as he might have been by
an accident in the well-known world, remembers, with a
measureless pathos, an event in the past to his credit,
recalled as an afterthought, and thrown in at the last
moment, a poor counter of " honour," to set against the
violence to which he has been driven by the whisperings
of things that have never existed.

And it is *we* who are intended to respond to these events,
as the Venetian, Lodovico, does, when he apostrophizes
Iago, describing him as :

" More fell than anguish, hunger or the sea ! "

The eloquence of that apostrophe is the measure of the
greatness of the heart that we have seen attacked and

overcome. We cannot take that as an eloquent outburst only : it was an expression of the author's conviction of the irreparable nature of the offence, because of the purity of the nature that had suffered. The green light of repugnance and judgment is thrown on to the small mechanical villain at the last.

Professor Bradley in his elaborate analysis of Iago says that many people have seen in Iago one of the traditional Machiavellis of the time ; but he repudiates that parentage for him. Yet it hardly seems a thing about which there can be any dispute. There is no question of Shakespeare's finding this *particular* duplicity in the figure of Machiavelli. But it is certain that Iago is a variety of the recognized stage Machiavelli type. Will anyone believe that if a philosophy of duplicity and ruthless mechanical intrigue, directed to the reaching of a definite material end, had never been written by Machiavelli : if Cesare Borgia had not supplied him with a living illustration and hero (as Napoleon was Stendhal's vast living confirmation and original) : and if the italian nature had not stood for *intrigue*, of a bold and relentless description, that Iago, the italian " villain " of this italian story, would ever have been created ?

In Act I., scene 1, he reveals himself at once, without the least delay or coyness, both to Roderigo and to the audience.

There is nothing that Iago says, in the displays of his mental workings with which we are accommodated, that would be inappropriate in the mouth of any solicitor, stockbroker, politician or man-about-town in England to-day, or in Shakespeare's day. He possesses the same pride in his *cunning*—tells you with a wink that *his* thoughts are not worn on his sleeve but in a deep and secret place, where they cannot easily be found.

There is something at once commonplace and maniacal, " normal " and mad, about the way he speaks of his hiding-place, his mind :

> " In following him, I follow but myself ;
> Heaven is my judge, not I for love and duty,

But seeming so, for my peculiar end :
For when my outward action doth demonstrate
The native act and figure of my heart
In compliment extern, 'tis not long after
But I will wear my heart upon my sleeve
For daws to peck at : I am not what I am."

The last words are the supreme bombast of such people. *I am not what I am.* The small and shoddy, when it meets its kind, knows it at once by this sign—namely, *that it is not what it is.* Both are the votaries of the goddess whose oracle these words convey. Shakespeare's own words—*I am that I am*—where in his *Sonnets*, through all the veils of his beautiful rhetoric, he is, as Wordsworth said, " unlocking his heart "—are similarly the supreme defiance of the rarest nature, for ever over against the dark equivocal crowds saturated with falsity.

When Robert Browning denied that Shakespeare was capable of such an action as " unlocking his heart " (as Wordsworth said that he did) he classed himself with more nicety than he knew. The romantically machiavellian and " detached " " *Robert Browning you writer of plays* " as he calls himself, with his social obsession (" the need of a world of men for me "), his vitalist habit of mind and proliferous spawning-powers, judged Shakespeare with that essential, romantic conventionality that he brought to all his judgments. So the " impersonality " dogma, popularizing the method of exact science, is, when applied to individual character or to the arts of life, an expression of the at once commonplace and demented cunning, pride in which is stigmatic of the man of the crowd of our day. But later in this book I give more attention to the subject of impersonality. I show how it is the characteristic myth of science, how in that sense it is a form of personality ; and how the instinctive and conscious mind is sacrificed to it.

The secret of Iago, then—if there could be any secret about Iago's nature for an intelligent spectator of the play in which he occurs, for he is as candid as it is possible to be to the audience and to everybody except his victim—is that this particular Everyman is the bluff, commonplace, quite unvillainlike, little "man of the world," mobilized to destroy a great shakespearian hero. Bossola is a complicated renaissance figure, but Iago is so great a creation because he is not that at all, but just the man-in-the street of any time or place since the emergence of *homo sapiens* on our scene. This plain man is, of course, deeply marked by professional, racial and other stereotyping effects of circumstance; and Iago, for instance, is the *blunt soldier*, and has other characteristics of his calling. But at heart it is one figure, the animal human average.

Most Shakespeare critics, however, when they come to write about Iago, use more or less the language of his wife Emilia on the discovery of his treachery, or of Lodovico, or Gratiano: his "motiveless malignity" is supposed to be motiveless because it is assumed to be so unusual and so deep. Professor Bradley scouts the idea that his own repeated explanation of his behaviour is to be accepted; and although he will not admit that it is motiveless, with Coleridge, he considers his villainy without parallel in its depth and degradation, and goes off hunting for motives of the most unusual sort (to match the *unusualness* of the crime).

He implores the reader to remember that Iago *under no circumstances* ever tells the truth! Should the reader forget that for a moment, one is almost made to feel he might find himself entrapped by this spartan dog as poor Othello was.

All this appears to me very far from the truth. The most obvious thing about Iago is that he never lies, and is as open (in his villainy) as the day, as we have already said.

He always tells the truth when speaking to the audience or to himself. It is a stroke of genius of Shakespeare to make him always called *honest*—when his actions are so deliberately dishonest, and yet when his nature, rough and direct, does, in another sense, perfectly answer that description.

The villainy of Iago did not seem to Shakespeare, from all appearances, very exceptional, although very black.

Also he accounted for it, fully, even, on several occasions, out of Iago's own mouth. In Act I., scene 3, Iago's soliloquy seems a very straightforward and reasonable explanation of why he intends "to pay out" his master:

> "I hate the Moor;
> And it is thought abroad, that 'twixt my sheets
> He has done my office: I know not if't be true;
> But I, for mere suspicion in that kind,
> Will do as if for surety. He holds me well.
> The better shall my purpose work on him.
> Cassio's a proper man: let me see now;
> To get his place, and to plume up my will,
> In double knavery,—How, how?—Let's see:—
> After some time to abuse Othello's ear
> That he is too familiar with his wife.
> He hath a person, and a smooth dispose,
> To be suspected; framed to make women false.
> The Moor is of a free and open nature,
> That thinks men honest that but seem to be so;
> And will as tenderly be led by the nose,
> As asses are."

That is a very close statement: or again (Act II., scene 1):

> "He'll prove to Desdemona
> A most dear husband. Now, I do love her too;
> Not out of absolute lust (though, peradventure,
> I stand accountant for as great a sin),
> But partly led to diet my revenge,
> For that I do suspect the lusty Moor
> Hath leap'd into my seat: the thought whereof
> Doth, like a poisonous mineral, gnaw my inwards;
> And nothing can or shall content my soul,
> Till I am even'd with him, wife for wife;
> Or, failing so, yet that I put the Moor
> At least into a jealousy so strong
> That judgment cannot cure."

Iago is a professional soldier, a "man of action," like Othello; and in a sense he is *simple*, like Othello. When he says the Moor is of a constant, loving, noble nature he admires those qualities. He does not sneer as he says it, their psychology has enough in common, just as their way of life has, so that, in spite of his immense respect for the tortuous, he can also admire the open and truthful.

Being in this sense *simple*, like Othello; and believing that Othello has cuckolded him, he reacts to this event in as violent and primitive a way as Othello does. He is, like Othello, very touchy where the faithfulness of his wife is concerned, and likes the idea of being pointed at as a cuckold just as little as Othello does. In other ways, also, Othello has treated him without very much consideration: but the ostensible plot of the play is really the revenge of the sex-vanity of a subordinate on his chief, the revenge taking the form of inspiring his chief with the same feelings of jealousy and wounded vanity that he has experienced himself.

But it is much more than a sex-revenge—*sex* in its way being as deceptive as *money* is in itself a human incentive. It is also, as it were, a *race*-revenge, the vengeance of the small nature upon the great nature.

To conclude the consideration of this question by returning to the conflict we supposed between the worldly soul of man and a champion of the superhuman idealism—the factor that has produced all those astonishing achievements that men have felt separated them from the other animals—where should we look for our champions? We have agreed that it would probably be from among Shakespeare's colossi that the champion on one side would be taken; though perhaps, because of the historic reference, and the magnificence of the traditional setting, the Antony of *Antony and Cleopatra* would be better than Othello. But if you were matching Othello or Antony in this way, who would you choose for the vulpine rôle?

Ulysses is a great myth traditionally representing " the world," but his cunning is almost heroic; and there would be the same objections to him, on those grounds, as to the jesuit. Yet (in a sense since they are real champions) it would probably be Ulysses, the jesuit, or the transformed shaman that you would choose. (The matching of a woman and a man is too unnatural.) You would not get the David and Goliath contrast in stature, but you would get a more exciting spectacle. The pathos of the " little pin " and the " good-bye king," the meanness of the instrument used to destroy all greatness, is perhaps too intense, in principle, for artistic expression. That is why tragedy is not the purest art. The contests of pure art would be like the battles of the norse heroes in heaven. They would ride back after the battle to Valhalla or some more congenial Elysium, the wounds and deaths abolished by magic at the termination of each day. Only heroes would participate ; and no reality would mar their vigorous joys.

PART VI
THE TWO KNIGHTS

CHAPTER I

THE CONTEST OF THE LION AND THE FOX IN SHAKESPEARE AND CERVANTES

IN the last part what I called in the preface the *master-subject* of Shakespeare's plays has been reached, and, I think, its essential nature exhibited. That is the form that all the deeper conflicts therein take. This was, of course, immediately and historically, the reflection of the struggle between chivalry, " celtism," christian mysticism, on the one hand, and the " scientific spirit " of the renaissance mind and of the modern world on the other. It was the struggle that gave such force and point to the work of Cervantes and Rabelais. And Shakespeare was more positivist than Cervantes, and less so I think than Rabelais : his was a mean position, but into this mean he gathered the excesses of his time as well. That is why with all his measure he had so much force.

The fact that this is also with Shakespeare, as with Cervantes and Rabelais, the master-*motif* of his work has not been given the salience it deserves. So far the *alto-fronto* type, originating or at least finding its rough archetype in *The Malcontent*, has received beyond doubt the most advertisement. The Hamlet-problem is the most obviously conspicuous one in all the mass of his plays. But there is, running through all of them and turned a hundred ways, another fundamental preoccupation of the mind, which is a universal problem but also a problem especially of his time —and now of ours. And Machiavelli (abused or ignored, in the nature of things, by every true machiavellian) is still the best textbook for much to-day being accomplished in the political field.

This preoccupation as manifested in Shakespeare could be styled the battle of the lion and the fox : the contest or the tragedy arising from the meeting of the *Simpleton* and the *Machiavel*, the Fool and the Knave. Othello is the most obvious instance of this preoccupation and nothing else ; but it springs up everywhere in Shakespeare's plays. Coriolanus, and Hotspur, Ajax, Hector, in varying degrees, are other instances of simpletons with whom, I think, contrary to what is generally believed, Shakespeare had little sympathy. Coriolanus is certainly not the hero, or the object of admiration, for Shakespeare, that he is generally supposed to be, any more than is the unintelligent and morbid chivalry of Percy. There is no love lost between these figures and their intelligent creator, as there is between Don Quixote and his. And it is at this point we once more will find how difficult it is to reconcile all the troubled elements, sometimes confronted on the same stage, in these creations. The sort of contradiction to which I refer is this, for example : that Hotspur and Coriolanus are as good physical heroes as Othello, but they do not apparently recommend themselves to Shakespeare : and therefrom their physical heroism itself seems to become disgusting or ridiculous. The quality in Antony and Othello that is capital for their dazzled creator, in the other two seems taken for granted, and now and then appears almost an offence. The cause for this seems to be in the fact that the latter heroes have not the necessary magnetism to transform their exploits into poetry, and to destroy in these the *real*. There is the stench of battle, and its " shop," about both of them ; mechanical, sanguinary, perspiring events are their inferior element, and they neither of them have Cleopatras or Desdemonas.

Coriolanus, a figure that occupies a great deal of space, is at no point allowed anything that could be described as charm. He is in a state of stupid tutelage, and remains a " boy " to the end. The Coriolanus of Shakespeare seems to have the qualities and defects of the english public-school boy, the really successful type of which has for its rationale a military or administrative objective, for which he is prepared by a castration of the imagination. Essentially also his training permits of no development : throughout life he remains the schoolboy he has been taught to be for

ever, so that at sixty the same jolly, healthy face shall be
there as at the beginning. No amount of physical courage
can compensate for the defects of dullness and meanness
inherent in such a system. And Coriolanus, who is crabbed,
sullen and pompous, has none even of the features that
redeem that.

If you were brought to accept that view of Shakespeare's
feeling about these two characters, only Coriolanus and
Hotspur, for instance, it would involve a radical modifica-
tion also of the generally accepted estimate of Shakespeare's
political tendencies. In short, the wedge successfully introduced at those points would bring to the ground the house
of cards of theologico-political shakespearian criticism
that has been built during a century (the first trans-
cendental stones of which were laid by Coleridge and
Gervinus), and which is being gnawed at to-day by most
contemporary critics. But it is always an open question
on *which side* the edifice will fall ; and my own inclination
would be to see it fall to a side favourable to Shakespeare.

If we turn our attention to his spanish contemporary,
Cervantes, we find again that whenever we get as near the
summits of human achievement as this we are in the presence of a very complex activity ; and for all the apparent
simplicity, at least in the result, that a *problem* is there for
us, as much in the motives as in the resultant incarnations.

The complexity of Cervantes is increased, I think, by the
fact of his long italian residence. There is something of
interest in this point in a book by E. J. Martinez (*Shakespeare en España*). Quoting Francisco A. de Icaza, on the
subject of *La Española Inglesa* of Cervantes, he writes:
" . . . que ninguno de los que intervienen en la accion son
personas de carne y hueso como otras creadas por Cervantes.
Hasta sus nombres, que nada tienen de ingleses y poco
de españoles, parecen denunciar que cuando Cervantes no
componia copiando directamente del natural, perdia mucho
de su personalidad artistica y recordaba demasiado la
urdimbre y contextura de las obras italianas."

When Cervantes had not nature to copy—when he had
to write, as in *La Española Inglesa*, of something he had

never seen and handled, all the life would go out of his work, and he would drop into imitation, instead, of the Italians, among whom he had lived and from whom he had learned his art, this writer says.

Was Cervantes' a sophisticated italian *eye*, imported into the " chivalrous " atmosphere of Spain (as in another art El Greco's was a byzantine eye); and was the parody of chivalry in *Don Quixote* the result ? And was this original impulsion frustrated and overwhelmed by the spanish and native nature of the writer ? Was it an alliance of the eye of Machiavelli, shall we say, and the spirit of the Cid ? In any case both were there.

A great admirer of Cervantes, Mr J. Fitzmaurice Kelly, writes (*Cervantes and Shakespeare*): " The spanish writer has not Shakespeare's depth of searching reflection and splendour of contrapuntal diction. But neither has the Englishman Cervantes' wealth of varied first-hand experience, his magnanimous charity and inimitable serenity." That probably sums up what most people would feel who were fairly familiar with both writers. They would feel that the " magnanimous charity " was lacking in the english poet : that the Spaniard had the more constant heart, and also a more original political insight.

" The wound that phantom gave me ! " says Don Quixote about the blow on his head he had received from the official of the Holy Brotherhood. His enemies are *phantoms*, because he is a phantom too. He has no trace in his nature of the raging reality of Shakespeare's figures, Timon or Lear, for whom, as even for Hamlet, enemies are only too *real*. But that is doubtless also because Don Quixote has the luck to be a phantom himself.

At first sight, then, *Don Quixote* appears as a mighty satire on something which, being such a great artist, Cervantes himself must have been (leaving *the Spaniard* out of the question).

All the chivalrous splendours of the Middle Ages, which redeem their " darkness," it was his destiny to " laugh away." Rabelais, it is true, did somewhat the same thing, although their objects were quite different ; only Rabelais dealt in impossible giants, whereas Cervantes took a very probable poor gentleman of La Mancha, as Defoe might have taken him ; and it was because of the natural *mise en scène* and the sober relative likelihood of the narrative, for one thing, that it was so much more effective.

Both again floated their great new ventures on a popular tide of romanesque fiction. Rabelais launched the gigantic satire of his time that he had slowly elaborated on a tide fed with such bombastic rivers as those of *Les faits et gestes du preux Goddefroy de Boulieu et de ses chevalereux frères Baudouin et Eustache, Robert le Diable, Fierabras, Les Quatre fils Aymon, Huon de Bordeaux, Lancelot du Lac, Ogier le Danois, Merlusine, Conquête du grant roy Charlemaigne des Espagnes, Morgant le Géant, Valentin et Orson, L'Histoire de Giglain, fils de Messire Gauvain ;* and (to run on from the *Inventaire de Jacques le Gros*) *Perceforestz, Meliadus de Lyonnois, Tristan, Giron le Courtois, Jourdain et Morgant, Merlin, Beufves d'Anthonne, Trébisonde, Perceval, Alexandre le Grant, Doolin et Fierabras, Gallien Restaure, Gerard du Frastre, Maquelonne, Jean de Paris, Jeoffroy Grant Dent, Belle Hélaine, Florimont, Melusine, Mabrian, Guerin et Mangist, Milles et Amis, Florent et Lyon.* The swarming of these chivalrous names will suggest to the eye the immensity of the literature of chivalries and enchantments *en marge* of which Cervantes and Rabelais lived, half-fascinated with its baroque empty magnificence, no doubt, and half of necessity mocking its lack of proportion and simplicity, and poverty of human meaning. " For the enjoyment the mind feels must come from the beauty and harmony which . . . the eye or the imagination bring before it. Nothing that has any ugliness about it or disproportion can give any pleasure " (*Don Quixote*). The gigantic, and a sort of poverty about impossible prowess or virtue, answer to this criticism.

The writer to whom I am principally indebted for my information on the sources of Rabelais—Jean Lattard— insists that it was not Rabelais' intention to *ridicule* the *chevaleresque* literature of France, but only to make use of its success for his own purposes. Indeed he cites La Noue

on the subject of the *Amadis* and similar books to the effect
that if in those times " quelqu'un les eust voulu alors blamer,
on lui eust craché au visage, d'autant qu'ils servaient de
pedagogues, de jouet et d'entretien à beaucoup de personnes."

But this seems to me to be talking as though the literature of chivalry contained nothing but one thing—that it was
chivalry itself, in short. It might be that both Rabelais'
and Cervantes' feeling on the subject of this contemporary
literature was that in the long run it was adapted in its
vulgarized form to make the chivalrous characteristics of
bravery, simple-heartedness, generosity, good faith and
exalted and romantic love, very ridiculous: much more so,
in fact, than any deliberate caricature of them could effect.
The popularization of the ideal of *aristocracy* by Nietzsche,
and its effect on many a little bourgeois, is a parallel of
interest. But how anyone can have thought that it was to
satirize a figure of that calibre that *Don Quixote* was written
is difficult to see.

For *Don Quixote* advertises and perpetuates chivalry,
does it not, far more than any *Amadis de Gaula* or the
Gesta of the Cid? And Cervantes betrays a tenderness for
this *hijo seco*, this mournful and stately child of his, in a
wild and commonplace world, which cannot be missed, and
which no burlesque can displace; and which is certainly not
the handling of political satire. The millionaire monsters of
roman satire, cheap and dull, swimming in a sewer of dis-
figuring luxury, are not on the same side of the battle as this
penniless, sober, solemn gentleman, setting out on a haggard
horse to relieve distress and uphold his empty dream.

For if Miguel Cervantes were *attacking* Don Quixote—the
very statement of this unnatural event disposes of it—it
would be the one lonely and conspicuous case of an attack by a
great artist on the poor, the unfortunate, the mocked-at, in-
sulted and despised. Which (applying the euclidean formula,
and remembering our earlier axiom that " Satire is always
directed at the fortunate and successful ") *is impossible*.

Therefore, if we had nothing else to guide us, we should
know that Cervantes was identifying himself with Don
Quixote, rather than with the world besetting his knight.

IN SHAKESPEARE AND CERVANTES

It would be identifying all that he admired most with his hero, at the same time that he understood its melancholy destiny : the laughter and mockery that he stirred up around this noble fiction he knew that violence alone could silence, and that for its depravity and foolishness the bitterest laughter would be too light a thing. And in that violence he was not disposed to deal. The violence that stamped out periodically all the foolishness was the rage of a thing of the same flesh and blood as itself, fighting it on its own material ground with material weapons. The rage behind the satire of Juvenal or Persius would easily take the form of a murderous violence and eclipse in one suffocating blow the image of itself that it hated. But the poor lunatic gentleman of La Mancha—no real rage ever came near him, at most the impatient buffeting of things he mistook for something they were not (as Roland, when he went mad, charged flocks of sheep in place of the infidel) : he is as remote from life as an image of the Buddha. He is one of the greatest productions of the western imagination : he is not a postulant but a complete initiate—but far more dissociated from his world than the high things of the asiatic imagination have been from theirs.

Taken as a satire, then, all the satire is concentrated not upon the palpable object of its activity, but just upon those assistants it conjures up to help it with its supposed victim. The stupid go-between, the half-hearted devotee, Sancho Panza, the faithful dog dazzled by something it cannot understand, its scepticism delivering constant assaults upon its infatuation, this fragment of the alien world sticking to the saint, is the focus for the satire in reality. The senseless turning of the windmills, even, is included in the mechanical personality of the homely and cunning spanish Hodge.

Sancho Panza's *catechism* under the tree outside Toboso, " Let us know now, brother Sancho, where you are going," has often been compared with Falstaff's famous *catechism* on the field of Shrewsbury. But it has never suggested, I believe, the natural conclusion of where we should look, in english literature, for our knight.

THE LION AND THE FOX

This is all the more so as *Henry IV.* is, as the german critic Gervinus says, that play where more than elsewhere the full power of the english " national poet " is associated with a theme inalienably english. (" The genius of a nation has never appeared on any stage in such bright cheerfulness," etc.) To match Cervantes (if it were a question of comparing the two artists) I should choose myself some play of Shakespeare's where this " national cheerfulness " played a less important rôle. And *Don Quixote* is too wide and too personal to be " spanish " first and foremost. But all allowances made, and conceding that *Henry IV.* is not *Shakespeare's* most significant work, though it may be *the national poet's*, and that you could get as *spanish* a production as *Don Quixote* without the great personal genius of Cervantes ; nevertheless these works can be confronted as peculiarly representative of their respective countries.

It may be as well to recall by reproducing it the well-known soliloquy of Falstaff :

" Can honour set to a leg ? no : or an arm ? or take away the grief of a wound ? No. Honour hath no skill in surgery, then ? no. What is honour ? a word. What is in that word, honour ? air. A trim reckoning !—Who hath it ? he that died o' Wednesday. Doth he feel it ? no. Doth he hear it ? no. 'Tis insensible, then ? yea, to the dead. But will it not live with the living ? no. Why ? detraction will not suffer it :—therefore, I'll none of it."

There is the characteristic reasoning, but with a rapider and more informed cunning, of Sancho Panza. Only the english Sancho Panza, if Falstaff is he, is ten times the size of the spanish one. He is also a *knight* ; so in a sense the rôles are reversed. He is a man of the world—a compendium of rosy vices, very pleasant and amusing : fallen on rather evil times, he displays himself as in reality a cutpurse, drunkard and sneak. And, without very much fancifulness, we could pursue the parallel, and show him surrounded (in Shakespeare's *Henry IV.*) with rather dull and boorish specimens of *real* chivalry, against which background he shows off to good advantage.

CHAPTER II

THE FORM RESPONSIBLE FOR THE MIND

IF we agreed to regard Shakespeare as composed, in more nearly equal parts than in the case of his great contemporary Cervantes, of chivalry on the one hand, and the modern positivist objective spirit on the other, we should be free to examine the nature of this chivalry and this disillusion separately. I think it would then be found that the chivalry, the afflatus of the grand style, has its origin in the manner and not the matter of his art. Shakespeare had an infinite love and compassion for the heroic figures of his art, or of anything naturally translatable into that world; but it is unlikely that the things of this world appeared to him to have any importance save as symbols of that. He recreated everything for himself, and his system balanced with nature to a nicety, and his work exhibited nature's system, too. In one system all was sublime sorrow and magnificence: in the other all was the squalor of infinite futility. He was as capable as any man, indeed more capable, of seeing Timon as a furious egotist, an insane spendthrift, whose particular weakness it was to love flattery and adulation, and who gave all his money away in order to obtain it. He knew that this hero could be regarded as a violent, lavish, egotistic fool, who spent his money like water, after the manner of many greek and roman magistrates, in order to be popular; and as a man too imperfectly sensitive to be troubled by the consciousness that this love and popularity was being bought. Then, his money spent, he turns on this world and charges it with "ingratitude" and a hundred vices which he had not before been concerned to observe.

In Timon's case this picture is entirely ignored: and in place of it a violent and mournful despair rises from a great nature, full of generosity in a time of awakening and immense astonishment at the vileness of the world—which takes everything and gives nothing, whose nature is poorer than any dog's, on whom no reliance can be placed, and on whom all love or compassion are only wasted. He is as lofty and spotless a nature as is Clermont d'Ambois ; a child like Othello, an outcast like Lear, a dying king. He is, in short, an inhabitant of Shakespeare's personal system. That personal system had no ethical bias, but was entirely an æsthetic phenomenon. Its goods and bads were the beautiful and the ugly. As such it was necessarily noble and immaculate, removed from the sphere of Thersites or Iago, made of different clay, and contrasted always with the actual world of men, and its figures provided with a suitable *pathos* at the hands of the crowd. They are in this way much more " moral " in their *effect* than the most powerful sermon or display of " principle " can be. Like Clermont d'Ambois, these heroes are usually metaphysical gods, strayed into our universe, very easy to deceive, as all noble natures are :

> " He was credulous :
> He would believe, since he would be believed ;
> Your noblest natures are most credulous.
> Who gives no trust, all trust is apt to break,
> Hate like hell-mouth who think not what they speak "
> (*The Revenge of Bussy.*)

Or you can compare the classical examples of this statement shown in the mirror of the intelligence of Swift's fabulous horse :

" And I remember in frequent discourses with my master concerning the nature of manhood in other parts of the world, having occasion to talk of lying and false representation, it was with much difficulty that he comprehended what I meant, although he had otherwise a most acute judgment ; for he argued thus : that the use of speech was to make us understand one another . . . now if any one said *the thing which was not*, those ends were defeated. . . . And these were all the notions he had concerning that faculty of lying, so perfectly well understood, and so universally practised among human creatures."

Where romantic sexual love is concerned, the heroes are inclined to depart also from the approved human standard —at least the Clermont d'Amboises or Hamlets are:

> " If there were love in marriage, so I would :
> But I deny that any man doth love,
> Affecting wives, maids, widows, *any women* :
> For neither flies love milk," etc.

Except when it is a destructive madness, it is absent, as a rule :

> " For where love kindles any knowing spirit,
> It ends in virtue and effects divine,
> And is in friendship chaste and masculine."

As the order of beauty is not an inferior thing to the moral order, so the fact that Shakespeare's *goodness* is æsthetic virtue, and not the emotion of the moralist, does not make it less pure or valuable.

Had Marlowe's " mighty line " not existed, Shakespeare might have drawn quite different characters—none for example like Othello or Timon. The matter of his art, or what he thinks and sees when not drunken with the grand style, is the mental material of *Troilus and Cressida*. And his mentality there contradicts categorically his mentality in many other plays. Nothing more disillusioned has been written about the traditional heroisms of the world than *Troilus and Cressida*. That is the pure intellect's true account of life. But even there Romeoesque love lifts up its head in the person of Troilus : and the non-heroic Fox (of the renaissance LION-FOX combination) in the person of the crafty Ulysses (moving amongst the inflated and ridiculous shapes of the homeric scene with the air of a private-inquiry agent—with a monotonous stealth and detachment) utters its craft with all the glamour of the grand style :

> " Time hath, my lord, a wallet at his back," etc.

THE LION AND THE FOX

Chivalry, even, finds its exponent, and its banner is upheld by Hector, however much it is "let down" by Achilles and the rest. Witness Troilus' remark to his brother :

> "*Tro.* Brother, you have a vice of mercy in you,
> Which better fits a lion than a man.
>   *Hect.* What vice is that, good Troilus ? chide me for it.
>   *Tro.* When many times the captive Grecians fall,
> Even in the fan and wind of your fair sword,
> You bid them rise, and live.
>   *Hect.* O, 'tis fair play."

But the great hero, Hector, succumbs, as every hero too purely lionlike must—whether he be Cæsar, Othello, Antony or Hector—to the craft and practice of some less heroic man. So Achilles with his myrmidons surprises him when he is unarmed, and he is killed " unfairly."

In a play like *Troilus and Cressida* the weakness of the grand style and of blank verse becomes peculiarly apparent. This weakness of the grand style (from the point of view of the *mirror-up-to-nature* theory of art, and also from the point of view of character-discrimination and a delicate adjustment and distribution of values) is a parallel one to that of *humour*. It transfigures everything at once, monotonously heightening it, so that it is impossible, in the midst of its splendours, to convey anything but the most elevated and dazzling perfections. The perfection of the *form* involves with it an elevation and perfection of *matter*. With Ulysses, for example, the intention is to convey a feeling of craft and " policy " ; and you would expect his utterance to be correspondingly circumspect, rather insinuating than grand. You would not expect organ notes to issue from his mouth as you would were it the mouth of Roland or Renaud. Yet, where Marlowe's *great line* is your medium, the moment he opens his mouth the organ begins, and no one, whatever his theme, could speak more grandly. Where Antony and Octavius Cæsar meet (*Antony and Cleopatra*, Act II., scene 2), and where an effort has been made to flatten and chill the blank verse, the following result is arrived at :

> " *Cæs.* Welcome to Rome.
> *Ant.* Thank you.
> *Cæs.* Sit.
> *Ant.* Sit, sir.
> *Cæs.* Nay, then.
> *Ant.* I learn, you take things ill, which are not so ;
> Or, being, concern you not.
> *Cæs.*   I must be laugh'd at,
> If, or for nothing or a little, I
> Should say myself offended ; and with you
> Chiefly i' the world : more laugh'd at, that I should
> Once name you derogately, when to sound your name
> It not concern'd me.
> *Ant.*   My being in Egypt, Cæsar,
> What was't to you ?
> *Cæs.* No more than my residing here at Rome
> Might be to you in Egypt : yet, if you there
> Did practise on my state, your being in Egypt
> Might be my question."

The six lines of dialogue belonging to Cæsar resemble Browning's interminable crabbed efforts on the same lines. Shakespeare would normally have written this in prose, but the very critical meeting of the two masters of the world had to be dignified by blank verse : and yet to be true to this instinct for the likelihood of the case it had to have the tone of prose. But in most cases he is unable to be so consistent. And Marlowe's *mighty line* swamps his characters in its reverberation. With *humour* similarly, or beneath its glow, it has often been observed that every character tends to become "lovable." Villainies and meannesses vanish, and satire loses its sting.

The perfection of the form, we have seen above, involves with it an elevation and perfection in the matter. It is from the ritual of art, in short, from its intoxicating rhythms, that these chivalrous dreams have ensued. All chivalrous realities similarly have ensued from such rhythms, in one form or another, if it is only the throbbing of a drum.

When, as in the present age, life loses its exterior beauty, and all the ritual of grandeur has become extinct, the intellect and character everywhere deteriorates. It is always the *form* that imposes the fact. But in its turn the form originates in some fancy or desire that seeks instinctively a ceremonious expression, just as an ardent mind seeks for itself a personal expression in some suitable medium.

And so there is "the prose" and "the poetry" of an individual or a nation's life; and wherever they meet, while the personality has life and youth, the poetry overwhelms the prose: the chivalry substitutes itself for the self-interest, a mystical religion for a "scientific truth," the Lion for the Fox. But the moment the drums stop beating the appeal of art weakens; the Fox resumes the centre of the stage, and the Lion withdraws, or perhaps his tail wagging from the wings is all we see.

CHAPTER III

FALSTAFF AND DON QUIXOTE

"THE wound that phantom gave me!" is an exclamation illustrating the quixotic attitude to the environing world, which, if it lends qualities to things they do not possess, restores in a sense the balance by not bestowing on any existence quite the harshness of the analytic eye of common sense. Don Quixote is of course one of the many demented characters inhabiting the region of great fiction. Hamlet, Lear, Othello, Timon are all demented or hallucinated, as so many of the celebrated figures in nineteenth-century russian fiction were. It is the supreme liberty that it is possible to take with your material. That it should be so often taken in the case of the great characters of dramatic fiction is the most evident testimony to the dependence on *untruth*, in every sense, in which our human nature and human environment put us. In the case of Muishkin, Dostoieffsky had to call in express and abnormal physiological conditions to help him incarnate his saint. And the natural heightening everywhere in Shakespeare is by way of madness. Since it is mad to behave in the way the hero does, he has to be maddened by some means or other more often than not in order to make him at all probable.

" The defeat of the hero " to see " the splendid triumph of his heroism " is in accord with the definitely tragic nature of the jest, and the movement of thought beneath the symbolization. That Don Quixote has not a ceremonious *pathos*, and that he only fights with *phantoms* which we know under homely shapes, does not make him any less a hero. Though Persiles and Sigismunda, for instance, could easily be confounded with the conventional heroes of Heliodorus—similarly connected with Thessaly—Don Quixote is, in literature, a lonely hero, and even in that responds to one of the chief requirements of tragedy, approximating at the same time to one of the conditions of madness.

The effect of Cervantes on the german romantics—G. Schlegel Tieck and Schelling—produced some interesting results. Some of their conclusions appear to me to correspond to the truth of the figure of Don Quixote.

"Schelling put into definite shape the formula of the new interpretation: he saw in *Don Quixote* the philosophical novel par excellence, in the great adventure of Quixote the universal conflict of the ideal and the real, and in the defeat of the hero the triumph of his heroism."

"For the rest, *Don Quixote*, interpretated from the romantic point of view, was in no way opposed to the spirit of adventure and mystical dreams, rather it exalted sacrifice and devotion to the Idea, and thus favoured every kind of religious and political initiative. And, on the other hand, romantic irony found in the spectacle of the eternal duality suggested by Don Quixote the justification of its smile and of its lofty detachment" (J. J. Bertrand).

You must not, the german romantics said, see in *Don Quixote* simply a good after-dinner laugh, a *bambocciata*.

"In the theory of universal discord, the principle [of the interpretation] is to be found. Schiller had adopted the hypothesis of the primordial disunity of the world, the result of which is the tragic antithesis in which we are struggling. Fichte opposed still more violently the self and not-self, and made familiar to contemporary thought this system of antagonism between life and the dream, the trivial and the ideal. Don Quixote is the symbol of this duality."

Such "romantic" explanations appear to be the only ones compatible with the great beauty of this book.

It was perhaps the long stay Cervantes made in Italy that enabled him to look at spanish life with detached and foreign eyes: but being an artist can alone have produced this condition in Shakespeare. And I think there is nothing in Shakespeare's work that makes him so *national* as Cervantes was. Shakespeare's laborious—and in a small

business way successful—life was not a fierce and youthful
episode, like Marlowe's. But he had his share of hardness
and effectiveness : which again, if you regard it as the most
exterior thing, and if you wished to trace it to the influence
of an environment, would be natural to people living in
a great and noisy town, in the midst of affairs, and of a
rapidly changing life. Whereas Cervantes had the idyllic
peace of the grave landscapes of his country as a background, and had round him the gentler agricultural life of
a " backward " people.

According to Kyd, Marlowe was " irreligious . . . in-
temperate, and of a cruel heart." He was involved in
seditious movements, was considered hostile to religion
and died in a brawl. Raleigh's departure in search of El
Dorado followed religious persecution and espionage.
Marlowe was caught up in the atmosphere of plots and
heroics of which that is an example. Kyd attributes to
Marlowe a document for which he, Kyd, was arrested, and
which is described as a " libell that concerned the State."
It was apparently the text of a placard (described by the
register of the Privy Council as *a lewd and mutinous libell*)
of which some had been stuck upon the wall of the dutch
churchyard. It is as well to remember on all counts that
Shakespeare was very much influenced by Marlowe, and
shared probably some, at least, of his habits and opinions.

Whether Falstaff (Shakespeare's " knight," as Don
Quixote was Cervantes') was only a whimsical invention
to amuse ; or how far certain more fundamental things—
and what things—were involved, has, like most of the
matters connected with this very rich and complex work—
overcrowded with startlingly real figures—been much discussed. Ulrici, for example, thinks that *The Merry Wives*
is a satire, from the bourgeois point of view, on chivalry—
Falstaff representing chivalry :

" The burgher class avenges itself pretty severely upon
Falstaff's knighthood, and his knighthood does not anywhere appear more miserable and unknightly than when
thrown into a basket among dirty clothes, when beaten as
an old woman and tormented and pinched as a *fantastic*

satyr. In fact, it seems to me that these three features might be found to contain as many metaphorico-satirical thrusts at the chivalry of the day."

Possibly every class—as it is supposed that every type of man—found its expression in this universal poet, and the new *magnificos* of London and the italianized courtier, and even the many-headed beast, could find something to please them. But with that mechanical type of criticism that could see in a figure like Falstaff the expression of a class it is difficult to agree.

Where Ulrici says that Falstaff is the " impersonification of the whole of this refined and artificial civilization "—and more closely still that he is a *child*, a *naïf*—he has, I think, established one of the important things about him. To this I will presently return.

This passage of Ulrici on Falstaff is, in full, as follows :

" He is, so to say, the symbol, the personification of that general state of human frailty which, without being actually wicked—that is, without doing evil for the sake of evil, in order to find satisfaction in it—nevertheless perpetually does evil (to a certain extent against his will) simply because it happens to be the most direct means of attaining what he calls life and happiness ; this, he believes, is not only actually arrived at by everyone, but ought to be allowed to be the aim of everyone. In so far Falstaff is a pure child of nature, and it cannot be denied that in *Henry IV.*, at least, he shows some sparks of that *naïveté*, gay humour and innocent good-nature, which is generally peculiar to the so-called children of nature ; but he is a child of nature who not only stands in the midst of, on many sides, an advanced state of civilization, but who— owing to the refined luxury of his enjoyments, the variety of his dissolute appetites, and the manifold devices he makes use of to gratify them—is, at the same time, the impersonification of the whole of this refined and artificial civilization."

If you imagine Shakespeare taking Falstaff all through his plays—or through as many more as possible—then we should have, still more, a central and great figure (which would also be an *idea*) to place beside Cervantes' knight.

"These scenes [the comic falstaffian ones in *Henry IV.*] fill almost one half of the whole play. In no other historical drama of Shakespeare's do we find such a total disregard of the subject. Here . . . the comic and unhistorical portions are so surprisingly elaborate, that the question as to their justification becomes a vital point. . . ."

It was not, according to Ulrici, "Shakespeare's intention merely to give a broader foil to the character of Prince Henry." Nor can it have been "Shakespeare's intention in *Henry IV.* merely to give a representation of the return of honour and of man's different ideas and positions in regard to it; and he has assuredly not introduced the Falstaff episode merely in order to contrast the representatives of the idea of honour—the Prince and Percy—with Falstaff, the negative counterpart, the caricature of honour and knighthood" (Ulrici, Book VI., chap. vii.).

Ulrici's solution is that the comic is set to dog the historic in *Henry IV.* on purpose to show up its influence: "It is intended to parody the hollow pathos of the political history [*i.e.* of Henry IV.'s reign]. . . . Irony is to hold up its concave mirror to that mere semblance of history which is so frequently mistaken for history itself, as being considered great and important only when it parades about in its purple mantle with crown and sceptre, haggles about kingdoms, or lays about it with the scourge of war. For all that which in the present drama appears outwardly to be historical action—rebellion, dissension and war, victory and defeat, the critics of political cunning, treaties and negotiations with their high-sounding speeches about right and wrong—all this was in truth a mere show, the mere *mark* of history. The reign was of historical importance only as a transition stage in the further development of the great historical tragedy, and accordingly could not be passed over."

So "to give a clear exhibition of this unreality [that of the proceedings of the 'born actor' Bolingbroke and his playful barons] this semblance, this histrionic parade, was

—conveniently or inconveniently—the poet's intention in placing the comic scenes so immediately by the side of the historical action, and in allowing them step by step to accompany the course of the latter."

Ulrici thinks that the contrast was necessary only because of the emptiness of this *particular* history, in short. It is very easy, in view of the so-called enigmatical play of *Troilus and Cressida*, and in the view upheld here of a great many other points in all the plays, to *extend* this estimate of Ulrici to the whole of Shakespeare's works.

CHAPTER IV

FALSTAFF

I WILL now show how all these various questions we have passed in review during the last few chapters can be combined, and how they each contribute to the fixing a psychical centre of control which is responsible for all of them. First of all, what I named *shamanization* must be reverted to : its effects will be found a necessary ingredient of one of the most celebrated attributes of Shakespeare—namely, his humour. How " worldliness "— which we have discussed—comes in always on the feminine tide of feeling is evident ; and how scepticism is not incompatible with courage, any more than it is with feminineness—indeed the contrary, since the female animal is very brave, but on account of different things to the male.

For those who are not familiar with the phenomenon of *shamanization*, still universally prevalent among the subarctic tribes, I will briefly describe it.

A *shaman* is a person following the calling of a magician or priest : and the word *shamanization* that I have employed would refer to a shaman (the most typical of them) who had in addition transformed himself. This phenomenon—that of sex-transformation—in our life to-day is so evident, and so widespread, that (unless we are never to refer at all to a thing that exercises such great social influence, and whose prevalence in one manner or another, principally by way of social suggestion, affects the general outlook on life) we should find some cliché that does not smell of the laboratory, or some word that does not belong to those latinizing vulgarities of speech depended on for popular discussion. On behalf of the word employed I have no ambitious views : it is only an inoffensive and convenient counter for my personal use ; and because around the figure of the shaman I have elsewhere gathered a number of observations on this subject, and it has naturally suggested itself to me in the course of use.

As to the phenomenon itself, of sexual perversion, I am not one of those people who regard it as insignificant, or harmless as a widespread fashion : though it is so very much involved with other things (which on the surface seem to have little to do with it) that it is meaningless to discuss it by itself. Its manifestations and effects are extremely different in different ages and countries : successful in Sparta, in Lesbos it might be an offence, and in Chicago a useless and unornamental one, where it would probably take on a curious mechanical intensity, and an earnest scientific air. It might add charm to the south of Russia, but make the arctic rigours of the north still more unendurable. In Rome, for example, its effects were coarse and disagreeable, whereas in Athens they even had the intellect as an ally, recommending them. These general reflections on the nature of perversion do not concern us here very much, except that it seemed advisable to record that partiality for its numerous adepts, and its effects as revealed in current social life, cannot be attributed to me.

Shamanism, then, returning to the custom prevalent throughout the north of Asia and America, consists generally in the reversal of sex : a man, feeling himself unsuited for his sex, dresses himself as a woman, behaves as a woman (usually adopting the woman's rôle also where some man is concerned), or by means of this sexual abnegation prepares himself for the duties of a magician. Women similarly abandon the outward attributes of sex and become men. (This is more rare, because it is obviously a less attractive proposition—and this does not take with it properly an enhancement of the powers of " mystery," as the other transformation does.)

Generally speaking, the process of shamanizing himself confers on a man the feminine advantages. It signifies either a desire to experience the sensual delights peculiar to the female organization ; or else an ambition to identify himself with occult powers. But it is further a withdrawal from masculine responsibilities in every sense, and an adoption of the spectator's rôle of the woman (freed further, in his case, from the cares of motherhood). That this is a very radical and even inversely heroic, or heroically inverse, proceeding is evident. If we now turn to a figure with which we have already dealt—namely, the "man of the world" (a figure with whom by implication Shakespeare is compromised, but from identification with whom this analysis should, in effect, rescue him)—we shall find that there is nothing that exactly corresponds to the transformed shaman. Like the latter, as it is his strategy to include among his numerous advantages those possessed by the woman, he has a tincture of the *shaman* in him. Hotspur (one of Shakespeare's lesser heroes) tells in a famous speech how he meets on the battlefield a shamanizing sprig of nobility, whom he describes as chiding soldiers carrying dead bodies near him "for bringing a slovenly unhandsome corpse between the wind and his nobility." This exquisite was not necessarily a wholly shamanized man, but possibly only a macaroni of the time. He would in that case be a "man of the world" of a very extravagant type, very extravagantly *shamanized*. He would have on the field of battle all the privileges of a woman, only frowned at—and perhaps hustled—by the blustering Percy.

It is at this point that, fully prepared, we can address ourselves to the subject that can be regarded as the centre one in Shakespeare—that of his *humour*.

The *humour* of Falstaff achieves the same magical result as Don Quixote's chivalrous delusion—namely, it makes him immune from its accidents. The battles he finds himself engaged in are jokes; his opponents, the Douglas, Colevile of the dale, are "phantoms" (of a different sort, it is true), just as Don Quixote's are. The contrast of these two knights is a contrast in two unrealities—two specifics to turn the world by enchantment into something else. One is the sense of humour, the other is the mysticism of chivalry; the first a negation, the latter a positive inspiration. The one, the magic of being *wide awake* (very wide awake—beyond normal common sense): the other of having your eyes naturally sealed up, and of *dreaming*.

The " sense of humour," again, provides us with an exceptionally english or american attribute of worldliness.

In Falstaff, Shakespeare has given us a very interesting specimen indeed of consummate worldliness, with a very powerfully developed humorous proclivity, which served him better than any suit of armour could in the various vicissitudes of his life. An excellent substitute even for a *shamanizing* faculty, and enabling its possessor to escape the inconveniences and conventional disgrace of being feminine—at the same time it provides him with most of the social advantages of the woman. The sense of humour is from that point of view the masterpiece of worldly duplicity and strategy. On the field of battle at Tewkesbury, Falstaff avails himself of it in a famous scene, and gives us a classical exhibition of its many advantages, and the graceful operation of its deceit. It does not cut off its practitioner from " men " of the rough " hero type," but on the contrary endears him to them. So it becomes even a substitute for courage. There is no lack that it does not cover. With it Falstaff is as safe on the battlefield as the shamanized noble noticed by Percy Hotspur.

So if Falstaff is the embodiment of a mass of worldly expedient, this is of course all directed to defeating the reality as much as Don Quixote's. He is a walking disease, but his disease is used to evade the results of that absence of a sense of humour which is so conspicuous a characteristic of nature and natural phenomena. The sense of humour is woven into a magic carpet ; with it he progresses through his turbulent career, bearing a charmed life. This " sense " performs for Falstaff the office of a psychological liberator ; it is of magic potency, turning the field of Tewkesbury into a field of play, and cheating death wherever they meet.

The man would indeed be a coward who, possessed of this magic, was seriously timid. Falstaff was evidently not that : yet Morgan thought it necessary to write a book defending his " honour " in this respect. " He had from nature," he said, " as I presume to say, a spirit of boldness and enterprise."

Being a humorous figure *par excellence,* it was not possible for him to be brave in the hero's way, any more than it would be proper for the circus clown to be an obviously accomplished athlete. Gaucherie and laughable failure is, in both cases, of the essence of their rôle. But boldness and enterprise—as far as that was compatible with the necessity of advertising a lack of courage—he possessed to a great degree.

Morgan begins his defence of Falstaff's courage by appealing to the fact that *actions* (by which people usually judge character) are a very misleading key : "The understanding seems for the most part to take cognizance of *actions* only, and from these to infer *motives* and *characters* ; but the sense we have been speaking of proceeds in a contrary direction."

So he appeals for the actions that were not there—and in the nature of things could not have been there—in his conventional pleading.

As to Falstaff being " a constitutional coward " (like Parolles or Bobadil) he says :

" The reader, I believe, would wonder extremely to find either Parolles or Bobadil possess himself in danger. What then can be the cause that we are not at all surprised at the gaiety and ease of Falstaff under the most trying circumstances ; and that we never think of charging *Shakespeare* with departing, on that account, from the truth and coherence of character ? Perhaps, after all, the real character of Falstaff may be different from his apparent one ; and possibly this difference between reality and appearance, whilst it accounts at once for our liking and our censure, may be the true point of humour in the character, and the source of all our laughter and delight. We may chance to find, if we will but examine a little into the nature of those circumstances which have accidentally involved him, that he was intended to be drawn as a character of much natural courage and resolution ; and be obliged thereupon to repeal these decisions," etc.

Morgan's affected defence (of Falstaff's physical courage) is successfully achieved—but at the expense of every psychologic requirement of the case.

THE LION AND THE FOX

Morgan makes a point of Falstaff's freedom from malice:

" He [Falstaff] seems by nature to have had a mind free of malice or any evil principle; but he never took the trouble of acquiring any good one. He found himself (from the start) esteemed and loved with all his faults, nay *for* his faults, which were all connected with humour, and for the most part grew out of it." So " laughter and approbation attend his greatest excesses."

This is of course the " man of the world " in Falstaff—the *anti-Machiavel* of the type of Frederick the Great. But the " good fellow " in Falstaff, as it is in anybody almost, was no more innocent than, actually not as innocent as, Machiavelli's " bad fellow " or *male persona*. There is, in short, much method in such sanity.

Morgan piles up his understandings of the plan of this character:

" We all like *Old Jack*; yet, by some strange perverse fate, we all abuse him, and deny him the possession of any one single good or respectable quality. There is something extraordinary in this; it must be a strange art in Shakespeare which can draw our liking and good will towards so offensive an object. He has wit, it will be said: cheerfulness and humour of the most characteristic and captivating sort. And is this enough? Is the humour and gaiety of vice so very captivating? Is the wit, characteristic of baseness and every ill quality, capable of attaching the heart or winning the affections! Or does not the apparency of such humour, and the flashes of such wit, by more strongly disclosing the deformity of character but the more strongly excite our hatred and contempt for the man? "

The nonsense into which the moralist critic leads the amiable eighteenth-century writer at least becomes palpable here—even if worthlessness does not become more palpable when associated with wit. That it is not good qualities, any more than great qualities, that " attach the heart " it is not necessary to say.

Falstaff is a " man of wit and pleasure," and could generally be described as a very good specimen of a " man of the world." But the same thing applies to him as to Iago: the

FALSTAFF

"man of the world" is never so dramatically and openly cynical as Falstaff, any more than he is so candid as Machiavelli. He is not dramatic at all. To come to one of the necessary conclusions in this connexion, if the *Machiavel* were an Englishman he would be like Falstaff. This laziness, rascality and "good fellow" quality, crafty in the brainless animal way, is the english way of being a "deep-brained Machiavel."

But Falstaff is a "child," too, a "*naïf*," as Ulrici says. A worldly mixture of any strength is never without that ingredient. The vast compendium of worldly bluff that is Falstaff would have to contain that. It was like "any christom child" that he "went away," Mistress Quickly says.

He is armed from head to foot with sly feminine inferiorities, lovable weaknesses and instinctively cultivated charm. He is a big helpless bag of guts, exposing himself boldly to every risk on the child's, or the woman's, terms. When he runs away or lies down he is more adorable than any hero "facing fearful odds."

His immense girth and stature lends the greatest point, even, to his character. He is a hero run hugely to seed : he is actually heavier and bigger than the heaviest and biggest true colossus or hero. He is in that respect, physically, a mock-hero. Then this childishness is enhanced by his great physical scale, so much the opposite of the child's perquisite of smallness. And because of this meaningless, unmasculine immensity he always occupies the centre of the stage, he is the great landmark in any scene where he is. It all means nothing, and is a physical sham and trick put on the eye. And so he becomes the embodiment of bluff and worldly practice, the colossus of the *little*.

PART VII
THERSITES AND APEMANTUS

CHAPTER I

DR BOWDLER AND THE ELIZABETHAN MIND

DURING the last few sections into which I have divided this essay I have had occasion to refer to several of the well-known masters of shakespearian criticism. The master-builders of this elaborate literature, english and german, during the last century, left us many valuable observations and a wealth of delicate insight. But what characterizes all of them is a sense you get of the great mental distance separating them from the object of their study. The whole structure, certainly, where the english critics are concerned, is unsatisfactory, because they were forced to adapt Shakespeare so much to their own time that they forced him out of his; whereas in reality he was hardly typical of either, but much less of theirs than of his own.

One of the stumbling blocks with them was always his fashion of approaching sex, and the "moral" shocks that any reading of his plays involved, especially for the english reader. It may be as well, before passing to the subject with which I close this book—the politics of the plays—to note the bad flaw in the traditional shakespearian criticism for which the unreal attitude to sex of the last century especially was responsible. Classical german Shakespeare criticism —that of Gervinus for instance—suffers less than english ; but it is not by any means free of a sort of euphuizing manipulation of the mind of Shakespeare, who was peculiarly incapable of anything but the completest equanimity where sex was concerned. He saw no difficulties where the Coleridges and Lambs would see a thousand.

As I have come to this subject only on a psychological or ethical issue, in search of the most fertile and apposite analogy I could find to contemporary problems, it is natural that the thing which I see with particular clearness is just the psychological or ethical inadequacy of the critics it has been my task to consult. The student with more technical or purely historical preoccupations would not be so apt to give that side its clear relief.

The whole critical writing of Coleridge and Lamb, for instance, is vitiated by the fact of their being so out of sympathy with the age in which this poet lived, and so, in one way, of this poet. And Gervinus is equally moralistic. With all the wonderful insight that they showed, especially Coleridge, into the poetry of Shakespeare, they seem constantly to be mistaken when they are writing about the mental architecture of their subject. The tone of the sermon is used, and excuses sought for, wherever questions of conscience or motive or any ethical issue is involved, which travesties or denaturalizes the thing in question. For this poetry, being *dramatic*, and dealing not with abstract beauty, but human passion, cannot be written about sensibly by a typical english moralist. Before the english democracy had settled for good into its prosing and canting there was a moment when it could produce such a figure as Shakespeare. But his earliest systematic critics were far into that latter time of congealed moralism, and hardly possessed the free use of their minds.

As an example of this I will quote—though it does not deal with Shakespeare—Lamb's note on *The Faithful Shepherdess*: "If all the parts of this delightful pastoral had been in unison with its many innocent scenes and sweet lyrical intermixtures, it had been a poem fit to vie with *Comus* or the *Arcadia*, to have been put into the hands of boys and virgins, to have made matter for young dreams, like the loves of Hermia and Lysander. But a spot is on the face of this Diana. Nothing short of infatuation could have driven Fletcher upon mixing with this 'blessedness' such an ugly deformity as Cloe, the wanton shepherdess! Coarse words do but wound the ears; but a character of lewdness affects the mind. Female lewdness at once shocks nature and morality. If Cloe was meant to set off Clorin by contrast, Fletcher should have known that such weeds by juxtaposition do not set off, but kill, sweet flowers."

This passage, with its hackneyed "fit to put into the hands of boys and virgins" and its offensive ring of the anglican pulpit, speaks for itself. The realities of the plays of which he is so well known an interpreter could not be even approached by a mind so poisoned with " virtue " as this passage shows it to have been. If you could meet the Marquis de Sade, or some voluptuary you knew to be an exclusive specialist in *sex* of one form or another, you would know that all his energy flowed into that, and that his view of life would be refracted and discoloured by that specialization—so intense as all specifically sex-obsession must be. In the same way that a profoundly bitten drunkard or drug-taker eventually becomes disqualified for any society not sharing his specialization, or disposed expressly for the glorification of that satisfaction, so any form of intensely personal sex-specialization, with its wide and shallow angle, and its deep pigmentation, makes general life a dream, and some maniacally assembled fragment its reality. The english moralistic obsession—also dangerously attached to *sex*, round which it ranges all its values—is a similar disability for a critic who in the course of his training has succumbed to it. Its manifestations—in *Comus*, for example, mentioned above by Lamb—are far more repulsive actually than any other sort of obscenity could be. (For anything which is *so much to do with sex* as puritanic chastity is, must be " obscene," being so much in the same world, and always in contact with its adversary.) Milton has succeeded in making of what he calls *chastity* something obscene. That is one of his principal achievements. It actually is calculated to *repel* by its stupidity and coldness as effectively as an over-hot sticky and strong-smelling obscenity could ever do. But we know what those satirists who attack and sicken our senses with some obscenity are doing : they are probably trying, by rubbing our noses in it, to cure us of an overfondness for it, which they think is a mistake. But what is Milton doing ? or, generally speaking, the english or american puritan spirit ? The puritan is actually trying to disenchant us with virtue by mixing it with sex, thus making it ridiculous and repulsive. Or if they are not guilty of that diabolic intention, they should be eternally execrated as the greatest sinners through stupidity, not malice, of whom there is any record.

If this is true of Lamb, it is also true of Coleridge and Gervinus to a less extent (though with Gervinus, naturally, being a German, the moral blemish is less implicated with sex). The age of Lamb and Coleridge was also that of Dr Bowdler, it must be remembered, and Shakespeare was the victim selected by the latter.

I have not space here to go further into this point, and the above passing note must serve to indicate my criticism.

I can now proceed to a scrutiny of the text of the plays with a view to extracting from them the evidence necessary for understanding the " politics " of Shakespeare.

CHAPTER II

CORIOLANUS AND ARISTOCRATISM

TROILUS AND CRESSIDA is the one play that
no shakespearian critic ever approaches without
a baffled "hem!" and a sense of treading on
dangerous ground. It is an eccentric integrant of the series
that will not fit in with the smooth picture he has been
able to compose elsewhere of his conventional hero. All
that he has said about the difference between Marston
or Tourneur or Webster and Shakespeare is upset by this
troublesome exception. *Titus Andronicus* he can say was
not written by Shakespeare, but *Troilus and Cressida* does
not offer him that escape: it is undoubtedly Shakespeare's.

But it is a contradiction usually, in his sense, of the rest
of his work—or at least of what that work can be made to
appear on the surface, and without it.

"The idea that Shakespeare, in some of the bitter and
trivial scenes of this play, is satirizing antiquity, is not
borne out by a closer acquaintance with his sources. . . .
This powerful and unmistakably shakespearian drama of
Troilus and Cressida may necessitate in the reader who
comes to it for the first time a revision of his generalizations
as to its great author; but the making him a closer student
of antiquity will not be among them."

The reader may have to revise his ideas of Shakespeare.
But he will not have to revise his idea of antiquity in consequence; or (to extend the application—for it is feasible
to extend it) of life itself. Even this great author, letting
down the whole concern (possibly) in this bitter play,
cannot bring down the perfections he satirizes with him.

"*Troilus and Cressida* offers one of the most difficult
problems in the range of Shakespeare criticism. . . . The
play is as foreign to Shakespeare's usual treatment of
classical subjects as it is alien to the pervading spirit of the

235

comedies that preceded it. *Troilus* resembles *Love's Labour's Lost* in an atmosphere of satire that makes the existence of contemporary allusion in it seem almost a necessity. But it differs wholly from that sprightly good-humoured comedy in its tone of cynicism and irony, and in the worldly philosophy and bitter wisdom with which it is weighted, especially in the part of Ulysses. We may dismiss the notion that *Troilus and Cressida* is a gargantuan satire on classical learning, a deliberate attempt to present in an unworthy and ironical light the memorable heroes of ancient Troy. Nor does the idea that this play is Shakespeare's contribution to what is known as the ' war of the theatres ' seem much more tenable. . . . It is certain that Shakespeare's *Troy* is absolutely un-homeric, and that the mediæval story, in the english dress which Chaucer, Lydgate and others had given it, sufficiently accounts for the departures from homeric traditions that have so troubled the critics " (Schelling).

And that is all : it is a nasty problem, the usual explanations are rejected, and there it is left. It is a very bad business. When Professor Schelling says that it is *alien to the pervading spirit* of Shakespeare's other plays that is true ; but is there not, if one looks carefully enough, a great deal of matter in the others—even *pervading* them to some extent—that makes them less foreign to this ironic play ? That is what I believe, in any case, and what, as far as I am able, I will show.

Troilus and Cressida, Professor Schelling says, is " the only play in which we feel that his [Shakespeare's] charity and equanimity for the moment failed him and turned to bitterness and cynicism." That is a statement that appears to me typically sentimentalist and untrue. For is it not possible to match out of *Lear, Timon, Hamlet, Macbeth*, the " bitterest " that can be found in *Troilus* ? The *cynical railer, altofronto* type, is one to which Shakespeare, far from being averse, seems particularly partial. Hamlet or Jacques provide incessant and deeply " bitter " examples. It seems beyond all contradiction that, however that statement affects your opinion of this gigantic poet, the *altofronto* mood was a permanent and characteristic one with him. That (accepting it, as best you can) you have to reconcile it with the " heroism " of his Antonys, Hectors and Othellos. No more than you can get a unity of time and place with Shakespeare can you get a unity of soul.

Before going further into this I will repeat the judgments at which I have arrived. In a sense, perhaps, Falstaff was Shakespeare's knight, as Don Quixote was the knight of Cervantes. For in the sphere of comedy, of tragi-comedy, that is the natural parallel. And Sir John is the antithesis of Don Quixote. But Shakespeare had another, and almost a separate, department ; and that was full of quixotic shapes. Timon, Coriolanus, Brutus, Hamlet, *are all Quixotes*. Only he sees them all, except perhaps Othello, more coldly than Cervantes saw his *hijo seco*, save when something like a sexual excitement seems to take possession of him, and he begins caressing and adoring his hero as though he were a woman—like another Antonio in front of a Sebastian, in *Twelfth Night*.

To take only one of these—and I will choose the one that introduces naturally the next point that we shall have to take up—Coriolanus. That is the great creation that establishes Shakespeare—for those who want to see him as such—as " the feudal poet." Coriolanus is the demented " aristocrat," the incarnation of violent snobbery. In that, as in most elizabethan plays, you get the invective against the " multitude." The spirit of Marston is found in it in full force ; though there is nowhere in it as convinced an " aristocratism " as terminates the following lines from *Antonio and Mellida* :

" O rotten props of the craz'd multitude,
　How you still double, falter, under the lightest chance
　That strains your veins ! Alas, one battle lost,
　Your whorish love, your drunken healths—your houts and
　　　shouts,
　Your smooth God save's, and all your devil's last
　That tempts our quiet to your hell of throngs ! "

THE LION AND THE FOX

But Coriolanus, as a figure, is of course the super-snob. Of all Shakespeare's heroes he is the coldest, and the one that Shakespeare himself seems to have felt most coldly towards. He was the child of Volumnia, not of Shakespeare, and one that never became anything but a schoolboy, crazed with notions of privilege and social distinction, incapable of thinking (not differing in that from the rest of Shakespeare's nursery of colossi), but also congealed into a kind of machine of unintelligent pride. He is like a nietzschean, artificial "aristocrat," with little nobility in the sense that Don Quixote caricaturally embodied the noble, but possessing only a maniacal intolerance and stiffness.

There is a hollowness in the "heroics" in Coriolanus. But no hero could ever expect to be quite safe with the author of *Troilus and Cressida*. The following description, for instance, of the behaviour of the little son of Coriolanus by a friend of the family is "true to life," but too true not to have been observed with a mind detached from any infatuation with the speakers. It is impossible that this picture of a little Coriolanus growing up "just like his father" is not meant to illuminate Coriolanus for us:

"*Valeria*. O' my word, the father's son; I'll swear, 'tis a very pretty boy. O' my troth, I looked upon him o' Wednesday half an hour together; has such a confirmed countenance. I saw him run after a gilded butterfly; and when he caught it, he let it go again; and after it again; and over and over he comes, and up again; catched it again: or whether his fall enraged him, or how 'twas, he did so set his teeth; and tear it. O, I warrant, how he mammocked it!

Volumnia. One on's father's moods.

Valeria. Indeed, la, 'tis a noble child.

Virgilia. A crack, madam."

"*Indeed, la, 'tis a noble child,*" is a remark that would certainly not pass the censorship in a despotic super-feudal state, or recommend its author to a nietzschean. And had Shakespeare wished to engage the sympathy of almost any audience with this fine little fellow he certainly would not have chosen such a pretty and also flimsy thing as a butterfly to show him wracking one of his " father's moods " on.

It would appear that Shakespeare means at this point to show us the true Coriolanus, a cruel and stupid child, and to show him to us through the eyes of what he conceived to be a typical member of this early roman society, Valeria, " dear Valeria "—" as chaste as an icicle," of the same composition as Volumnia. So it would appear, and why should we not accept that as Shakespeare's intention ? But there are, of course, many reasons why such things should be bowdlerized, as it were, by the critic. But Shakespeare is full of scandalous matter that has to be hushed up. When the critic arrives at certain passages in *Lear* or *Macbeth* (as regards *Troilus and Cressida* he ignores the whole thing as far as possible) he will refer in a sober voice to this little " lapse from sanity " of Shakespeare, and then hurry on. Edgar's remark about his father's blindness in the fifth act of *King Lear* is one of these :

> " The gods are just, and of our pleasant vices
>   Make instruments to plague us :
>   The dark and vicious place where thee he got,
>   Cost him his eyes."

That is one of Shakespeare's more notorious " lapses." *Troilus and Cressida* is one vast " lapse," and *Timon* is almost another. But, in spite of these disturbing phenomena, the improper nature of much that is spread everywhere through all the plays is denied or ignored. And so in process of time whole plays, like *Coriolanus*, have received an interpretation that is contradicted everywhere in the play itself. Sir James Robertson, for instance, in writing of *Coriolanus*, treats Valeria and the chip-of-the-old-block episode as follows :

" It was probably a circumstantial accident that gave us, in addition to those incomparable portraits of women, yet a third, that of Valeria, who . . . has strictly nothing to do with the action of the play save to suggest anew, by her account of the boy Marcius, how even admirable women may miseducate children. Shakespeare is careful to insist on her nobility and charm by putting a warm eulogium of her in the mouth of Coriolanus; but had before introduced her as enjoying the episode of the child rending a butterfly in pieces."

He had indeed " before introduced her " in the act of enjoying the spectacle of this promising young chief engaged in a characteristic roman sport, and preparing himself for the martial preoccupations of the life that awaited him. But we are not to suppose that Shakespeare meant her to be anything less than noble, and possessed of the greatest charm. Indeed has he not been " careful to insist on " this in a " warm eulogium of her in the mouth of Coriolanus " ? (The " warm eulogium " referred to is, of course, when Coriolanus later describes her as " an icicle.")

Now this in manner and in matter is very typical of english shakespearian criticism. If the play is read with any interest and attention, this version of Sir James Robertson's of a charming " lady of great nobility," in the case of Valeria, will be seen as what it is—the deferential euphuism of a highly respectable upper-servant of the old english school. That large class of able middle-class men, domiciled in universities, of the type of the correct and snobbish family solicitor, usually ending life with a few irrelevant honours, is responsible as a rule for Shakespeare criticism. Sir William Robertson is better than that, but still is of that genus of critics. Shakespeare, both in the circumstances of a rough and bitter life, and in the vigour and recklessness of his mind, will not fit that social framework. So, as we have said, most Shakespeare criticism comes to be a mild adaptation and bowdlerization, the sort of meaningless respectability of the english professional man smeared over everything that looks too stark, or that would seem to make it difficult to describe Shakespeare subsequently as " with a kindly twinkle in his eye," or as " a gentleman ": " gentle " alone (" gentle Shakespeare ") would not be regarded as possessing any particular relevance.

So the Valeria episode is explained by Sir James Robertson as showing how " even admirable women may

miseducate children." And there is an end of it : it means
nothing more than that : it is an unfortunate episode,
undoubtedly—it leaves an unfortunate impression : but
it is introduced by the poet after one of those incessant
readings of Montaigne (in which he seems to have spent
most of his time), and is a little burst of educationalist
enthusiasm—nothing more ! The picture is paradoxically
put into the mouth of *a most charming and well-bred woman* ;
which again may have been intended by this most ingenious of poets to show how strong *custom* is, and how it
may induce even the most gracious of gentlewomen to let
slip a few remarks that might be misunderstood by someone not familiar—ahem !—with the *natural kindliness* that
is such a characteristic of the nobility and gentry—ahem—
of any land or period of history !

This episode of the little budding Coriolanus is, however, with the utmost consistency, typical of the play and
Shakespeare's treatment of Coriolanus from beginning to
end. It is an astonishingly close picture of a particularly
cheerless and unattractive snob, such as must have pullu-
lated in the court of Elizabeth, and such as the english
public-school and university system has produced ever
since. He is a fearless and efficient leader in war, with every
opportunity of training, and the stimulus of self-interest, to
be such—and nothing else. In every other respect he is a
glum, vain and extremely peevish dog, always abusing
a crowd of supers for not incessantly flattering him, and
furthering his interests and those of Volumnia ; with ex-
hortations to deeds of matchless heroism, for which, if they
performed them, they would receive nothing but further
abuse, bearing largely on the respective diet of the carefully
kept dog in the fine marble kennel and the ill-kept dog in
the mud one. Both these species have their faults, and
Coriolanus is allowed to hit off those of the rabble with
sufficient force ; as when he chides them :

> " He that depends
> Upon your favours swims with fins of lead
> And hews down oaks with rushes. Trust ye ? Hang ye !

With every minute ye do change your mind,
And call him noble that was now your hate,
Him vile that was your garland."

But since his own small senatorial crowd prove themselves equally undependable, and are separated by almost as wide a trench from his demented ideal of authority, this abuse remains a Timon-like outpouring of unreason from the point of view of life's realities. Menenius Agrippa, Cominius or Titus Lartius are the real workaday " aristocrats," and are as much strangers to an ideal of inflexible authority as are the people themselves : and naturally veer to the popular side when this quixotic doctrinaire pushes them to uphold the letter of their superiority.

In war the " thunder-like percussion " of his " sounds " is a martial rhetoric Shakespeare was very capable of measuring. And therewith Aufidius sounds the machiavellian note—which caused Coleridge so much embarrassment : when the volscian leader says that as he is unable to beat him fairly, as " man to man," he must " potch at him some way," a volscian soldier remarks, " He's the devil ! " referring to Coriolanus ; and Aufidius replies :

" Bolder, though not so subtle. My valour's poison'd
With only suffering stain by him,"

and we then get the Achilles-Hector situation, with the same frantic and luscious sensuality of strife that is reproduced in the battlefield rivalries of the greek and trojan captains, and in the case of Hotspur and Prince Hal.

The confrontation of Coriolanus and his mother, Volumnia, in Act III., scene 2, is the most characteristic of the piece, and gives the true interpretation of Coriolanus. He is shown there as the child, drilled into a second nature which goes on mechanically obeying. His mother—whose ultra-roman despotism has been shown in other scenes—has coached and formed him into the madman he is. Then, when he comes fresh from acting on her teaching, to his own undoing, he is suddenly, with a naïve confusion, confronted with his mother's disapproval. And the obedient schoolboy, rebuked for doing what he has been taught to do, turns with baffled reproach on his teacher :

" *Coriolanus.* I muse my mother
Does not approve me further, who was wont
To call them woollen vassals ; things created
To buy and sell with groats, to show bare heads
In congregations, to yawn, be still, and wonder,
When one but of my ordinance stood up
To speak of peace or war.
                    [*Enter* VOLUMNIA]
                         I talk of you :
Why did you wish me milder ? Would you have me
False to my nature ? Rather say I play
The man I am.
    Volumnia. O, sir, sir, sir,
I would have had you put your power well on,
Before you had worn it out.
    Cor. Let go.
    Vol. You might have been enough the man you are,
With striving less to be so."

This scene between Coriolanus and his mother is the key to the play : it shows Coriolanus as the rigid and hypnotized schoolboy influenced in his most susceptible years by a snobbish and violent parent, and urged into a course of destruction, which, the machine of an idea, he mesmerically pursues : it is now too late even for the master-mind to pull him up.

The scene to which this critical confrontation of the mother and son should be compared is the last scene of all, when he is killed by Aufidius and his followers. The word with which he is dismissed from the scene of this world is " Boy," and he is shown as resenting it very much indeed.

" *Aufidius.* He has betray'd your business, and given up,
For certain drops of salt, your city Rome
(I say ' your city ') to his wife and mother ;
Breaking his oath and resolution, like
A twist of rotten silk ; never admitting

Counsel o' the war ; but, at his nurse's tears,
He whin'd and roar'd away your victory ;
That pages blush'd at him, and men of heart
Look'd wondering at each other.
   Cor. Hear'st thou, Mars ?
   Auf. Name not the god, thou boy of tears !
   Cor. Ha !
   Auf. No more.
   Cor. Measureless liar, thou hast made my heart
Too great for what contains it. Boy ! O slave !—
Pardon me, lords, 'tis the first time that ever
I was forc'd to scold."

But during the ensuing lines he goes on repeating " Boy ! "
—which epithet appears to have entirely overpowered him :

" *Cor.* Cut me to pieces, Volsces ; men and lads,
Stain all your edges on me.—Boy ! false hound !
If you have writ your annals true, 'tis there,
That, like an eagle in a dove-cote, I
Flutter'd your Volscians in Corioli :
Alone I did it.—Boy ! "

" Boy " is almost the last word of Coriolanus. The action
of his little son as described by Valeria is one of the things
that anyone would chiefly remember in the play, and is the
thing in it to which the critics naturally turn, and which
they have to explain away to fit their substituted picture.
And the child-parent situation is the mechanism of the
piece in any case. Since we possess a great deal of evidence
as to what Shakespeare thought of military glory and
martial events, we have no reason to suppose that the
military heroics in *Coriolanus* are of a different order to
what they are elsewhere. There is the curious demented
sensuality that he is fond of attributing to military rivals,
but which is not an element calculated to increase the
atmosphere of respect at their feats of daring : it even
makes them—the Hotspurs, Achilles, Hals and so forth—
a little ridiculous. As to this feudal poet's courtly leanings,
I do not think they are proved. He is quite ready to sup-

CORIOLANUS AND ARISTOCRATISM

port his characters when the moment arrives for them to abuse the "many-headed multitude" (which was the usual term—"we have been called so of many," the Citizen in Act II., scene 3, says). Shakespeare no doubt agreed with all the abuse his puppet Coriolanus was called upon to hurl at the roman crowd. It would very nearly describe what Shakespeare probably felt about the London crowd of his time, and especially as he came in contact with it at the theatre. But from this to supposing that he had discriminated between this crowd and that other smaller crowd to which Coriolanus belonged—the crowd that thronged the more expensive seats of the Bankside theatres—is a long step of snobbish unreason and self-deception that we have no right to assume Shakespeare at all likely to have taken. For him *l'un vaudrait l'autre*, I expect. For it was human nature about which Shakespeare wrote, and he did not write on a tone of morals, nor on one of class-prejudice or class-illusion.

Coriolanus is no more a play to exhibit the virtues and destinies of the aristocrat (with a strong propaganda for a severe oligarchical form of government, and a strong snobbish illusion about the graceful advantages of the aristocratic life) than it is a play of educationist propaganda, whether for or against a certain type of training. It is a play about a conventional military hero, existing as the characteristic ornament of a strong aristocratic system. Shakespeare was neither for or against him, on propagandist, feudal or nonfeudal grounds. He was quite ready to curse the crowd with him : and he was equally ready to examine with as little pleasure the child of a harsh practical system, abusing his many advantages, and showing to perfection how the top, as likewise the under, dog is unsatisfactory and foolish, the one very nearly worthy of the other—the violent, dull, conceited leader, and the resentful but cowardly slave. Meantime the play is charged with a magnificent rhetoric, as wherever any character utters Shakespeare's blank verse. Coriolanus speaks frequently like a god : also the *altofronto* tone is adopted by him from time to time, as by most Shakespeare heroes—his banter and bitterness

THE LION AND THE FOX

being often just the same as that of Hamlet, Timon or Lear. But that is Shakespeare's own voice and manner that you hear, the central surge, that, wherever the music he is making excites him, comes out and is heard. What belongs properly to Coriolanus is not meant by Shakespeare to be attractive: he shows none of the sympathy for him that he does for Othello, Antony or Timon. Yet he is cast for the lion part; and Shakespeare gives him, as remarked above, his portion of magnificent music. Also he has to the full one of the great requisites of the shakespearian *lion*; he is completely helpless, childlike, truthful and unfortunate. So it is the rôle, rather than the figure filling it, that would set the tragic organ playing.

The *fox* is there too; the tribunes Sicinius and Brutus supply the Iago element very adequately, except that no unpopularity is concentrated on them.

CHAPTER III

APEMANTUS AND TIMON

THE cast of *Troilus and Cressida* includes all the heroes of the homeric cycle : you see them all in turn engaged in their characteristic heroisms. Troilus is, of course, the hero of the play : he is introduced in his own famous and beautiful words, as follows :

> " But I am weaker than a woman's tear,
>   Tamer than sleep, fonder than ignorance,
>   Less valiant than the virgin in the night,
>   And skill-less as unpractis'd infancy."

The " croak " of Thersites echoes through the whole play like an invention of Poe's, choosing a bust of Pallas for a perch. His voice is the same as that of Lear, Hamlet or Timon—that is when these characters get out of hand and give the shakespearian critic trouble. But the voices of Lear, say, and Thersites are identical :

" *Thersites.* How the devil luxury, with his fat rump and potato finger, tickles these together ! Fry, lechery, fry ! "

" *Lear.* To't luxury, pell-mell ! for I lack soldiers.—
Behold yond simpering dame. . . .
That minces virtue, and does shake the head
To hear of pleasure's name ;
The fitchew, nor the soilèd horse, goes to't
With a more riotous appetite."

" *Ther.* That same dog-fox, Ulysses, is not proved worth a blackberry. They set me up, in policy, that mongrel cur, Ajax, against that dog of as bad a kind, Achilles : and now is the cur Ajax prouder than the cur Achilles, and will not arm to-day."

" *Lear.* A man may see how this world goes, with no eyes.

247

Look with thine ears : see how yon justice rails upon yon
simple thief. Hark, in thine ear : change places; and, handy-
dandy, which is the justice, which is the thief ? Thou hast
seen a farmer's dog bark at a beggar ?

Glos. Ay sir.

Lear. And the creature run from the cur ? There thou
mightst behold the great image of authority : a dog's
obey'd in office."

The personalities are not the same, but the voice beats
out its repulsion in the same way. Thersites is the black
sheep of the *altofronto* type : but when any shakespearian
figure is approaching his *pathos* he drops into the *altofronto*
type of gibing. Lear's is bellowed and Thersites' spat.

Shakespeare, like Cervantes, was occupied always with
cases of insanity, we have agreed : that could be said to
be a great characteristic of his. And we have compared
Muishkin's epilepsy (which is a pretext or something provided to account for his saintliness) to Lear's madness.
And madness accounts for the nihilism that surges up in
every tragedy of Shakespeare, once the characters have
become " mad " enough with suffering. Their " madness "
is for an Englishman the necessary excuse. Such wildness
would have seemed unnatural if it had not been labelled
pathologic. Thersites, as a horrible clown, is allowed to
express without embarrassment a great and neglected vein
of truth, the nihilistic truth of what we see, looking with
our ears or otherwise. It is as outcasts, as men already in
a sense out of life, and divested of the functional machinery
of their rôles (which would necessitate their being *objects*
only—things *looked at* and not *looking*), that speak objectively—an objective, and not a functional, truth. Lear,
Hamlet, Timon, Thersites, and so forth, are in the position
of disincarnate spirits, but still involved with and buffeted
by life. Their " truth " is an angry one usually, but they
have the advantage of having no " axe to grind."

Thersites is always in that unfortunate position : Lear
and Hamlet only become so when they grow demented :
or rather (as we usually meet them first when they are

APEMANTUS AND TIMON

already in this prophetic condition), we assume that if undisturbed by calamity they would be respectable members
of society, and not have, much less express, all these horrible
thoughts. It is this *assumption* of conditions that do not
exist at all in the plays (for, as just remarked, in a tragedy
the figures from the start are usually very excited) that is
usually the basis of english shakespearian criticism. The
remarks made by a whole sequence of characters in shakespearian tragedy are the ravings of madmen, it would
imply. They have no relation to the settled mind of their
great author, but are unfortunate aberrations in which he
is compelled to deal: being (for some reason best known
to himself) a democratic writer, disposed to choose tragic
themes. (What makes a man a hangman? What causes
him to adopt the profession of tragic dramatist? Both
are highly respectable people, if successful, very devoted
servants of the community. It is impossible to say.)

A man is either (1) a philosopher, or (2) not a philosopher:
or he is (1) mad, or (2) not mad. Where (in shakespearian tragedy) a man becomes *mad*, he shows a strange
tendency to become what we usually call a *philosopher*.
That is to say, of course, he is transformed, and becomes
somebody else. Should any character in a play of Shakespeare's, *before he went mad*, express himself as, let us
say, Schopenhauer constantly was in the habit of doing,
a scandal would at once ensue—or if not a scandal, a
disturbing *problem* would have been posed for the english
shakespearian critic. Under the stress of some great
emotion, or belaboured by some particularly evil circumstances—like Job—even the best of men is apt to make
remarks that he will subsequently regret. But in cold
blood, and in his sober senses, no man—or no gentleman,
which is the same thing—ever says, or thinks even, things
of that description.

This situation is justly parodied by Shakespeare in the
squabble of Apemantus and Timon. Apemantus (who,
contrary to what it is usual to affirm, has the best of
the argument) comes to Timon to put him out of conceit
with himself. Timon gets angrier and angrier: and at

length they part in a storm of mutual abuse. Apemantus (described as "a churlish philosopher") argues with Timon that he is only imitating him, Apemantus, and other cynics, because he has been *forced* to this by circumstances, and has not elected to live "the philosophic life" of his own free choice; and is indeed very "churlish" and disagreeable about it. What the churlish philosopher says is, of course, quite true : and the contempt of Apemantus for the spiteful worldling, stealing the thunders of Diogenes to bombard his old associates, who are neither better nor worse than himself, is justified. Or rather it would be justified if we were not assured that there was a streak of generosity and *naïveté* in Timon that saved him from fulfilling the rôle suggested to us for him by Apemantus.

It is usually said that Apemantus is introduced by Shakespeare, with his invariable resourcefulness and tact, to contrast Timon with this cynic philosopher, to the disadvantage of the latter, and to enable us to see how superior Timon was to such people, and to relieve our minds on a point on which they might have been uneasy. For otherwise we might have said to ourselves that after all Timon is only a cynic philosopher !—and "cynic" is an unpopular word.

This explanation is on a par with many others of a similar order. In reality it seems much more that Apemantus is introduced, and is intended, to occupy the position of the nihilistic chorus or the *fool*, who gives the show away—just as Thersites is constantly at the elbows of the achaian overlords to remind us what human life in truth is, lest we should be dazzled by their helmets or their glittering names. There is little parallel otherwise between Thersites and Apemantus (who only pays a flying visit to the hero) : but his rôle is a revelatory and truth-bearing one. The reason for it could be that without such a voice giving *the other side of the case*, and showing where Timon's advocacy is apt to break down, the spoilt-child bellowings of Timon would arouse answers in the audience, perhaps : for the answer to this very one-sided heroism is too palpable to be missed ; and for the success of this figure a vent must be provided for criticism. Apemantus could be regarded, from this point of view, as the chorus, or the critical *vent* of the audience, baiting with dangerous arguments the dying god, and accusing him of plagiarism:

> " men report
> Thou dost affect my manners. . . ."

And he describes this affectation of Timon's as:

> " A poor unmanly melancholy sprung
> From change of fortune."

The melancholy outburst of nearly every shakespearian hero could be described from this standpoint as " unmanly," or at least highly unreasonable, and as the wild bellowing of the spoilt-child of fortune, fallen on evil times from the height of tragical *hubris*.

Apemantus reminds Timon that his flatterers still "*wear silk, drink wine, lie soft, hug their diseased perfumes*": and he recommends him to return to his vomit:

> " Shame not these woods,
>
> .   .   .   .   .   .
>
> Be thou a flatterer now, and seek to thrive
> By that which has undone thee : hinge thy knee,
> And let his very breath, whom thou'lt observe,
> Blow off thy cap ; praise his most vicious strain,
> And call it excellent."

And his principal argument is expressed in the lines:

> " If thou didst put this sour-cold habit on
> To castigate thy pride, 'twere well : but thou
> Dost it enforcedly ; thou'dst courtier be again,
> Wert thou not beggar.
>
> .   .   .   .   .   .
>
> Thou shouldst desire to die, being miserable."

Timon arguing with Apemantus is a typical shakespearian hero arguing about his rôle. All shakespearian heroes being the result of the conventional tragic drop from *hubris* and happiness to misery and disaster, it is always mechanically assumed that it is this rapid and unexpected fall that shakes out of them the marvellous music of the shakespearian blank verse, and the dark fury of their gibing. It is further assumed that humanity in general—unless taken up aloft a certain way by the devil, and allowed to have a godlike peep around it, and then cast down again from this dangerous height—is incapable of such things. But the situation in reality, where Shakespeare's plays are concerned, lacks the simple definition of this accepted formula. For the " great line " invented by Marlowe, the music of verse, and the soul of Shakespeare, complicate it to such an extent that confusion is inevitable. But disentangled as best it can be, this is how it must be read.

First, there is Timon's reply to Apemantus. It is the logical reply of the protagonist of a tragic performance. What he answers quite directly and with truth is somewhat as follows: " *You*, Apemantus, are not the hero of a tragedy, nor ever will be. But I, Timon, am. Therefore, in order to produce the effect, as you know, it was necessary that I should be very rich or eminent in some way, and then suddenly lose all my money or my social position." He argues that his *cynicism*, unlike that of Apemantus (which is natural, inborn cussedness), is the result of this unexpected and undesired obvention. For :

> " I, to bear this,
> That never knew but better, is some burden."

This very reasonable complaint could hardly be met otherwise than with sympathy. But he proceeds then to deny to Apemantus the right to be a cynic, because Apemantus has never been rich, like him, and so has nothing to complain about :

> " Thy nature did commence in sufferance, time
> Hath made thee hard in't. Why shouldst thou hate men ?
> They never flatter'd thee : what hast thou given ?
> If thou wilt curse, thy father . . .
> Must be thy subject ; who, in spite, put stuff
> To some she beggar and compounded thee."

APEMANTUS AND TIMON

Apart from the abuse with which Timon accompanies these remarks, Apemantus could hardly be expected to agree to the latter part of this statement of his. Timon asks him : " Why should you hate men ? They never flattered you ! " To which probably Apemantus would reply : " That is why I hate them ! "

Apemantus' message to Timon is much as follows (taking it on from the last rejoinder) :

" It is just because you have something to complain about now, because any man in your position would complain, and still more because you—just like most other men similarly placed—when you were comfortable showed no sign of disgust with life, nor showed any aptitude nor disposition to ' see through it,' that I am expressing contempt for your present attitude. That is why I am objecting to your affecting the life of the *cynic*, now that you can't do anything else : whereas when you were wealthy, and lavished your money on a crowd of sneaks and fools, and were imbecile enough to enjoy their lip-service, such an existence as that you at present live would have aroused your mirth or astonishment. You are not a master at all of your destiny : you go where you are pushed, drop where you are dropped, roar and bellow when you are hurt, purr or wag your tail when you are stroked, and so on. You are not a philosopher in short ; and you are at present in a false position, for you are pretending to be one. In reality you should be back in Athens, in ' the world,' where you belong. I came out here to see if it were true that you were engaged in this travesty of the cynic life, and find that in effect it is true. You are still, as ever, a *fool*. You should either drown yourself or return to your natural element, not *shame the forest*."

That is more or less what he says. To this Timon can find no reply. He is a puppet of a certain sort, and he sticks to the logic, or rather to the traditional functions and uses, of that sort of puppet. " I have been full of *hubris*. I have been cast down. I complain," he says ; and there is the end of it. That is what " tragedy " is about. Apemantus does not think much of tragedy, or the poetry of its spoilt children in adversity ; and has a strong professional objection to their stealing the thunders of the cynic philosopher : and is prepared even to pursue them into their adversity and rebuke them for it. Timon, on the other hand, does not believe in cynic philosophy, or any other philosophy, without *tragedy* : he does not believe that philosophy can exist without tragedy ; and he thinks that to have the right to gibe and bellow you must have been either a king, a field-marshal or a millionaire first : *dropped* from that height (in which you will have displayed *hubris*) : and then, as the day succeeds the night, or as you put a penny in the slot and the figure works, you will utter the organ-notes of shakespearian despair, and almost certainly give an exhibition of the *altofronto* Hamlet technique. For Timon is very conventional : that is because he is a puppet, mechanically worked, and seeing nothing beyond his mechanism—which is the traditional mechanism of the european formula for tragedy.

But *we* must be aware of several things undreamt of in Timon's philosophy. We agree more with Apemantus than we do with Timon. We know, for instance, that ninety-nine per cent. of human beings—however *high up* you may transport them, however much insolence they may deploy when they discover themselves so *high up*, and however far you drop them *down*, and however much despair they may feel as they strike the bottom—will never show the least tincture of philosophy. They will never, we know, make even a tenth-rate tragic hero ; and will neither produce, automatically, an organ-music like Bach, nor a mournful and gigantic rhetoric like that of Timon. They will say, " Ah, this is too bad ! This is cruel ! What have I done to be treated in this way ? Oh, I am miserable ! I wish I were dead and out of it." A few would be a little more musical, but most would articulate something like that. At the best (and at the worst) they will speak with that ter-rible cold vibration of self-conscious " emotion " that the typical english actress produces when, as St Joan, or some other distressed heroine, she gets the tragic drop. They will *boo*, in short, like a cultivated and self-conscious cow

APEMANTUS AND TIMON

(this last word not intended offensively, for most english actors *boo* as well as english actresses), nourished in the matter of emotional expression on the anglican pulpit.

We know therefore (however much we are told that it is the *drop* of a normal man or woman that causes the great afflatus in a shakespearian tragedy) that that is not so. Emotional beauty of diction, depth and strangeness of philosophical understanding, are not produced by this means; any more than Shelley's verse or Kant's philosophy is produced by dropping a person over the edge of a cliff. But the scientific *sans gêne* which characterizes our attitude of mind to-day will enable us to get a closer view of this perplexing phenomenon, even, than our reasoning so far has given us. For we can say: "Was the man who wrote these plays himself a tragic hero? What was the nature of his experience?" etc. And we should find that Shakespeare himself was neither a prince nor a wealthy man, but on the contrary a very poor and humbly placed one: who, like Apemantus, had never any chance to *drop* from anywhere, and consequently, according to Timon's reasoning, had no occasion to hate his fellow-men. In spite of this handicap, he seems to have understood very well the nature of grief, to have possessed a mind of a philosophic cast; and—being a matchless artist—he was able, as we know, to perform these tragical operations far better than they ever happen in life.

Shakespeare's knowledge of the ins and outs of human character was so wide, and he displayed such a varied power and self-restraint in portraying different sorts of men in a lifelike way, that people are inclined to forget, perhaps, that the art of the drama, and all its purgational greek rules of jealous gods (and envious audiences), of revenge for grandeur, and of well-turned and melodious death, is a game: and that what is enacted in a heroic play bears very little resemblance to *life*. In none of its details is it the least *likely*. Timon would probably, after a life of overeating, have caught a cold immediately in his damp cave, or been at once prostrated with rheumatism. Lear was similarly an exceptionally hardy old man in the play : in real life he would have died from exposure without the assistance of the Atte. Hamlet's *shortness of breath* is one of the many things that make him a likelier figure. But no Prince of Denmark ever thought at the level of Montaigne, or expressed his thoughts in the language of Shakespeare.

Within the great latitude of this framework of possibilities, governed by its own æsthetic laws, and not at all subordinated to the laws of life, it is easy for such a poet as Shakespeare to manœuvre with great freedom : to slip himself into the place of the hero, and out again, to infinitely enliven the tedium of the reality or to depress it at will, to be both Apemantus and Timon. His attitude to his characters was that of the actor : it is evident which characters he enjoyed most playing : and as he was in a sense *playing to himself* it is possible also to know which sort of character he most professed *to be*—or *was*. Although wonderfully supple and detached, there is a voice that is Shakespeare's and there is a character that is his. His greatest heroes gibe like Thersites (the *altofronto* type), and his most embittered chorus-work is grandly direct and stings like truth. It is the overdoing of the *impersonal* mirror notion, as we started by saying, that has obscured this fact.

CHAPTER IV

THERSITES AND THE HEROES OF THE HOMERIC SAGA

RETURNING to *Troilus*, we have in Thersites, in the actual incidents of his part in the play, a useful parallel to Falstaff. I am aware that to see any analogy between the " kindly," bluff, fat knight and the terrible Thersites will not recommend itself at first sight. But they are not so different as their disparity in bulk, and the outward amiability of the one and viciousness of the other, would lead you to believe. First of all, in Ulrici's account we have seen how it is quite possible (whether we accept the explanation or not) to regard Falstaff as deliberately invented, and set in the midst of the pageant of english history, to *show up*, to dog and ridiculously parallel, the history which the play is ostensibly written to celebrate. But Thersites is similarly thrust into *Troilus and Cressida*, and made to shadow and insult the homeric heroes for a similar purpose.

When Thersites meets Margarelon, a prince of the opposing host, on the battlefield (Act V., scene 8) the following conversation ensues:

" *Margarelon.* Turn, slave, and fight.

Thersites. What art thou ?

Mar. A bastard son of Priam's.

Ther. I am a bastard too ; I love bastards : I am a bastard begot, bastard instructed, bastard in mind, bastard in valour, in everything illegitimate. One bear will not bite another, and wherefore should one bastard ? Take heed, the quarrel's most ominous to us : if the son of a whore fight for a whore, he tempts judgment : farewell, bastard. [*Exit.*

Mar. The devil take thee, coward ! [*Exit.*"

Falstaff's attitude to situations of danger, and his

behaviour on the field of Shrewsbury, are similar to this. Thersites could scarcely have indulged in his soliloquy on the subject of honour, for he was a more uncompromising figure, and would have considered such Sancho-Panzaism as beneath him. The reigning attribute of Thersites is intellectual pride : and it is from the point of view of this intellectual pride that he views his heroic associates, scorning their simple satisfactions, and the naïve view of themselves that pushes them to their martial antics. Their spite and untruthfulness is also visible to him : and when they accuse him of these shortcomings, in a fury he belabours them with his tongue.

As an example of his *intellectualist* approach to the episodes of the trojan war, in which he found himself involved, and its semi-divine personalities, the following passage gives a good idea :

" *Achilles*. Come, come, Thersites, help to trim my tent ; This night in banqueting must all be spent.—
Away, Patroclus.   [*Exeunt* ACHILLES *and* PATROCLUS.

Thersites. With too much blood and too little brain, these two may run mad : but, if with too much brain and too little blood they do, I'll be a curer of madmen. Here's Agamemnon,—an honest fellow enough, and one that loves quails : but he has not so much brain as ear-wax : and the goodly transformation of Jupiter there, his brother, the bull,—the primitive statue, and oblique memorial of cuckolds ; a thrifty shoeing-horn in a chain, hanging at his brother's leg,—to what form, but that he is, should wit larded with malice and malice forced with wit, turn him to ? To an ass, were nothing ; he is both ass and ox : to an ox, were nothing, he is both ox and ass. To be a dog, a mule, a cat, a fitchew, a toad, a lizard, an owl, a puttock, or a herring without a roe, I would not care ; but to be Menelaus,—I would conspire against destiny. Ask me not what I would be, if I were not Thersites, for I care not to be the louse of a lazar so I were not Menelaus.—Heyday ! spirits and fires ! "

All the advantages of heroic bodily strength, the central fact of the saga-world of Homer, are ridiculed, " described only as the rude and clumsy right of the stronger," as Ulrici says. Many theories as to the generating causes of *Troilus and Cressida* have been advanced, as was remarked in the last chapter : for it is considered always as a very dreary play for Shakespeare to have written, a scandalous and difficult one to account for, that will not fit into the conventional picture that is usually drawn of him. As he is such a great poet that it is necessary to adopt him as the *national* poet (although Lord Tennyson would have been a much more suitable figure—or Lord Verulam) he must be edited into a myth with a " kindly twinkle in his eye " and with the usual attributes of a successful middle-class professional man. In many ways Shakespeare lends himself to that. He wrote plays that can be turned into children's pantomimes in a way that *The Faithful Shepherdess* could not be : he equipped with grandest blank verse in a most " loyal " manner a whole series of english monarchs ; and if his unfortunately published *Sonnets* contain a disagreeable ambiguity, on the whole his attitude to matters of sex was reticent. *Pericles* and *Titus Andronicus* are, each in different ways, disagreeable things to be mixed up with : but their authorship can be infinitely disputed. *Troilus and Cressida* is, however, an insurmountable obstacle.

This is how Professor **J. S. P. Tatlock** acquits himself of the critic's difficult task : " To the modern reader all other questions about the play seem insignificant compared with these. What did Shakespeare mean by it ? What was his feeling toward its transactions and characters ? Was its tone determined by external conditions or his own state of mind ? Many readers find this play and *Timon of Athens* the most distasteful of all his works. . . . Why does he seem to turn Chaucer's sympathy into scorn, Homer's serenity into discord, and his heroism into pettiness ? "

Some of the answers found for these questions are as follows : Shakespeare was satirizing chivalry ; or else, contrasting the pagan ethic with the christian. Personal hostility to Chapman excited his wrath against the great poet whom Chapman had translated. On the other hand, he may have been expressing his sentiment of rivalry toward the greatest poet of antiquity by parodying him. None of these answers bear examination, Professor Tatlock says. The apology most frequently offered is that the play dates from "a period of gloom and bitterness in Shakespeare's own life." The "apples of Eden were proving apples of Sodom . . . humanity, which earlier and later seemed to him kindly in its folly, touching in its weakness, and grand in its will, seemed to consist only (as one critic has said) of fools who are cheated and knaves who cheat."

If the play is contemporaneous with *Measure for Measure* and *All's Well that Ends Well* it is near the opening of the massive and unrelieved group of tragedies with which Shakespeare completed his work.

However Professor Tatlock can, of course, find no consolation in that. "We cannot believe," he protests, "that one of the best-balanced and most self-controlled natures that we know of in all history, in the prime of its power, yet past its first youth, was thrown for years into such disorder and morbid self-expression. Yet here is *Troilus and Cressida*. Why this seeming blight on the most harmonious and most kindly of poets ? "

So Professor Tatlock rejects the theory that accounts for the bitterness of this play of the middle period (coming just before the great tragedies) on the score of a (temporary) exhaustion of the flood of human kindness that is traditionally supposed to well up from the shakespearian depths.

The conclusion come to finally is that *Troilus and Cressida* should be regarded as a historical play in the elizabethan sense ; its author approached it from the mediæval standpoint, not the classical, and so, whereas for us it is a very shocking performance, for him it would be a very jolly affair indeed, full of both chivalry and humour.

So Professor Tatlock disposes of this unique stumbling-block thus : Shakespeare's *Troilus and Cressida* quite naturally favoured the Trojans and belittled the Greeks, because the mediæval peoples of western Europe all believed themselves descended from the Trojans. Sir John Harrington's *Metamorphosis of Ajax* and the *Ajax* of Sophocles necessitated the treatment of Ajax. Ajax could not be a hero for anyone familiar, as Shakespeare was, with those accounts of him. Pandarus had already long ago given a common noun, pander, to the dictionary. Cressida and Helen were stock whores of Babylon. Thersites—who " appears at first to seem as an ever-debasing chorus, tearing off the veil and calling things by their true and foul names "—comes straight from the second book of the *Iliad* : so he could not be otherwise. Achilles " cuts a worse though naturally a less vivid figure in Caxton than in Shakespeare."

Shakespeare, having decided for some reason to do a play about Troy, could not have written it differently to what he did, and the " kindly " outlook of the national poet is once more safe for democracy, the approved benevolent mask returned to him by this benevolent american professor.

And yet a new and attentive reading of *Troilus and Cressida* will not satisfy the student that the anomaly is explained by this " simple historic method." It may occur to him to ask : Why should it be explained away, in any case ? Why should this obsession of a " kindly " english poet be perpetuated, however that may appeal to a kindly american critic, or be required by the more conventional reader of his plays ? The " kindliness " of the emersonian mask did not exist in Shakespeare's day ; and had it done so, it is unlikely that it would have attracted him any more than the semitic features of a horned Mephistopheles.

The *Troilus and Cressida* is one of his two satires (*The Merry Wives of Windsor* being the other), and is one of the greatest of his plays. But it is not, like Middleton's *Game of Chess*, an exercise on an antique model. In its many-sidedness it shows how irresistible the personal element was in his work. We have his individual signs all over it. For example, Hector and Achilles reproduce the martial pairing, accompanied by the same curious sensuality, of Coriolanus and Aufidius, or of Hotspur and Hal.

" *Achilles.* Go call the writer hither, sweet Patroclus :
I'll send the fool to Ajax and desire him
To invite the Trojan lords, after the combat,
To see us here unarmed : *I have a woman's longing*,

THE LION AND THE FOX

An appetite that I am sick withal
To see great Hector in his weeds of peace ;
To talk with him, and to behold his visage,
Even to my full view."

There is the same interpretation of the sensuality experienced towards each other by champions on opposite sides
in war ; the terms of love employed to express the quality
of their heated rivalry.   Then there is the *altofronto* technique ; there is the spotless image of a Romeo's chivalrous
love, but the inconstancy of the heroine is added to dis-
figure that side of it.   M. Fagus sees in it a triple satire :
(1) against women ; (2) against anarchy ; (3) against the
Greeks.   That the play was written against the Greeks
in their capacity of Learning's favourites, as the gods of
the renaissance, of which Shakespeare was tired of hearing
the praises, that it was written against the enemies of the
Trojans to whom as an Englishman he supposed himself
related, this critic does not say : but women certainly are
generalized about.   In Hector we have a very good model
of the simpleton of the military type of Shakespeare's heroic
nursery.   And Achilles is the military villain of the type of
Aufidius, with whom other plays familiarize us.

From this point of view *Troilus and Cressida* is a rendez-
vous of shakespearian characters.   It throws a similar
light on the probable political leanings of Shakespeare as
does *Coriolanus* : removed like it to a distant time, but
more open and less conjectural for us.

PART VIII

RENAN'S *CALIBAN* AND CHAPMAN'S *DUKE OF BYRON*

CHAPTER I

RESEMBLANCES IN THE POLITICAL AND ETHICAL CANONS OF SHAKESPEARE AND CHAPMAN

IF *Troilus and Cressida* presents an insoluble problem for the shakespearian critic desirous of bringing out the " good fellow " and the " kindly twinkle " in the cryptical eye of the national poet : then the political problems that lie hidden in the profundities of Chapman are no less striking. He lends himself, like Shakespeare, to the most contradictory interpretations ; he gives such a dashing critic as Swinburne many a fall, and the wariest has his moments of vertigo. In *The Revenge of Bussy* there is the Hamlet-problem of action and non-action as much as in *Hamlet*, and in *Bussy*, the *Revenge* and the *Admiral Byron* there are all the baffling and " sinister " twists which make *Troilus and Cressida* such a hated region for the shakespearian critic.

George Chapman was no exception to the rule of machiavellizing of the elizabethan mind. The craft in statecraft and the problems of policy were even more present to him than to Shakespeare. He was imbued with a deep curiosity about the fortunes of the Lion when engaged in a conflict with the Fox. To this description can certainly be added, in every case, a childlike interest in the methods of acquiring this potent duplicity and the manner of its use. Indeed Chapman was in many ways the most interesting of all the elizabethans in this respect ; and that is why I have chosen him here for reference. For he was one of the only tudor or stuart dramatists—as noted in Part VI., when Shakespeare's philosophic propensity was discussed—who possessed an intelligence that could in any way be ranked with that of his greatest contemporary. In Chapman there is none of the *fremitus* of great emotional depths, or the infallible roar and surge that greets you as you approach a play of

Shakespeare ; or the intoxication of beauty, which to some
extent makes the thought less evident. His plain and
didactic manner, on the other hand, leaves his thinking
starkly apparent. Saintsbury, in praising Chapman, says
he was free of what he calls " the fatal philistinism in
taste and in politics, and in other matters, which has been
the curse of our race." He was certainly that, and on
the political side has given the usual critic a good deal of
trouble. He even disturbed Swinburne. But Swinburne
accounts for this equivocal vein in Chapman on the score
of the sophist temper. He would have been forced (and
perhaps willing) to call Shakespeare a sophist too.

Swinburne says about Chapman : ". . . it is among the
schools of greek poetry that we must look for a type of the
class to which this poet belongs. In the great age of Greece
he would have found a place of some credit among the ranks
of the gnomic poets, and written much grave and lofty verse
of a social and political sort in praise of a powerful conservative oligarchy, and in illustration of the public virtues
which are fostered, and the public vices which are repressed, under the strong sharp tutelage of such a government. At the many-headed beast of democracy he would
have discharged the keenest arrows of his declamation, and
sought shelter at need from its advance behind the shield
of some tutelary Pittacus or Pisistratus " (Swinburne,
Contemporaries of Shakespeare).

This picture of Chapman as an enthusiastically conservative partisan of the usual middle-class type—*plus
royaliste que le roi*, like Nietzsche, more " aristocratic " than
any aristocrat—is not confirmed even by Swinburne's subsequent misgivings. Swinburne's misgivings on the score
of Chapman's sophistical proclivities are curious enough to
deserve especial attention. Speaking of the popular failure
of the *Revenge*, he writes : " This latter curious and cour-
ageous abuse of intellectual dexterity may perhaps have
contributed to the ill-success of a play which in any case
must have disappointed, and that apparently by design
and of malice prepense, the expectations appealed to by
a title seemingly devised to trade upon the popularity of

SHAKESPEARE AND CHAPMAN

Bussy d'Ambois, and make its profit out of the artificial
capital of a past success. . . . It is not likely that a writer
who must have been old enough at the age of thirteen to
feel and to remember the shock of the first tidings of the
hideous twenty-fourth of August 1572—that an English
poet and patriot of the stalwart type, which from all that
we know of Chapman we might expect to find always as
nobly exemplified in his life and writings as in those of
such elder and younger contemporaries as Spenser and
Jonson—should have indulged any more personal sentiment
in those eccentric trials of intellectual strength than a way-
ward pleasure in the exercise and exhibition of his powers
of argument and eloquence ; but there was certainly in his
nature something of the sophist as well as of the gnomic
poet, of Thrasymachus as well as of Theognis. He seems
to feel a gladiator's pleasure in the swordplay of boisterous
and high-handed sophistry, less designed to mislead or
convince than to baffle or bear down his opponent. We
can imagine him setting up almost any debatable theorem
as a subject for dispute in the schools of rhetoric, and
maintaining his most indefensible position with as much
energy and crossing of argument as his native force of
mind could bring to the support of his acquired skill of
fence. We can perceive that in any such case he would
argue his point and reinforce his reasoning with no less
passion and profusion of thought than if his heart and
conscience were enlisted on the side which, in fact, he had
taken up by mere chance or defiant caprice."

Swinburne visualizes Chapman " the English poet and
patriot of the stalwart type " as a sort of old sea-salt
crossed with a Juvenal, the Homer-Lucan of the rugged
tudor stage ; a bearded weatherbeaten man of sixty and
odd years, as he was when these plays were written, in a
saucerlike ruff and with an eye seemingly accustomed to
screw itself up, winking against the homeric spray driven
backwards in his translations ; brimming with every
sturdy and civic virtue ; and having so permanently
visualized him, he is somewhat surprised to find ethical
peculiarities in the most famous of his plays that demand

explanation. But not only are the *morals* (the famous puritan morals of the characteristic old british sea-salt) in some unaccountable way *wrong*—much more fundamentally wrong than Swinburne's hysterical and girlish naughtiness : unfortunately his religious scruples as well seem to have been in some disarray, causing him to hobnob with papists who at the same time were assassins. The Guise of Chapman's history, unaccountably well treated, is one of the notorious French family that more than followed the italian machiavellian model, " surrounded by italian minions and poison distillers, buffoons and moneylenders." Had Swinburne gone further on this track he would have found much evidence to suggest that *loyalty to the Crown* may not have been among Chapman's virtues. It would not be at all difficult, for that matter, to question the " innocence " of *Andromeda Liberata* : and it is even difficult to see how Swinburne can have respectably upheld this innocence after having noticed to some extent these anomalies elsewhere in Chapman. " *In some cases, indeed, it is hard at first to determine,*" Swinburne says, " *whether the author meant to excite the sympathies or the antipathies of his audience for a good or a bad character ; the virtue of the heroine collapses without a touch, and friends and foes change sides with no more reason shown than that the figure of the dance requires it.*"

In *The Duke of Byron* we get all the elements, in the subject, for testing this view of Chapman's " duplicity." For Byron is a traitor who has once been a patriot. So we have in the central figure a natural overlay and duplicity to start with.

Swinburne says : " It has been observed that the por-trait of the traitor Marshall is overlaid with so many touches that the outline is completely disguised." Here again, as with Swinburne, you get a critic (who has never probably dreamt of any real duplicity of motive or in-stinctive process in Chapman) experiencing the uneasy sense of something *disguised*. The suppression of this play (*Byron*) at the instance of the french envoy, and the arrest of three of the actors, was not wholly on account of the

treatment of the gallic court. The popularity that prior
to its suppression it had enjoyed had floated certainly on
the artificial tide " of a seditious element " as well as an
anti-gallic one.

Swinburne speaks of Chapman's " *taste for extravagance
of paradox and shocks of moral surprise.*" He also alleges
Chapman's " passion for paradox," and accounts for the
contrast between the *Bussy* and the *Revenge* as follows :
" In the argument, the action, and the characters of this
poem one chief aim of the author was apparently to sever
all expectations that might be excited by its title ; and by
way of counterpart to produce a figure in all points opposite to that of his former hero." Chapman even had to
invent a brother for Bussy to arrive better at this, I believe.

Swinburne also notes the oddity of Clermont appearing
as the " creature " of Guise, one of his brother's principal
murderers :

" Guise is made rather a pleasant figure than otherwise,"
and gives the impression of being one of the author's
favourites : and this strangely enough—for Guise, as the
author of the massacre of St Bartholomew, would be
expected by the pit-public to be roughly handled.

Finally Swinburne notes : " *His delight throughout these
historic plays is to put into the mouths of his chief speakers
some defence of the most preposterous and untenable proposition, some apology for the most enormous and unpopular
crime that his ingenuity can fix upon for an explanation or
excuse.*" Byron has a panegyric on the policy and person
of Philip II. Clermont vindicates the massacre of St
Bartholomew, etc.

Swinburne sums up the results of these uneasy investigations as follows : " *No external ground for conjecture by
what original impulse or bias of mind the genius of Chapman
was attracted to the study and representation on an english
stage of subjects derived from the annals of contemporary
France, or what freak of perverse and erratic instinct may
have led him to bring before a protestant audience the leading
criminals of the catholic party under any but an unfavourable
aspect*"; also " we have no means of guessing whether

or not any conscious reason or principle induced him to present in much the same light three princes of such diverse characters as the first Francis and the third and fourth Henrys of France."

It is to show that without " external ground of conjecture," by a careful comparison with elements (amounting actually to a method) in his other plays, we can arrive perhaps at the correct interpretation, that I am writing this of course. But I was led to it first of all by noticing in the much more highly fused and complex mind of Shakespeare these same curious contradictions. And in examining his contemporaries for further light on this, I found that this historic group of Chapman's supplied the required enlightenment. Swinburne has confirmed, by his obvious uneasiness and wish to justify Chapman, my own feeling of an ethical negation, consorting with the nihilism that breaks out so often in Shakespeare, percurrent in the entire mind of the national poet.

Finally, as to Swinburne's estimate of the poetic personality of Chapman, the following lines express it with his usual eloquence: " At every page some passage of severe beauty reminds us with how great a spirit we are called to commune, and stand in the presence of how proud and profound a mind . . . when these [his faculties] are displayed in their full strength and clearness, the study of them gives us some taste of the rare and haughty pleasure that their owner must have taken in this exercise."

In his *Preface to Shakespeare* Dr Johnson says, in speaking of the age of Elizabeth : " The contest about the original benevolence or malignity of man had not yet commenced. Speculation had not yet attempted to analyse the mind, to trace the passions to their sources, to unfold the seminal principles of vice and virtue, or sound the depths of the heart for the motives of action."

We know what Dr Johnson was referring to in his own time, but this passage is effectively meaningless when contrasted with the evidence we are reviewing. It was in the most conspicuous way the reverse of the truth. He also commits himself to the following characteristic analysis:

SHAKESPEARE AND CHAPMAN

" From his [Shakespeare's] writings, indeed, a system of social duty may be selected, for he that thinks reasonably must think morally ; but his precepts and axioms drop casually from him ; he makes no just distribution of good or evil, nor is always careful to show in the virtuous a disapprobation of the wicked ; he carries his persons indifferently through right and wrong, and at the close dismisses them without further care, and leaves their examples to operate by chance."

This describes the procedure of both Shakespeare and Chapman very well, where " vice and virtue " is concerned. They did not neatly distribute them, to say the least ; there was a certain confusion at all points :

" *Epernon.* Oh, of what contraries consists a man !
Of what impossible mixtures ! vice and virtue,
Corruption, and eternnesse, at one time,
And in one subject, let together loose ! "
                                (Tragedy of Duke Byron.)

I will now quote a few passages from Chapman's principal plays showing how closely in the almost unique preoccupation I have attributed to him—namely, " the contest about the benevolence or malignity of man," which Dr Johnson says the elizabethan was not interested in or had not formulated—he resembles Shakespeare ; and how the same obliquity or duality is apparent in both.

First, this passage from *The Revenge of Bussy* (Act III., scene 1) sets forth the machinery of the tragic situation :

" And Demades (that pass'd Demosthenes
    For all extemporal orations)
    Erected many statues, which, he living,
    Were broke, and melted into chamber-pots.
    Many such ends have fallen on such proud honours,
    No more because the men on whom they fell
    Grew insolent and left their virtue's state ;
    Than for their hugeness, that procured their hate ;

And therefore little pomp in men most great
Makes mightily and strongly to the guard
Of what they win by chance, or just reward."

Similarly in the *Bussy* (Act V., scene 1) the following
lines provide the same lesson, with appropriate noting of
the advantage of " mediocrity " :

                  " But usually
[Nature] gives that which she calls merit to a man,
And belief must arrive him on huge riches,
Honour, and happiness, that effects his ruin ;
Even as in ships of war, whole lasts of powder
Are laid, men think, to make them last, and guards them,
When a disorder'd spark that powder taking,
Blows up with sudden violence and horror
Ships that, kept empty, had sail'd long with terror."

That is the important commonplace (namely, that of
the penalty of scale or " hugeness ") which it is well to give
precedence to in these quotations, since they hinge, equally,
on this ordinary tragic machinery, and the opposition of the
Lion and the Fox. There is a penalty, too, for the Fox,
of course : though this penalty is not included as necessary
in the piece, except where, as in the case of Iago, it is
required by the audience. Only the penalty peculiar to
the Lion, for being a Lion, is regarded as beautiful and
pathetic, and is necessarily shown us :

" Yet, as the winds sing through a hollow tree,
  And (since it lets them pass through) let it stand ;
  But a tree solid (since it gives no way
  To their wild rage) they rend up by the root ;
  So this whole man, . . .
  (That will not wind with every crooked way,
  Trod by the servile world), shall reel and fall
  Before the frantic puffs of blind-born chance,
  That pipes through empty men, and makes them dance."
                      (*Bussy*, Act V., scene 1.)

That is the description of the fate of the " white man "
or " whole man " (the opposite to what is called in these

plays "a fragment," Achilles' favourite epithet when addressing a subordinate).

Beneath are a few of the Duke of Byron's remarks as he is preparing to be a traitor:

" *Byron.* There is no truth of any good
To be discerned on earth : and by conversion,
Nought therefore simply bad : but as the stuff
Prepared for arras pictures is no picture
Till it be form'd, and man hath cast the beams
Of his imaginous fancy through it,
In forming ancient kings and conquerors,
As he conceives they look'd, and were attired,
Though they were nothing so : so all things here
Have all their price set down, from men's conceits,
Which make all terms and actions good or bad,
And are but pliant and well-colour'd threads
Put into feigned images of truth :
To which, to yield and kneel as truth-pure kings,
That pull'd us down with clear truth of their gospel,
Were superstition to be hiss'd to hell. . . .
We must have these lures when we hawk for friends,
And wind about them like a subtle river,
That, seeming only to run on its course,
Doth search yet as he runs, and still finds out
The easiest parts of entry on the shore ;
Gliding so slyly by, as scarce it touch'd,
Yet still eats something in it."

The Duke of Byron is such an astonishingly living figure—arriving on the scene of Chapman at the end of a life of heroism, and so affording you a spectacle of a " Machiavel " of the Chapman pattern in the making, and whom subsequently you see dying as a very confused personage indeed, but bursting with vitality to the last—that he is the best of the Chapman heroes to take as an illustration. His machiavellism is creative and almost virtuous :

" We must reform and have a new creation
    Of state and government, and on our Chaos
    Will I sit brooding up another world.

I, who through all the dangers that can siege
The life of man, have forced my glorious way
To the repairing of my country's ruins,
Will ruin it again to readvance it."

Lenin, converted into a hero of drama, both machiavellian and heroical, might explain himself in that way.
Byron's is the most protracted and extraordinary death or
pathos of any elizabethan hero, and all the more remarkable in its reality because he is a soiled and spoilt hero. He
feels this, and that his death is unnecessary, and that is why
he takes so long in accepting it.

"*Vitry.* My lord, you make too much of this your body,
Which is no more your own.
  Byron. Nor is it yours ;
I'll take my death with all the horrid rites
And representments of the dread it merits ;
Let tame nobility and numbèd fools,
That apprehend not what they undergo,
Be such exemplary and formal sheep ;
I will not have him touch me till I will."

When the archbishop says to him,

" Look upward to a world of endless light,"

he turns on him (the still a little bit be-foxed lion) and
exclaims :

" Ay, say, you talk of upward still to others,
  And downwards look, with headlong eyes, yourselves ! "

The frailty of *personality* is returned to and emphasized.
Harley says as he watches his agony :

" He alters every minute : what a vapour
  The strongest mind is to a storm of crosses."

And Byron himself says later :

                              " Like a man
Long buried, is a man that long hath lived ;
Touch him, he falls to ashes."

SHAKESPEARE AND CHAPMAN

He seems to regard his transformation into a traitor and a " Machiavel " as *witchcraft* ; it is quite natural for him to account for it in that way : but his personality, although so real, is very vacillating.

Now to turn back to *Bussy* and the *Revenge* from the *Admiral Byron* : where Monsieur is talking to Clermont d'Ambois, or earlier to Bussy, and suggests an exchange of opinions, in which each should reveal his most in-edited view of the other, in the actual exchanges (very full where Bussy is concerned) the advantage is more on the side of Monsieur than his adversary. Monsieur finds things to say about Bussy that with educated audiences would be more telling, and that in eloquence and truth have received as much of Chapman's care and, seemingly, partiality, as the accusation of italianism and treachery coming from this older of the " idealist " brothers.

Monsieur, in the *Bussy d'Ambois* of Chapman, plays Thersites on this occasion to Bussy's achaian hero, Achilles or Ajax, just as Apemantus does to Timon in *Timon of Athens*. But the results of this queer and sudden bargain between Monsieur and Bussy to open their minds to each other, and display in each the picture recorded, is of a different nature to what we get from the " croaking " of Thersites, or the argument between Apemantus and Timon. It is almost a bargain also that Chapman strikes with the reader to open *his* mind, and show what he really feels about his hero, Bussy. And I believe that what we are listening to is a similar thing to what would be heard if Shakespeare had, adopting this device of Chapman's, unlocked his. If Shakespeare had agreed to set down in the form of vehement dialogue what he truly thought about Coriolanus or Hotspur, for instance, we should, I am sure, have got something very similar to this outburst of Monsieur. In both there would be the same contempt for physical strength, the hero of war, the broiler or duellist, the Ajax or Hotspur or Bussy. And yet, in complete contradiction to this, an admiration for the courage and aplomb of the machine (the " wild horse " or " tiger "), to match the contempt for the rest of the chivalrous make-up.

" *Monsieur.* . . . I think thee then a man
That dares as much as a wild horse or tiger ;
As headstrong and as bloody ; and to feed
The ravenous wolf of thy most cannibal valour,
(Rather than not employ it) thou wouldst turn
Hackster to any whore, slave to a Jew
Or english usurer, to force possessions,
And cut men's throats of mortgaged estates ;
Or thou wouldst 'tire thee like a tinker's strumpet,
And murder market-folks, quarrel with sheep,
And run as mad as Ajax ; serve a butcher ;
Do anything but killing of the King :
That in thy valour th'art like other naturals
That have strange gifts in nature, but no soul
Diffused quite through, to make them of a piece,
But stop at humours that are more absurd,
Childish and villainous than that hackster, whore,
Slave, cut-throat, tinker's bitch, compared before ;
And in those humours wouldst envy, betray,
Slander, blaspheme, change each hour a religion ;
Do anything but killing of the King :
That in thy valour (which is still the dunghill,
To which hath reference all filth in thy house)
Thou art more ridiculous and vainglorious
Than any mountebank ; and impudent
Than any painted bawd ; which, not to soothe
And glorify thee like a Jupiter Hammon,
Thou eat'st thy heart in vinegar ; and thy gall
Turns all thy blood to poison, which is cause
Of that toad-pool that stands in thy complexion,
And makes thee (with a cold and earthy moisture
Which is the dam of putrefaction,
As plague to thy damn'd pride) rot as thou livest ;

.   .   .   .   .

To thy friends' slaughters like a screech-owl sing,
And do all mischiefs but to kill the King."

Bussy's reply is to describe him as a full-dress " Machiavel."

"*Bussy*. . . . I think you are (at worst)
No devil, since y'are like to be no king ;

.   .   .   .

That you did never good, but to do ill ;
But ill of all sorts, free and for itself :
That (like a murdering piece, making lanes in armies,
The first man of a rank, the whole rank falling)
If you have wrong'd one man, you are so far
From making him amends, that all his race,
Friends, and associates, fall into your chase :
That y'are for perjuries the very prince
Of all intelligencers ; and your voice
Is like an eastern wind, that where it flies
Knits nets of caterpillars, with which you catch
The prime of all the fruits the kingdom yields.
That your political head is the cursed fount
Of all the violence, rapine, cruelty,
Tyranny, and atheism flowing through the realm.
That y'ave a tongue so scandalous, 'twill cut
A perfect crystal ; and a breath that will
Kill to that wall a spider.

.   .   .   .

And, for your life, the thread of that was spun
When Clotho slept, and let her breathing rock
Fall into the dirt ; and Lachesis still draws it,
Dipping her twisting fingers in a bowl
Defiled, and crown'd with virtue's forced soul."

That is the ordinary machiavellian picture of the elizabethan mind. In *The Revenge of Bussy* (where you also have from Tamyra (Act I., scene 1) a sympathetic declaration of feminist doctrine) *force*, in that case the unjust, the irrational rule of force on the part of the husband, is adversely reflected on. In the *Revenge of Bussy*, however, Baligny is the chief machiavellian figure ; for a prince could not help being a *Machiavel*, whereas a noble or commoner could pass on occasion into the neighbouring class of Hero. This is how

THE LION AND THE FOX

Baligny recommends himself to his king, reciting a credo of a highly machiavellian nature:

> " *Baligny.* . . . Your highness knows
> I will be honest; and betray for you
> Brother and father; for, I know, my lord,
> Treachery for kings is truest loyalty;
> Nor is to bear the name of treachery,
> But grave, deep policy. All acts that seem
> Ill in particular respects are good
> As they respect your universal rule.
> As in the main sway of the universe
> The supreme Rector's general decrees,
> To guard the mighty globes of earth and heaven,
> Since they make good that guard to preservation
> Of both those in their order and first end,
> No man's particular (as he thinks) wrong
> Must hold him wrong'd; no, not though all men's reasons,
> All law, all conscience, concludes it wrong.
> Nor is comparison a flatterer
> To liken you here to the King of kings;
> Nor any man's particular offence
> Against the world's sway, to offence at yours
> In any subject; who as little may
> Grudge at their particular wrong, if so it seem
> For th'universal right of your estate:
> As being a subject of the world's whole sway
> As well as yours; and being a righteous man
> To whom Heaven promises defence, and blessing,
> Brought to decay, disgrace, and quite defenceless,
> He may complain of Heaven for wrong to him."

Baligny is seen to be, as Henry describes him, a "virtuous" man, of the type perfected in the Company of Jesus, and dreamed of by Machiavelli, obsessed with the mechanical order of the universe, and a fanatic of authority. He is quite willing to *let the dead bury their dead,* and to

> " *voir mourir*
> *Mère, enfans et femme,*"

in the interests of the King, the emblem of authority. With this last quotation from the *Revenge* I will terminate the evidence from Chapman bearing on his attitude to the problem of good and evil, the hero and the "Machiavel," the question we have been trying to resolve where Shakespeare is concerned.

CHAPTER II

RENAN'S *CALIBAN*

ERNEST RENAN'S play *Caliban* (described by him as *a philosophical drama continuing "The Tempest" of William Shakespeare*) is the most interesting creative contribution to the criticism of Shakespeare, especially with regard to his probable political tendencies, which we have been especially investigating in this essay. Renan tells us that his play was written during a holiday at Ischia, principally in the early morning. "The philosophy which springs from the hours of the newly born day," he remarks in his preface, "is that of the grasshoppers and larks, which I think never have a doubt that the sunlight is most unaccountably sweet, like a most excellent gift, and the whole living earth a most agreeable dwelling-place." The play is of course full of the ideas suggested by the "natural magic" of Shakespeare's most "magical" play. Prospero is made to explain his function as follows:

"*Prospero.* I am sure I am the instrument of a will that seeks expression. Nature does not comprehend itself, my Ariel. For instance, thou little bird of the blue, what didst thou realize of thyself before I drew thee from the great universal chaos in which thou wast lost, by summoning, gathering and massing together in diaphanous mould thy scattered elements? Salt is in all the wide sea and it is incessantly striving to set itself free. Life is in every atom of air, and the smallest leaf on the tree, in its dim consciousness, is eagerly drinking it in. We work as they do by an analysis and synthesis, tearing asunder and building together. That is science. I wish to be master of the spirits of nature and to give a distinct personality to each. Such is the aim and desire of all my investigations.

RENAN'S *CALIBAN*

Ariel. Those spirits, then, are forces lost in nature, existences which one cannot see in the pure state unless science extract them.

Prospero. That is it. All that which strives, but has not hitherto realized itself by expression " (*Caliban*, scene 2).

Prospero is Shakespeare's only philosopher-prince : a prince who attempts to govern by magic, and naturally, as Shakespeare is his creator, by " celtic " magic. He is perhaps the best projection of Shakespeare's personality ; he has none of the vividness or peculiarity of Hamlet, nor is he in any way a hero, but only a prince, who at the same time is a magician—an early theoretic example of the combination of the rôles of king and magician. Also it is the question of *government by magic* that is the subject of Renan's play. When the *Tempest* closes, this magical personage is left supreme, returning to take up his proper position as Duke of Milan. There is no political cloud on the horizon of Shakespeare's magical island. Caliban is nothing but the slave and servant still, Prospero still the ideal master.

But in Renan's play all this is very rapidly changed. In touch with civilization, Caliban learns to " see through " his master's magic, and through his master too. And the illusions by means of which he has been kept in servitude, now that he can get behind them, make him more furious and vindictive even than he was on the island.

" *Caliban.* He has deceived us, and of all humiliations deception is the most irritating, since it implies a weakness on the side of the deceived. Those little devils which made me fall into fits in the thunder, those little apes which tantalized me by their grimaces, those mad cats which gnawed my legs—that was all horrible, *but what is worse*, it was *not true*. Ah ! villain, that injury I will never forgive thee—never. When the people perceive that their rulers have led them by means of superstition, thou shalt see what a doom it will bring down upon their old-time masters. That hell, by which they terrified us, never existed. Those monsters on which Prospero's prestige rested were all imaginary, but they tormented me as greatly as if they had been real. Prestige! wait a little, and you will soon see that it has vanished into thin air."

The magical origin of Prospero's kingship, at least on the island, is then at length understood by Caliban. He sees the source of the power of such men as Prospero over such men as himself. Their power is a magical bluff, a conjuring trick. And then Renan brings out very well the inevitable line that the revolted Caliban takes. Eventually Caliban enlightens the populace also, pointing out to them the weakness of this tyrant, and indicating the sources of his power. He stirs up an insurrection, and is proclaimed reigning duke in place of Prospero. And in the outbursts of revolutionary wrath the object of the especial hatred of the insurrected, instructed by Caliban, is the *books* from which they see that the power to enslave them came. It is the *books*, more than the person of the magician, that must be destroyed. It is the Grand Inquisitor in the *Karamazov Brothers* (or the Bishop of Beauvais, if you like, in Mr Shaw's *St Joan*) being turned on by the enlightened populace, furious at having been caught with such a childish machinery: with, of course, the results foreseen by the Grand Inquisitor, or his author, Dostoieffsky.

Ercole says (*Caliban*, Act II., scene 1): "In reality men only respect those who grind them into the dust and kill them. When fortune has given them a sage for their ruler they cry out: 'Fie on it! what a humiliation!'"—which is also word for word the opinion of Machiavelli.

The milanese courtiers at the garden fête express themselves in the purest machiavellian vein. Prospero remains to the end the hero of Shakespeare's imagination, but Caliban grows up and transforms himself. As the representative of the proletariat, the great citizen, Caliban, is no longer a monster. One of the women-characters, Imperia, describes symbolically how Caliban can become Ariel:

"Take the butterfly which is less an animal of itself than it is the blossom of another animal. The butterfly is the highest expression of the worm, as the flower is the perfect fulfilment of the plant . . . suddenly the crawling, stupid creature has become winged and ideal and possessed of a purely aerial life."

Caliban, the earth-worm, whose triumph is predicted in this strange supplement to *The Tempest*, does not become a butterfly, but he becomes much less hostile to Prospero, and becomes without effort a typical "*grand ancêtre*." The power of the people is celebrated, for it is found that Prospero's magic is useless against them. But one un-flattering reason is given for this, at least by Prospero: for it is said that they are immune from magic because they were insensitive and believed in nothing. They probably could not even see the Olympians, if the heavens were opened for them. This play is at all events an interesting philosophic deduction from one of the greatest works of the european imagination.

CHAPTER III

SOME CONCLUDING OBSERVATIONS

THE result of this examination of the evidence relative to a very curious feature of the elizabethan mind, which we have just concluded, is of interest in very different ways. I will now briefly indicate these.

First of all the heroic tudor drama is as purely mythical as any. But it was not an organized, semi-religious, state affair ; and so it can be said to have been the expression of *individuals* much more than is the case with most dramatic art. It was attached to no great tradition : it sprang up accidentally, and flourished for a very short time with considerable difficulty : and it was part of the great revolutionary movement of the renaissance.

The divine *impersonality* of Shakespeare has clearly marked and easily recognized limitations. In so far as it existed, it was the result probably of a balancing at the basis of his intellect of two worlds which met in him (as the most perfect instrument of their meeting), and in a sense cancelled each other. One was the world of chivalrous romance, and the other the world of positivist nature that has triumphed since his time. He was in the position of a man whose parents belong one to one nationality, another to another, and who in consequence stands apart somewhat from the interests of both. Another generation on one side or the other, and such detachment would not be possible.

Of the sense of the stability of the personality required by the moralist these poets had no idea. Into the moralist's " good " so much " bad " would be mixed, and into his " bad " so much " good," that, since they were not producing paradigms of vice or virtue, designed to influence opinion, but only a picture of a conflict between these two abstractions, in an intermediate zone, of objective reality, they could only record tendencies, and not complete wholes.

SOME CONCLUDING OBSERVATIONS

But the tendency would always be to imperfection and evil:

> " O all ye virtuous powers, in earth and heaven,
> That have not put on hellish flesh and blood,
> From whence these monstrous issues are produced,"

the Duke of Byron exclaims. " Flesh and blood," to their more strained observation, was an evil enchantment: and anything like a harmony or unity was impossible for them. Saint or hero was only a convenient expression for something less of this world than usual—that was the only standard of relative perfection—there could be no other.

But there is one aspect of all these difficulties that has been seldom touched on, for reasons not far to seek. The personages that form the natural stock-in-trade of the tragic drama are kings, generals, statesmen and so forth. But the poet who presents them to us is not one of these people himself: his experience is very different to theirs, and his tastes differ the more widely from theirs the greater poet he is. Shakespeare, for example, seems to have been the reverse of a combative personality in his life; he was " gentle " and " sweet," and " nature's child." These are more appropriate epithets for the saint than for the man of action. Yet he was supposed to enter fully into the interests of all those violent and usually, compared to him, foolish personages.

With this we arrive at the root of the " impersonal " fallacy. All the talk of the " impersonality " of such-and-such a work of art is the purest romanticism: and it is a similar romanticism actually to the exaggerated sentiment about " personality." The admired " impersonality " of an outlook is even, it could be said, the admiration for a certain form of " personality ": of a personality of such power that it can completely efface itself. For it evidently is not an admiration for a Nothing. It is an idea of an age of miracles, its reputed operation is of the nature of a conjuring trick, and it is saturated in the sentiment for the marvellous. It is actually as impossible (as it is undesirable) for an artist to be " impersonal " as it is for a " tree " to be neither an oak, nor a birch, nor a pine, nor any known tree, but the abstraction "tree." There are only different ways of being personal; and one of them is that admired method of insinuation whereby a particularly compendious pretended reality enables its creator to express himself as *though he were nature*, or a god. But it is never as nature, or as the god responsible for this world, that a great creative artist speaks; nor does he ever identify himself with this other actuality. Artistic creation is always a shut-off—and that is to say a *personal*—creation. From the point of view of the evidence we have just traversed I will resume and develop this statement.

The "impersonal" fallacy appears in the light of a genial bluff; it is a similar device to that whereby a man hunting a seal will cover himself with the skin of a dead seal, and, disguised in that way, stalk his prey. The "impersonality" of the artist is as simple a device as the primitive bull-roarer employed to frighten the women and children of the primitive tribe.

The artist pretends to be nature: neither men's wits nor senses are very sharp, and they are easily deceived. They say: "Why that *is* nature." In the same way the philosopher claimed to pursue and to capture *truth*, with complete detachment. The system he presented was not a "personal" system, he always said, *but the truth*: and for a long time he was believed. But to-day his version of his function is no longer accepted. The analysis of science has taught people to recognize the individual and his personal bias, at the heart of the philosopher's system: just as a seal by experience might learn eventually to recognize the hunter hidden beneath the skin in which it was being stalked. Art, being of less practical importance, or thought to be, than philosophy, is allowed to go on with its pretence, and even to enrich itself with some of the trappings of the other defunct superstition. But its pretence is exactly of the same nature. And of course the critic of the philosopher, the "impersonal" adept of positive research, is just as vulnerable, and can always be "hoist with his own petard."

SOME CONCLUDING OBSERVATIONS

Under these circumstances, fashionable superstition as it is, the use of the pretence of "impersonality" is unsafe, and, as analysis of artistic process becomes more close and exacting, is liable to be exploded at any moment. Therefore, if we place the virtue we find in a great creative artist in this attribute of impersonality, not only our critical picture of him, but what we hope to effect by it, is liable to be upset. It would be as well under these circumstances for the critic to make a business-like retreat from that position. And it is my object here to show that nothing would be lost by that withdrawal.

Another reason of course for the adoption of this disguise of "impersonality" is to be traced to the natural contempt of men for their fellows. For they are surrounded by "persons," and there are few among them that they can feel anything but contempt for : so it is natural for them not to have much faith, or to take much interest, in a thing avowedly the utterance of a *person*. It is, especially, contemporary disbelief in the efficacy or importance of individual character, that makes the disguise almost essential. How they can ever bear to witness a creature with a poll covered with hair, two eyes, two nostrils, a mouth, a pneumatic chest, and so on, singing to them in a concert-hall is difficult to understand. But a sensitiveness as regards the peculiarities of the human physique is not a strong point with most people, the necessary veil of illusion being tightly drawn over that. But the *human character* is provided with no such palladium or rosy disguise.

The "impersonal" fallacy, again, is closely connected with the implicit non-recognition of status for the creative artist. The artist is in the nature of things more "abstract" than the "man of action." But when it comes to poetry, it is this more volatile and profounder man who is looked to, to be the poet of this more concrete and superficial one. For the man of action cannot be his own poet or recorder ; he is too busy "acting." This situation has never been properly examined, or indeed hardly considered at all.

What can such a man as Shakespeare think of all this mass of crude and confused *action* that it is his task to depict ? He is bound to come to the same conclusion as one of the only intelligent historians, or a sane man asked to write out the furious dreams of lunatics for the purposes of mental diagnosis. The one man who is never depicted in a tragedy is the poet or the philosopher, except in a subordinate rôle. This is for the same reason that the functioning of the normal mind does not offer the same opportunities for (often dramatic) diagnosis as the insane.

The one qualification that the life-history of a person must have to make it fit for tragedy is that it must abound in and express *action*. The really tragic hero must be *demented* : and there is nothing strange in all shakespearian colossi being demented, as was observed at the time we were reviewing them : where there is only *action* enough the person becomes demented automatically.

But it is impossible to be both a poet and a man of action, to be Homer and Hector, or Shakespeare and Cæsar ; for, as we say, the man of action's self-expression or " poetry " is his *action* (whereas, we could add, the traditional poet's—or that of the epic poet, like Shakespeare—is other people's actions) ; it is natural, we should also say, or even necessary, that the poet should be " impersonal." For he has to fit into the lives of his subjects and not they into his. The heroic appetite, even, of Hesiod is too much of something that is Hesiod's. The great *actions* must be harmonized and seen in the mirror of a dream, and its surface must be as smooth as glass. The vacuity of Shakespeare's face, even, is the receptive face of such a mirror, or a symbol of that inner condition that it was his function to affect. So to think of Homer as written by a woman, instead of by the blind and frowning Zeus of the Baiae bust, is, evidence apart, not such a wild notion.

Beneath the unruffled surface of this mirror, however, a drama is being enacted, too—namely, what could be termed the *drama of the mirror*—an Alice-through-the-Looking-Glass-like life. What is generally forgotten is that Shakespeare himself is a greater *hero* than any of the figures he depicted : that actually in spectacular glory and renown no physical achievement could surpass his. And yet he is *nobody* in his life ; neither a norman king, a norman noble, a general or a statesman. He is a little actor, classed by the police of his day with " sturdy beggars and vagabonds." Christ's origin is not more singularly humble. He was at least well placed to have some of Christ's thoughts about the " oppressor " and " the proud man."

To be a poet to-day (or in Shakespeare's time) is to be a tuneful writer of laments, principally connected with sex-experience ; or the chronicler in some form of the heroic deeds of soldiers, royalties and statesmen. Since the numerous men and women fulfilling those duties in Shakespeare's time were very like those engaged in similar occupations to-day ; or in combative, speculative finance —which is our equivalent for much that was then not so palpably connected with money—he can hardly have formed more favourable opinions of such personages than an outside observer, above the average in intelligence, would to-day. The only reason that we suppose he did is that he has been labelled at one time " the feudal poet," and we are still inclined to be romantic about those " spacious " days, and forget that, if nothing else, they had a renaissance, and we have not.

In spite of the placid and " gentle " surface of this *mirror* of a man, we know the storms that raged beneath it ; and we know that he must, personally, have suffered as much from the world about him as any of his heroes. If we take one of his great tragedies, *Timon of Athens*, for instance, and see what happens, in reality, in the progress of the play, the point of this protracted argument will be apparent. The Timon that a dispassionate observer would see (without the intervention of Shakespeare's poetry) would be the Timon seen by Apemantus. Shakespeare saw that one also—as he shows by means of the discourse of Apemantus. But Timon has to be sacrificed, to become *nothing* in a worldly sense, from having been *everything* ; he has to suffer heroically and have a *pathos*. This does not happen to most men of the world—they know too much, are too prudent, or merely sufficiently lucky, in ordinary circumstances, to escape this degradation. In Timon's case, or Lear's, it was due expressly to some violent or child-like kink. It is when these figures *fall* to abjection that they reach the region of the Christs. But what is not so readily admitted is that that is also the region of the Shakespeares. If these figures had no *pathos* and humiliation they would never be clothed, as they are invariably by Shakespeare, for these occasions, in the most grand and mournful rhetoric of perhaps any poetry in the world. *Antony and Cleopatra, Othello, Lear, Timon*, and the rest, are all splendid masterpieces, all reproducing the same music of extinction and unbounded suffering. They are a gallery of sunsets : they are dream-storms in a single soul, with a piling up of vaster and vaster burdens with ever more colossal figures to carry them.

In this way the contradictions of these tragic creations have their immediate explanation. Shakespeare was, by reason of the tragic side of his dramatic function—the "Shake-scene" side—something of a "mute" and something of an executioner. His only interest in these great ones of this world was on account of their violent ends and the ceremonies arising in connexion with those events. Their worldly life, unclouded by catastrophe, did not interest him at all. So he was rather a pious and discreet executioner of feudal personages (but one showing great gusto) than a "feudal poet." And he had his favourites. No mother could have treated these more tenderly.

As the painter is fixed by opinion and public taste to the imitation of tables, lamp-posts, lord mayors, society beauties, regulation "still-lifes," and so forth—although in reality his interest in these things *as such* is often very slight (his interests may plastically be of a more abstract description)—in the same way a dramatic poet is fixed to the personages of the world of action. He has to make his world of thought out of elements of action, which in themselves and in their natural setting are almost meaningless. If a painter were able to make, and did, pillar-boxes and lamp-posts *think*, and *feel*, and subsequently or at the same time cause their thinking and feeling to issue in speech like the music of the spheres, he would then be doing what

SOME CONCLUDING OBSERVATIONS

Shakespeare did. The action was the *being* the pillar-box or the lamp-post: the thinking, feeling and speech was Shakespeare's always, when the great interior action started, and the thing became transformed into a person. As action, in the sense used above, is function merely, it is when these figures turned from their function at last, and became alone, that they became a person. But without the personality of Shakespeare they would, from the moment of their functional demise, have ceased to exist. He gave them a short and brilliant existence, posthumous to the death of their function. He and the art he had perfected, especially that of heroic blank verse, performed this together.

PART IX.—APPENDIX
SHAKESPEARE AND RACE

CHAPTER I

RACE AND THE PERSON

SOMETIMES the fashionable error of the moment is to neglect the factor of race, as though there were no such thing as race, but only classes or nations or empires; and sometimes it has been the fashion to exaggerate that factor, as though there were not such a thing as persons, but only races. *Class* in these adjustments is, of course, the great rival of *race*: it is also a very much easier thing to fix. Race is for the most part too obscure a force for us to be able to organize it into anything coherent, so it is perhaps rightly ignored. In an art-form like elizabethan drama, if the race factor could be got at, it might tell us a great deal more than anything else—as it goes deeper and farther back—about the impulses at work in it, giving it its peculiar physiognomy. But it is the one thing that it is impossible to chart. We can only argue, rather uncertainly, from the results, and inductively work back to a supposed origin; where some particular idiosyncrasy, oddly flowering and challenging our curiosity, suggests a new road to the virgin regions behind us.

These remarks apply of course to Shakespeare as well as to his contemporaries. But our contention here is that they apply differently and less. At this point it may be well to ask if, to start with, we are prepared to deny the significance of race altogether? That—from what has been said above—is evidently not the case. A man's *race* is the most interesting thing about him, usually—*class* is a parvenu category compared to it. But Shakespeare's race (not his nation), if we knew it, would *not* be the most interesting thing about him.

The belief on which I am basing my statement here can be summarized as follows. Not only genius, as we call the greatest development of conscious personality, but all personality, is raceless for all practical purposes : for the characteristic work of personality is to overcome the mechanical ascendancy of what is imposed on it by birth and environment. So, since it illustrates itself essentially by triumph over race, class and fashion, these things are rather what it is *not*, than what it *is*. It is, however, true that in this struggle it uses aptitudes and forces that it derives from the things it is destined to combat.

In Shakespeare's case there is less temptation than in that of almost anybody to occupy ourselves with where he came from : for where he got to is a matter of such great and universal interest that it would be sure to dwarf his origins, as it dwarfed his immediate environment. However far back you went down the stream of his blood, you would not be likely to meet anything so worth your attention (however picturesque) as himself.

We can suggest more clearly what we mean, perhaps, by other examples. Supposing you were talking to an enthusiast for " french civilization," the fact that Flaubert was " a Frenchman " would be very much in Flaubert's favour. But most Frenchmen, as everyone who has travelled in France must have rapidly discovered, are very much like Bouvard and Pecuchet. Therefore, in dragging in " the Frenchman " in Flaubert's case, you would be arriving at this surprising result : you would be advertising Flaubert on account of his racial or national association with Bouvard and Pecuchet ! It would surely be far truer to say that it would be reasonable to be a little endeared to the average Frenchman on account of his fellow-countryman, Flaubert; or because he spoke the language of Racine. This is the extreme personalist-position, the opposite to the first one to which you would be committed in the above illustration—namely, that in which you ended by congratulating Flaubert on belonging to the same stock as Bouvard and Pecuchet.

This is a very painful subject : I will not dwell on it, else I might take the average Swede (who in the past has got a good deal of advertisement out of Ibsen, for instance, whom in his lifetime Sweden exiled and did its best to destroy), and by turning to the German, the American, the Russian, the Persian, or the Welshman we should find that there was the same tale to tell. For example, too great an insistence on the latter's nationality (in the case of your chosen hero) would ultimately result in your finding that he had become involved with that "welsh wizard," Mr Lloyd George.

The foregoing remarks in no way dispose of the interest in race for us: all they are designed to do is to put us on our guard where unbridled racial romanticism is concerned, and to hint at the ridiculous situations we inevitably arrive at if we pursue that enthusiasm too far. If it were suddenly announced, with a wealth of proof that it was impossible to controvert, that Shakespeare was a Chinaman, I should of course know at once—in the present state of science and politics and with what I know of the press—that it was intended in England to establish some sort of alliance with China. I should expect to see the announcement followed by a clever forgery described as a "recently discovered play of Shakespeare's," with as many points of resemblance to the philosophy of Confucius as Hamlet has to Montaigne. But supposing I heard, and *believed*, that Shakespeare was a Chinaman, I should then feel no surprise; it would require no readjustment at all in what I thought about him. For I should know that he must be as unlike most Chinamen as he was unlike most Englishmen. But because you say that the position of an individual such as Shakespeare to his race-class-time context is exactly that of the child to its parents, it does not mean that you deny the beauty and propriety of filial love; nor that you would deny that the outward appearance of every creature roughly follows the lineaments of father and mother. It would only involve a suspicion that very strong race-characteristics in an individual, in their face, gait or mental disposition, probably means, at all events to-day, that they are not the highest examples of their kind; that had they been more creative and mentally active they would not have been content *to repeat*—even physiologically: nor would they have followed mechanically the rules laid down by nature and humdrum tradition.

But race is a very great reality : and were we not dealing with such a figure as Shakespeare we should certainly not have been compelled to go into all these uncomfortable details. How amusing it is, for instance, to speculate whether the pictorial attainments of the modern Jew has its rationale in the turanian intermixture, showing itself so often in the features of jewish immigrants. Or, again, renaissance Italy is one great ethnologic question-mark. The largely oriental slave-population of Rome far out-numbered the native Romans, and these along with the hordes of slaves employed on the latifundia must subse-quently have left huge deposits of human stocks, opposite to those provided by northern invasion.

Any analysis of a great creative period—and we are concerned with that too—must have this chaotic spot in its centre: the incalculable factor of racial intermixture. For it needs only a few men, or even one man, to give a novel turn and a strange power to a supposedly "national" move-ment. In a mind like Shakespeare's a whole necropolis comes to life. And he made a good use of his ghosts. In such a risorgimento who is to say what ultimately is the value even of Stratford-on-Avon and the Bankside theatre business ? The special conditions we have applied to the individual must also be applied to any exceptional creative group; the same alibis must be, perhaps, employed. The strangest ghosts must have trod those elizabethan stages, as they always assemble wherever life becomes suddenly incandescent.

CHAPTER II

THE DEPERSONALIZATION OF SHAKESPEARE

TO enter in any serious way into the question of *race*, or seek a scientific support for these few remarks, is not at all my intention here. That would be a very complicated business indeed; but it would also be quite outside the interests of this book. In the great writers whom Shakespeare has attracted, and who have provided him, each in turn, as a tribute, with a new spell of immortality, the question of his racial origin often occurs. Renan says, for instance: "It would be curious to ascertain how much of the Celt there is in the former of these poets [namely, Shakespeare]." Lord Morley remarks that if it had not early come in contact with the Celt, "germanic England would not have produced a Shakespeare." Matthew Arnold writes: "Shakespeare's greatness is thus in his blending an openness and flexibility of spirit, not english, with the english basis."

Of all the means at the disposal of anybody bent on accounting away Shakespeare, or any figure disturbing as he does by its unsupported appearance the neighbouring world, there is no more effective one than that of *race*. Race can be made to explain so much that otherwise seems to demand some form of hypostasis. No one so much as Shakespeare requires this unsubstantial substance to account for his towering and hanging in the air, for no reason, where mostly everything is flat.

The explanation that science may some day be in a position to offer, to account for such a phenomenon, is not yet available. The form it will no doubt take will be to reassure people by showing that it is quite *natural*, although it looks so unnatural, that a solitary person, without assistance, should simply *grow* like that and not need to be built, like a cathedral. It will perhaps be proved to them that

THE LION AND THE FOX

it is quite possible for Nelsons to *grow* their own columns, that it is quite in order, that the monumental is an uncomfortable and even ridiculous position : and that if you see one shooting up there is no occasion to be indignant. For genius and its queer habits, its monstrous results, no hypostasis is required. The phenomenon of great personality—such a rare one that it always comes as a shock—will meet all the requirements, they will be informed in the science column of their newspaper. All the troublesome " Others abide our question—thou art free," the " self-scanned, self-schooled, self-honoured, self-secured," so highly displeasing in any case to our age, and at no time popular or satisfactory, with its smack of the miraculous and uncontingent, once the formula has been found by science, will be accepted like Thule, the Magnetic Pole, or the Atom, and the popular mind will be at rest. At present that point has not yet been reached.

It is as a factor in the programme of depersonalization, then, that this question is approached here. If a whole race could be found to have conspired in such a result as Shakespeare, then such a monstrosity would no longer offend. Or if such greatness can be transferred to the shoulders of a race—for preference an ancient race, lost in the mists of the past, its greatness exalted to suit the occasion—then in a sense " greatness "—that dimensional epithet that serves us when we are referring to some defaulter by excess from the human canon—has been explained : or rather, pushed so far back, and so dispersed, it no longer requires explaining.

It is the privilege of such a community as Arnold described in his books against the Philistines to lay bare the existence of such a thing as genius, which in happier surroundings might hardly be suspected. That is a very useful function, and Shakespeare seems almost to have been specially designed for England. He is the greatest poet in the world ; and here he is, pat, just where he ought to be, in the middle of an extensive plain, with nothing in the surrounding landscape to provide the slightest physical explanation of how he got there. When in the midst of such a community as the Saxon-English such a personality as Shakespeare arises, then there *can* no longer be any doubt at all—there is such a thing as a *person* after all, and in spite of most people's persistent wish that that may be disproved.

But there is one way in which you can dispose of this personality even then, and at the same time deprive the flat community of the privilege of producing him: one way remains. You can turn him into a *Celt*. At least that is what can always be done in England, rather in the way that Nietzsche turned himself into a *Pole* to account for his appearance among the Germans. But, although Pole and Celt are accepted as quite good counters, there is really no resemblance between them at all, for whereas the Poles are a nation, the Celts are a figment of the brain. Or rather, there was once a tribe that we call Celts; but what is meant when we say a " Celt " to-day is nothing to do with that, and is strictly a thing that does not exist.

Many great writers, however, such as Arnold and Renan, have firmly believed in the existence of the " Celt "—or have appeared to do so. And indeed there was a very considerable and celebrated literature to confirm them in their belief. They could also go to small highly conservative countries where the inhabitants would tell them that they were, among other things, " Celts." Indeed in Renan's case the evidence must have seemed even more conclusive; for he actually *came from* such a country himself, and was himself convinced that he was a " Celt." Yet to-day we know, and should have known all along, had we used our eyes, that the " Celt " does not exist, nor ever has.

CHAPTER III

THE "CREEPING SAXON" AND THE "CELT"

HOW this myth has been built up is very curious. If you wish to study its evolution you cannot do better than go to Arnold's *Celtic Literature*. There you get this delusion presented in perhaps its craziest and most magnificent form. You get in Arnold, in its purest form, the pseudo-racial contrast, as net as a theophrastian type: you get his "creeping Saxon" on the one hand (to whom a considerable reality must certainly be conceded), and on the other hand, what is known as a "Celt." Now, if you generalize a little arbitrarily about the Saxon, push him into his corner, insist on him, show him at his worst, as the eternal *Philistine* of Arnold's criticism, then certainly you would seem to require something or other in the way of race to account for the Arthurian Cycle, Shakespeare, Taliesin, Ossian, and so on. But, to meet this need (provoked by the obstinate presence of the Saxon), the "Celt" is an absurdity. The best way to show this will be to juxtapose a few passages from Arnold. In the first group which I will now reproduce he is describing what he understands by the "Saxon." In the second he is describing what he calls the "Celt."

The Normans, with their "strenuousness, clearness and rapidity, the high latin spirit . . . hated the slowness and dullness of the creeping Saxon" ("For dullness, the creeping Saxon," is a line in an old irish poem).

"Of the steady-going German nature the bane is, as I remarked, flat commonness; there seems no end to its capacity for platitude . . . it is only raised gradually out of it by science, but it jogs through almost interminable platitudes first." The english nature, however, "is not raised to science." In this it has not the ultimate reward

of the infinitely jogging German. Its compensation for
this is that something in it, whether " celtic " or norman,
" seems to set a bound to its advance in platitude."

The germanic nature, the saxon basis in the Englishman,
has for its constant accompaniment " the humdrum,
the plain and ugly, the ignoble: in a word *das Gemeine,
die Gemeinheit*. . . . The universal dead-level of plainness
and homeliness, the lack of all beauty and distinction in
form and feature, the slowness and clumsiness of the
language, the eternal beer, sausages and bad tobacco, the
blank commonness everywhere, pressing at last like a
weight on the traveller "—it is that germanism " against
which Goethe was all his life fighting ": and that is the
germanism that is in the Englishman, and which produces
the " Creeping Saxon."

The dazzling advantages of the " Celt " over his old
enemy, the saxon Philistine, Arnold next enumerates:

" Its [the celtic nature's] chord of penetrating passion
and melancholy, again, its titanism, as we see it in Byron,
what other european poetry possesses that like the English,
and where do we get it from ? The Celts, with their vehement reaction against the despotism of fact, with their
sensuous nature, their manifold striving, their adverse
destiny, their immense calamities, the Celts are the prime
authors of this vein of piercing regret and passion—of this
titanism in poetry."

The " Celt " has " that in him which cuts him off from
command of the world of fact," but " his mere eye is not
less sharp, nay, it is sharper, than the Latins." *Style*,
Arnold suggests, is the key to the celtic genius: ". . . the
Celts have it in a wonderful measure . . . Celtic poetry
seems to make up to itself for being unable to master the
world and give an adequate interpretation of it, by throwing all its force into style, by bending language at any rate
to its will, and expressing the ideas it has with unsurpassable
intensity, elevation and effect."

The " natural magic " of Shakespeare (Arnold's phrase)
is the celtic magic. The greek genius gives us *beauty*: the
celtic genius *magic*. The celtic sensibility found in nature

a source of romantic power that, Arnold thinks, is the property of the " Celt " :

" As the saxon names of places, with the pleasant, wholesome smack of the soil in them—Weatherfield, Thaxted, Shalford—are to the celtic names of places, with their penetrating, lofty beauty—Velindra, Tyntagel, Carnarvon—so is the homely realism of german and norse nature to the fairy-like loveliness of Celtic nature.

" And as in material civilization he has been ineffectual, so has the Celt been ineffectual in politics. This colossal, impetuous, adventurous wanderer, the Titan of the early world, who in primitive times fills so large a place on earth's scene, dwindles and dwindles as history goes on, and, at last, is shrunk to what we now see him. For ages and ages the world has been constantly slipping, ever more and more, out of the Celt's grasp. ' They went forth to the war,' Ossian says most truly, ' *but they always fell.* ' "

There are the two natures contrasted—the " Saxon " and the " Celtic." Before going any further, it would be useful to note a great discrepancy between this last picture of the *Titan of the early World* (who is the " Celt ") and Renan's idea of the " Celt." Renan's " Celt " is St Patrick ; Arnold's is Ossian.

The Celts, who imposed their poetical motives upon the whole of Christendom, which they changed from top to bottom with their chivalry, were for Renan quiet and humble natures, immaculate saints, the first christians : " The decided leaning of the celtic race towards the ideal, its sadness, its fidelity, its good faith, caused it to be regarded by its neighbours as dull, foolish, and superstitious. They could not understand its delicacy and refined manner of feeling. They mistook for awkwardness the embarrassment experienced by sincere and open natures in the presence of more artificial natures."

But Renan's account of the " Celt " is in every way different to Arnold's.

" What strikes one at a first glance in the imaginative composition of the celtic races, above all when they are contrasted with those of the teutonic races, is the extreme mildness of manners pervading them. There are none of those frightful vengeances which fill the *Edda* and the *Niebelungen*. Compare the teutonic with the gaelic hero— Beowulf with Peredur, for example. What a difference there is! In the one all the horror of disgusting and blood-embrued barbarism, the drunkenness of carnage, the disinterested taste, if I may say so, for destruction and death; in the other a profound sense of justice, a great height of personal pride, it is true, but also a great capacity for devotion, an exquisite loyalty. . . . The primitive man of teutonism is revolting by his purposeless brutality, by a love of evil that only gives him skill and strength in the service of hatred and injury. The cymric hero, on the other hand, even in his wildest flights, seems possessed by habits of kindness and a warm sympathy with the weak."

The poem of St Brandon is the typical example of this " celtic " refinement issuing in romantic expression.

" This fantastical nature created expressly for another humanity . . . makes the poem of St Brandon one of the most extraordinary creations of the human mind, and perhaps the completest expression of the celtic ideal. All is lovely, pure and innocent; never has a gaze so benevolent and so gentle been cast upon the earth. . . . It is the world seen through the crystal of a stainless conscience; one might almost say a human nature, as Pelagius wished it, that has never sinned. The very animals participate in the universal mildness. Evil appears under the form of monsters, wandering on the deep, or of Cyclops confined in volcanic islands; but God causes them to destroy one another, and does not permit them to do hurt to the good."

That is Renan's " Celt," and it will be apparent that it is a very different one to Arnold's.

Arnold is, however, temperamentally under the spell of "titanism": he is a man-worshipper, as it might be called —which is traditionally "feminine." And has not Arnold himself, in one of his best-known poems, referred to his own "feminine" characteristics unambiguously enough?—

> " *Have I not wished—what woman more ?*
> *This starting, feverish, heart away.*"

THE LION AND THE FOX

So with him we know *à qui nous avons à faire,* for he has enlightened us. The sensibility of the celtic nature, however, for him has "something feminine in it": the "Celt" is, where the feminine idiosyncrasy is concerned, "not far from its secret." How he reconciles this with the *Titan of the early world* is difficult to see, except that the Titan "always fell."

Renan's idea seems to be that the ruling class amongst the "Celts" were the Ossians, and all the rest were as he describes them above. The "titanic" element would thus be accounted for on class grounds. But *class* in primitive society always involves *race.* Into this, however, he does not go : for he is satisfied that all are "Celts."

We can now return to Arnold's contrast of the Celt and the Saxon. Ethnologically, it is true, Arnold's book is worthless : he was not even a great student of celtic literature. He only went to the "Celt" hurriedly, on a political mission, to get ammunition for his war with the "creeping Saxon." But although this was nothing more than a raid, and Arnold was not quite clear himself about what the "Celt" was, he saw, where nobody else has, then or since, a very deep comedy in progress. Incidentally he supplied us with a superb "celtic" nonsense-book.

CHAPTER IV

CHIVALRY

THE only thing in german or latin Europe possessing mysterious power and expressing itself with a lovely faultlessness—whether you call it " celtic " or leave it merely as an exhalation having its seat along the western fringes which were the extreme landmarks of the ancient world, influencing the people who settled there like some drug in the air—is saluted by Arnold. That he salutes it by the name of " Celt " is unfortunate : but what he says, apart from this, is admirably true.

It was that *strength in mystery*, like the inhuman strength of a demented person, that caused the " celtic " peoples to create, and enabled them to launch, the notion of chivalry —the only great spiritual creation of Europe—which the democratic renaissance, arising in the mercantile republics of Italy, superseded. Chivalry was a sort of christianity adapted for the use of the aristocrat ; but the accommodation was so dexterously managed that it left no traces of its humble origin, and indeed turned the tables on the levelling evangile, cutting off the noble from the common man more effectively than anything less lofty and immaterial could have done. Neither the most massive external pomp, nor crushing physical force, could have achieved the separation of one sort of man from another so completely as this airy impalpable aloof " gentleness." As a heaven-sent gift, in the shape of a patent of nobility so much more convincing than their own patents, the otherwise rather rough-and-ready norman, spanish or german nobility seized on it with delight. All a man had to do, then, was to call himself " gentle " and all was well. This was the great " celtic " patent ; for the pigments that went to the making of the magic dress, the cunning beauty of the materials, all the genius for style, lavished upon these chivalrous patterns, represents a work that is unmatched in Europe.

It is strange that the european world should have received these opposite gifts, as they were in a sense—christianity and chivalry—both from a small, politically insignificant and defeated people—at the asiatic extremity from the Jews, and at the western extremity from what we call the " Celts."

The cymric and gaelic tribes, not being nations, and having none of the burdens of policy and aggressive expansion of an ambitious and successful nation, were able to pursue to some extent an " ideal " life. At the time when they finally launched their poetical productions—or rather when the Normans "took up" and popularized them—they had developed a human ideal of mixed bardic and aristocratic detachment and inactivity, which the long leisures of their political unsuccess had been used to ornament and perfect, and which contrasted in a surprising way with the prosaic expression of their teuton neighbours. It was a very great novelty, and as this platonic picture sank into people's minds it had the effect of " showing up " the brutality and commonplace that had been of course the conditions of the success of the peoples who had overcome these dreamers.

This enforced idleness and inertia of the Celt, owing to his being locked up in his mountains and islands in the extremity of the world of his time by the victorious norse and saxon population, is invariably stressed, as accounting for what happened. But would the same result have ensued had you locked up the Saxon ? However much you squeezed him it is unlikely that he would have exuded arthurian romances. If you take a parallel in general experience, it is commonly said that " adversity " is good for people. Although certainly a human wreck, however dilapidated, is less disgusting than a sleek and prosperous, insolent and shining, human being, it does not generally (as the christian religion did) make poverty *active*, and give it a value enabling it to meet success on equal terms. It is seldom you see a man who has become very poor putting his new condition to the uses indicated by St Francis. Instead of filling it with apocalyptic activity like a flagellant, he confines himself to the mechanical merit of destitution, for the most part. So all nations when they have been finally defeated in war do not burst into song at once, or retaliate by becoming christians at once, with a superb revolutionary philosophy—like the Celts or like the Jews.

Renan gives as the principal reason of the universal success of celtic romance its *abstractness*. It was the disincarnate quality of the fastidious knightliness of welsh myth that enabled every country to adopt it at once; whereas had it, instead of moving so steadfastly in an ideal world of no-nation and no-time, possessed the specific national flavour of Robin Hood, it would have crossed frontiers with more difficulty. Its other-worldliness, unlike the christian, of course, but giving it similar advantages, disarmed every national antagonism. It was as spirits, not as men, that these patterns of knighthood descended upon Europe.

Again, they effected their descent in every case *alone*: they not only had not a nation behind them, they had not even a squire. They were too poor in fact, as we know, to possess such feudal furnishings: but as they were all poets this was natural. So their knight-errantry passed all the usual political nationalist obstructions. With their manners of very great princes, these poor and solitary dreamers passed into every court and fortress, paladins reminiscent of Christ. So the secret of the celtic success was that, whatever the reason, they had disposed of all trace of race, of feudal machinery, and indeed terrestrial reference altogether.

In bidding such an eloquent adieu to this mighty spiritual influence (against which he did not wish to bring to bear any qualification, except that it was accompanied by an *ineffectualness* in politics and business), for all his shining praise, Arnold seems at the last to be betraying it. He contrasts first of all the *titanism*, the rebellious *striving*, of the Celt, with the humdrum *commonness* and docility of the German and Saxon, his constant adversaries. And then he goes on to show how in the end this *titanism* is tamed and vanquished by the *philistinism* that he has loaded with stinging epithets.

He shows the magnificent spirit of the "Titan of the early world" broken at last by what? By the small ridiculous saxon shopkeeper, or the heavy german fool, the genius of the modern industrial world. And, after all the almost unmeasured praise he has lavished on these things that are perishing, he places himself, at the end of his essay, or seems to do so, on the *winning side*, the side of the Philistine, on whom he has lavished all the resources of his formidable scorn.

"Out of the steady humdrum habit of the creeping Saxon, as the Celt calls him—out of his way of going near the ground—has come, no doubt, flourishing with its genuine marks only in the German fatherland, Great Britain and her colonies, and the United States of America. . . . This stereotyping habit leads at last, as I have said, up to science, up to the comprehension and interpretation of the world. With us in Great Britain, it is true, it does not seem to lead so far as that: it is in Germany, where the habit is more unmixed, that it can lead to science."

The English are, it will be recalled, *incomplete Philistines* because of the strain of "celtism" in them. It is on account of this strain of "celtism" that they will probably perish. Whereas the German, the *complete* Philistine, without any of that destructive admixture of "celtism," will gloriously succeed.

But even in the anglo-saxon world—not destined *quite* to reach, on account of "celtism," the germanic consummation in *science*—what benefits have come from philistinism? "What conquests has it not won?" He, Arnold, who is "often supposed to be Philistinism's mortal enemy," hastens to correct that impression:

"How it [anglo-saxon philistinism] has augmented the comforts and conveniences of life for us! Doors that open, windows that shut, locks that turn, razors that shave, coats that wear, watches that go, and a thousand more such good things, are the invention of the Philistines."

The irony, as you see, gleams in the midst of his recantation. The " flat commonness " of the german mind, in the homeland of the supreme Philistine (merely to travel in which so oppresses the traveller at last, like a dead-weight, that he is " impatient to be gone "), produces *science*. And through that democratic force everyone, every little Philistine, will *ultimately*—where no " celtism " enters into their composition to interfere with this highly desirable process—arrive at "the comprehension of the world "—the docile, obedient, devout, scientific understanding of how the machine works. Instead of the gallant insurrection against "the despotism of fact," the superb and visionary " celtism " of the past, there will be a docile and respectful assiduity in following the interminable technical details, enumerated endlessly, it would seem, as though by a verbose mechanical genius of godlike stature, showing the gaping little Philistine over the Works.

CHAPTER V

THE PLAIN UNVARNISHED CELT

BEFORE passing behind Arnold's façade of rhetoric and introducing you to the astonishingly humorous piece that is to be found in progress there, we had better for a moment turn to the plain unvarnished Celt, and see how he differs from Arnold's "Celt" and Renan's St Brandon. This is Professor Perry's account of him :

"The Celts, like the Teutons, never invented anything ; the whole of their culture shows signs of derivation from the Mediterranean. Moreover, their countries of origin had previously been tenanted by peoples of the Bronze Age, who possessed a culture obviously derived from peoples of a higher civilization than themselves. The original Celts, as we know them, were a boundary folk ; originating in a centre where remains of older peoples exist, and they obviously derived the whole of their culture from the Mediterranean, with the exception of their horse-riding habits " (*The Growth of Civilization*).

The Teutons and the Welsh, who were such powerful enemies of the Romans, got even their martial energy, he thinks—following in this Professor Chadwick—from contact with the roman army organization.

The Teuton, Norseman and the Celt were a closely related group of kinsmen. Their enterprise was principally of an impulsive, barbarous and destructive sort ; they were not inventors but borrowers. What you can say of one, you can say of all ; except that the Norseman was more energetic and adaptive than his teuton cousin : and the Celt was also a more enthusiastic borrower, probably, than the German.

With this statement of Professor Perry it will be useful to compare a similar one on the subject of that other

THE PLAIN UNVARNISHED CELT

ingredient of the "english" character with which Arnold deals—namely, the norman. The Normans were of course those Norwegians—as they would be to-day—or Vikings, whose black piratical ships, as they passed the coast of France, filled Charlemagne with such forebodings: who eventually became the masters of Normandy and England and for a time of Calabria and Sicily; and whose neighbours, the Swedes, under the name of Varangians, founded the first russian kingdom. These Scandinavians, as we have seen, Arnold supposed—leaving it to others to prove it—to have a touch of the "Celt." This does not save them, however, from being described by Professor A. H. Johnson (writing a little after the middle of last century) as Professor Perry to-day describes the Celt and the Teuton:

"The northmen never seem to have been original, never to have invented anything; rather they readily assumed the language, religion, ideas of their adopted country, and soon became absorbed in the society around them. . . . In Russia they became Russians; in France, Frenchmen; in Italy, Italians; in England, twice over Englishmen—first in the case of the Danes, and secondly, in that of the later Normans. . . . Nor is this all," he continues; "they borrow everything, make it their own, and their presence is chiefly felt in increased activity and more rapid development of institutions, literature, art. Thus, while they invent nothing, they perfect, they organize everything" (*The Normans in Europe*).

The same account of the Normans—almost to the same words—is supplied by Professor E. A. Freeman:

"Little of original invention can be traced to any strictly norman source; but no people were ever more eager to adopt from other nations, to take into their service and friendship from any quarter men of learning and skill and eminence of any kind.

"In Ireland his [the Norman's] power of adaptation caused him to sink in a way in which he sank nowhere else. While some of the norman settlers in Ireland went to swell the mass of the English of the Pale, others threw in their lot with the native Irish, and became, in the well-known saying, ' *Hibernis ipsis Hiberniores.*' "

These adroit borrowers are the near kinsmen of the Celts —great borrowers as well—inventing nothing, preferring to live by preying on the world, loving violence, including herds of men on the footing of animals in the great hunting-system of their lives, possibly the first in history to have this idea, or having it perhaps at the same time as the Semites in Akkad. Their god was a Valfadir or Battle-father ; and they imagined a heaven that was not a happy hunting-ground, but a happy battlefield.

These turbulent characteristics, however, we must assume, did not go so deep as at first sight would appear, at least in the case of the Normans and Celts. The latter became transformed, in Ireland, to the most characteristic christian lambs in the whole of Christendom, as Renan insists : and the Normans gave themselves up willingly, as successful men, to the intricate pleasures of litigation, which Professor Freeman says was their other great obsession, going hand in hand from the start with their martial tendency. Thus William the Conqueror arrived in England surrounded with as many lawyers to prove the legitimacy of his proceeding, as soldiers to enable him to point concurrently to the *fait accompli.* So it always was with the Norman, according to all accounts : he was armed from head to foot with arguments to legalize every crime that his strenuous life necessitated.

The Norman, the Celt, the Teuton, the Achaian was an ideal " conqueror." " *Libera nos a furore romanorum,*" christian Europe prayed, considering the Viking merely as a storm or a pestilence. But they were a storm that was willing to accommodate itself and to learn, at bottom, and which would willingly light up the landscape with its lightnings. No one could wish on the whole for a better conqueror. If submitted to without fuss, and if impressed at all with his new subjects, he was admirable.

He was an ideal patron, guardian and nurse of the conquered. Where, indeed, the conquered possessed a good type of civilized life of their own they would not know that they had been conquered at all—he could guarantee. Sicilian life has never flowered so peacefully and well as with him in charge of the practical side of it: the arts were ideally protected, with no trace of interference. Then he took few women with him (even that he borrowed from the conquered). That may have something to do with his rapid assimilation, and makes him still more ideal.

Of *non-interference*, that secret of the art of happy government, the last traces of which has disappeared to-day, the Norman was the great master. His political egotism was a *simple* one, a *physical* one. It had no pretentiousness and no fanaticism. Its physical health and equanimity was extremely beneficent. Only when confronted with a character very like his own, of kindred race—like the irish " Celt "—and of a fiery and contentious disposition, did he become an actual tyrant.

The " ideal conqueror " of the norman—and probably achaian—sort is a rather odd fish, we must however agree. And as to what rank to assign, in human affairs, to these ideal conquering races, there will no doubt be many opinions yet. A typical member of one of them is very genial and pleasant: very " amused " by the delightful " artistic " and " brainy " habits of the curious natives which indulgently he encourages, up to a certain point, but of course no further. Their totemistic carvings, and curious brightly coloured *objets d'art* (which of course are not of value in the sense that a hundred-thousand-pound portrait by Van Dyck would be), will be put in museum cases for his herd, with a grin of civilized superiority, to gaze at. He is self-complacent; but having " for reading and thinking no great turn," he has a sort of naïve schoolboy awe of it, which he dispels with his grin—on which he falls back whenever impressed beyond the limits proper to a ruling race or class. Yet heaven help any country conquered by people with " a great turn " for such things. The hardy, illiterate pirate is even *gentler* in the end—as the Lombards were found to be, with some surprise, by their italian subjects, beneath their ferocious beards.

The Norman's is evidently not a great civilizing rôle,

any more than the anglo-saxon world-conqueror's has been. But the Anglo-Saxon has not shown the fineness of the Norman. It is a heavier hand that he has stretched over the countries he has taken.

Arnold saw very well the significance of the anglo-saxon "independence" and self-assertiveness; the peculiar type of hard conceit and will to enfranchisement of the northern man, how it was accompanied with a rather deceptive docility. In a nature both cold and slow it is obvious that considerable periods must elapse before this unreflecting will-to-selfhood can be broken. He did not perhaps see the uses of this narrow and frigid obstinacy, so dependable because so dead. The repose provided by it, like the massive walls of a workshop, he ignored, insisting always on the imprisoning nature of those walls, and never allowing for the isolation and security this deadness, at its best, could provide. He talked as though he wanted all the world to be in restless movement round us. Nevertheless it is difficult to dispute that in practice european enterprise has left the world much harsher, uglier, and more inhuman than it found it.

"The same sensibility [that responsible for their feeling for nature] made the Celts full of reverence and enthusiasm for genius, learning, and the things of the mind; *to be a bard, freed a man*—that is a characteristic stroke of this generous and ennobling ardour of theirs, which no race has ever shown more strongly. . . . The Celt, undisciplinable, anarchical and turbulent by nature, but out of affectionate admiration giving himself body and soul to some leader, that is not a promising political temperament, it is just the opposite of the anglo-saxon temperament."

Arnold's "Celt," "out of affection and admiration giving himself body and soul to some leader," does not resemble the Anglo-Saxon, it is certain. Arnold insists on this. "It is," he says, "just the opposite of the anglo-saxon temperament, disciplinable and steadily obedient within certain limits, but retaining an inalienable part of freedom and self-dependence."

THE PLAIN UNVARNISHED CELT

In this german or anglo-saxon docility, in the midst of which is an irreducible, unconvertible core of egotism or self-will, which keeps back something always, lies a certain duplicity and lack of generosity which is one of the least amiable german or anglo-saxon characteristics. For what it keeps back is usually not worth keeping back. It is the peasant hoarding of a pound or two, transferred to the spiritual plane. It is this small hard core of egotism that is accountable for the type of " freedom " and " independence " of a widely diffused and widely shared sovereignty, that is the european stock-type. It is this core of a man that is his heart : and also it is his political identity card.

The " plain unvarnished Celt " which we set out in this chapter to examine, in contradistinction to Arnold's brilliant, poetical, paladin, is now a little more defined. He is a very different creature from what Arnold saw when he said " Celt." What, then, is the explanation of Arnold's " Celt " ? For that in some sense such a person existed is certain, since we have his songs and legendary romances as witnesses of his reality.

The explanation most generally accepted to-day is that of the Elliot-Smith-Perry-Rivers school, which supposes that the ancient race settled in England and Ireland before the arrival of the Celts was of mediterranean stock, possessing the mediterranean culture, and its solar symbolization and cults. The nordic " conquerors " coming down on top of this race were very much affected by it : and with their genius for borrowing, and adapting them selves, became more what the other people were than they were themselves, giving their name " celtic " to the result. That, in a few words, is the answer that a great deal of anthropology to-day would give. But with that we should at once get into such a very controversial region that this mention of what seems to me the best substantiated theory must suffice. The " small dark people " in the celtic countries would be these original inhabitants : the big norse-looking people would be the susceptible nordic (celtic) deposit. Where this original population was thickest, in the west, into which it was driven, it has had most effect. The Irish and Welsh are therefore more " celtic " than the English. But " celtic " is as obvious a misnomer as " saxon " would be for something that is very different from both.

CHAPTER VI

ARNOLD'S LITTLE FARCE, NOW FOR THE FIRST TIME RESCUED FROM ITS IRONICAL SETTING FOR THE ENGLISH-SPEAKING PUBLIC

FROM the treacherous polished surface of Arnold's prose (its body clouded for its reception) I will now expiscate that laughing idea which we have been preparing to examine. It is the idea of two island neighbours and strongly hallucinated brethren, the Irishman and the Englishman, the Celt and the Teuton (both in the baleful grip of " celtism," which stands between them and success in science, or any exact, unemotional study), involved in a curious fratricidal strife and tangle of romantic misunderstandings. There is, however, in Arnold's essay a very formidable under-tow that, unless the reader were warned of its presence beforehand, would be apt, at the end of the discussion, to leave him floundering. The ironical equivocation is a very peculiar one : it lends a great deal of force to his argument : and to seize this double meaning will in itself strengthen the student's hold on the subjects that occasioned it.

Arnold is not himself at all the dupe of the " celtic " notion : his whole essay is written to expose it. Yet he accepts the conventional nomenclature of " Celt " for all that type of expression and sentiment that had been popularized under that name, and which is so opposite to the usual german way of seeing and feeling. While pointing out the true relationship of the Irishman and the Englishman, he nevertheless attributes to the " Celt " all those spiritual qualities associated with what we call the celtic peoples. He proceeds to display the abyss existing between the " celtic " and the german nature : one (the " celtic ") a brilliant, romantic and " titanic " nature : the other, slow, flat, common and unheroic. But it is a strange thing that it should not have occurred to him to account for this extraordinary disparity between two such close kinsmen as the Teuton and the Celt. They should love each other, he suggests, because they are close kinsmen. Yet surely, from Arnold's account of these respective kinsmen, near relations can never in history have been so dissimilar!

Did Arnold in reality perceive that to some extent he was talking nonsense; and was his easy acceptance of the mistake, simultaneously with his exposure of it, a further ironical confusion: or was it necessary, in order to load the " creeping Saxon " with his scorn, to leave the " Celt," his enemy, in technical possession of all those qualities that show up so brilliantly against the british background?

At all events in his picture of the " titanic " Celt there is this confusion: that he is confounding the " celtism " (that has nothing more to do with the plain, unvarnished Celt than with the Saxon) with the martial, ossianesque, norse characteristics. That racial pride and individualism that resulted in an aggressive conception of personal freedom and personal importance is european; norse, celtic and german. The " titanism " of the " colossal, impetuous, adventurous wanderer " of the early world was similarly norse, celtic and german, as much one as the other. It was about the Viking that Arnold was speaking; and his " early world " was the warlike period of the great migrations and settlements of nordic peoples, which later Professor Chadwick named the " Heroic Age." He confuses this colossal blue-eyed seaman with the supernatural delicacy of " celtic " romance, as we have seen: and we all, to this day, to some extent, do the same; so we cannot blame him. But it is not sure that he did not see the situation more clearly than it answered his purpose at the moment to discover.

He says to his almost unbelievably stupid audience that they, Saxons or Teutons, were admittedly closely related to the Celts: therefore, he said, it was absurd of them to oppress as though they were the last of " foreigners," and to be so vindictive about, the Irish. For there was no such racial disparity as was popularly supposed between the English and Irish. The Irish, because they are " Celts," he says, are politically ineffectual : but he hints also that the English may not be so effective, really, as they believe, and that their political success may be short-lived.

"Nay, perhaps, if we are doomed to perish (Heaven avert the omen!) we shall perish by our Celtism, by our self-will and want of patience with ideas, our inability to see the way the world is going ; and yet those very Celts, by our affinity with whom we are perishing, will be hating and upbraiding us all the time."

There is the heart of the irony in this extraordinary essay. Seeing when it was written, this ironically conceived scene has a prophetic claim. Taking Arnold's pessimistic view of the deadly effects—where political and practical affairs are concerned—of this " celtic " emanation, then, what would have happened would be this. The successive waves of invasion represented by the Celt and Saxon would have passed into Britain. The first wave would come down on to the so far for us anonymous and racially unclassified people already established there, receive some contribution of blood, and at once fall under the enervating spell of what we call " celtism." The hardy celtic stock was never good for anything afterwards. They continued to ride out to war : but, in Ossian's words, " *They always fell!* "—that was, they had become " celtic." Their saxon kinsmen had no difficulty in locking them up in a corner of the country. From there, by this time saturated with " celtism," they exuded it ; and with the help of the subject-race, who had spiritually mastered them, they manufactured the great romances. The Saxon benefited rather than otherwise— sustained of course by the hard-headed latinized Norman —by the " celtic " effluvia. But not for ever! The norman element and influence, never very thick, thins and then disappears. At last, like the Celt, the Saxon must succumb to this terrible other-worldly potion (from the same factory as the witcheries that unknit lives in the story of Tristan and Yseult), which makes everything ineffectual that it touches.

The picture of these two neighbouring tribes of Teutons (more or less) perishing side by side with each other, of the same mysterious complaint (one, the " creeping Saxon," supposing he has caught it from his neighbour); neither recognizing the other as his brother and close kinsman (as Arnold implores them to do) but loading each other with abuse, is one of the highest comedy, that it is strange no one should have seized on. For very little observation is required to see that the celtic-saxon contrast contains somewhere a portentous flaw.

During the martyrdom of the Lord Mayor of Cork I had had several opportunities of seeing considerable numbers of irish people demonstrating among the London crowds. I was never able to discover which were Irish and which were English, however. They looked to me exactly the same. With the best will in the world to discriminate the orderly groups of demonstrators from the orderly groups of spectators, and to satisfy the romantic proprieties on such an occasion, my eyes refused to effect the necessary separation, that the principle of " celtism " demanded, into chalk and cheese. I should have supposed that they were a lot of romantic english-people pretending to be irish-people, and demonstrating with the assistance of a few priests and pipers, if it had not been that they all looked extremely depressed, and english-people when they are giving romance the rein are always very elated.

This is of course purely a matter of looks : in outward appearance, confining ourselves to that, it would be difficult to imagine two better specimens of Viking than Mr Bernard Shaw and Mr James Joyce, say. It would require an extremely romantic temperament indeed to see much difference between Mr Shaw and an average rather fine-looking Swede, Scot or Dane, were it not for the language, and the rôle imposed on Mr Shaw at his birth of being a " Celt." The power of sentimental suggestibility possessed by the Saxon, patented by Mr Shaw in *John Bull's Other Island*, and repeated in the person of Haines in *Ulysses*, would even be inadequate for that task. Provided Mr Shaw were not allowed to speak, the Saxon would not be able to pick him out in the police-yard from among a dozen other ancient or modern Norsemen. All his geniality (in dumb show) would be in vain. The Saxon would merely think it was a " jolly old Swede," or an especially " kindly " Norwegian, or a sort of pickwickian Dane.

Apart, however, from the near kinship of the Teuton and Celt, the east of Ireland was colonized by the Norsemen almost as much as was the east of England. Dublin was more a norse town than anything else, the Norsemen of Dublin and of Bristol (a town founded by norse colonists) were in close touch, and there, as in King's Lynn, Grimsby and elsewhere, norwegian was largely spoken until well into the fourteenth century. In blood there is probably very little difference between the majority of the inhabitants of Ireland, Wales, and the north, east and south of England ; not so much difference, at all events, as, religion apart, to create a riot, or an animosity based on pigment and smell. But that statement must be qualified, in the case particularly of the highlands of Scotland, Wales and the west of Ireland, to include a very dark type of person, who certainly would seem to require explaining on other grounds than those of slight differences between specializations of teuton stock : and with those " little dark people " we are no doubt in the presence of this prestigious minority responsible for all the " celtism " in the wide world. What a political responsibility !—but, meanwhile, it is not usually they that play the part of the " Celts." It is the Viking like Mr Shaw, or the Spaniard like Mr de Valera.

If the picture Arnold draws is a true one—of the two close kindred disguised, by one accident and another, of culture and of speech (one much more deeply tainted than the other with what we will agree to call " celtism "), so that they neither recognize each other, and both sink to their common doom locked in a death-struggle—if that, allowing us to anticipate by a few years the " doom," is a trustworthy account, then the following elucidations would suggest themselves to an impartial observer.

Just as the German (as Arnold would see it) in the Englishman, with a haunting feeling that he *is* a rather unromantic creature, predisposes him to feel an intense pleasure when he is taken for a Spaniard, a gipsy, a Pole or a Chinaman—he does not discriminate, *anything* strange: so it may be that the real Celt (not the mythical " Celt "), being so closely related to the Teuton, may share this failing of his kinsman. Only in his case nature has so arranged things that all he has to do is to pretend to be a " Celt ! "—that is to say, " Celt " in the sense of that mysterious something that produced all the wonderful romances of chivalry, haunting popular music, sun myths, dolmens, etc. So disguised (even from himself !—for he too has been taken-in long ago) he has had no difficulty in imposing on his simple saxon kinsman, who regards him with the greatest awe, as a " foreigner " of the deepest dye, and most alien blood ; according him alternately his dog-like admiration and wolf-like hatred, the latter of which is naturally reciprocated ; for it serves, on the side of the Irishman, to keep up the illusion of a *difference* which exists only in the imagination of these two over-romantic relatives. This account of the irish-english situation is a very different one, it is unnecessary to say, from that which Shaw made so popular in his plays. But it is in many ways very much more comic, and hardly yields to the conventional and generally accepted one on the tragic side. Is it not perhaps the true one ? It is what Arnold's account, corrected by later ethnologic research, would lead us to accept.

The whole structure of " celtic twilight " and racial romance is really the work of the Irish : the Welsh and Scots have little to do with it. It is entirely a little temperamental affair between the English and the Irish, that centuries of political disputes have in no way disturbed. It is Arnold's picture of them indeed, only a rather more bitter buffoonery than he cared to show it. Actually in the case of the more energetic sort of Irishman we are probably in the presence of our old friend, the Norseman, transformed with his well-known assimilativeness into a perfect " Celt." The Irish share to a remarkable degree many of the most marked characteristics of the English : they have—a little intensified and heightened, perhaps, owing to the romantic facilities for satisfying it in their more obscure tribal past—the social snobbery of the English. They share to a marked degree the anglo-saxon prudery and sentimentalism. And, most characteristic of all, they share with the English their intense snobbery about the *Irish*, which, of course, they both call the " Celt."

In consequence of the existence of this confirmed mis-understanding—so sedulously fostered, of course, by the Irish themselves—it has been a constant source of surprise on both sides of the Irish Channel that Englishmen like Swift, established in Ireland, should (making abstraction of their gifts, if that were possible) have so perfectly answered to the " celtic " ideal. Of course had it been realized that most Irishmen were in the same situation—namely, that they were, just as Swift had been, benefiting (where like Swift they had the genius to do so, which is an important condition) by something no more " celtic " than it was ingævonic or norse—then naturally such things would have provoked no comment. It will not be necessary to remind the reader that the modern Irishman, led by Shaw, repudiates both the sentimental and the ineffectual, unpractical imputations found above. The irish-american business man is pointed to, his great energy and success, to controvert this picture. The tables are turned, the senti-mentalism of the Saxon or German is contrasted with the good sense and unemotional wit of the Irish. The *difference* is maintained in its full integrity, but its qualities reversed. There is a measure of truth in the Shaw account of the able and business-like Irishman. For he is no doubt (as in the case of Shaw himself) either a Scotsman or a Norseman, with the original energetic qualities of the norman nature better preserved in Ireland, which is out of the way, than in modern England—though disguised, of course, beneath a " celtic " patina.

Like the people in cymric legend one of whose eyes has been rubbed on something belonging to the fairies, and who afterwards with that eye see everything truly, whereas with the other they see everything as most people do ; or who with the one eye see a splendid palace and with the other unmodified eye they see only a hovel ; so possibly

THE LION AND THE FOX

Shakespeare may have had access to the same magical objects as other Saxons, Celts, Picts, Danes and so forth, and rubbed his eye by accident in the way people do in the welsh legends. But after having half made of him a Lord Chancellor, to satisfy british class-snobbery, it would be the consummation of the ridiculous to wish to make him a Celt, as Renan suggests should be done, to satisfy the queer race-snobbery about something that does not even exist.